D1528329

Land tenure on Southern California Indian reservations is one of the least understood aspects of the entire United States reservation system. Currently in Southern California thirty-three reservations and many public domain allotments (Indian homesteads) operate under several different types of land tenure, each with its own history and its own set of rights, limitations, and socioeconomic implications. Since 1953 these lands have been subject to the laws of California in most important respects, but exceptions are made on the basis of the "traditional" or "tribal custom" ownership and use status of unallotted lands. Legal interpretations have depended at least in part, and will continue to do so, on the meaning of "tribal custom"—what it was and is in Southern California.

In *Pushed into the Rocks: Southern California Indian Land Tenure, 1769–1986,* Florence Connolly Shipek offers the results of her thirty years of research and testimony as an expert witness for the Indians struggling to regain and maintain control of their land. In tracing the historical ownership and use patterns, Shipek illustrates how a case is made. Her major concerns are to establish what the "tribal custom" is and to offer a practical guide to tribes and consultants involved in land-use planning or litigation. A professor of anthropology at the University of Wisconsin-Parkside and first holder of the Rupert Costo Chair in American Indian History, University of California-Riverside, 1987–88, Florence Shipek recorded *The Autobiography of a Diegueño Woman, Delfina Cuero* (1969).

PUSHED INTO THE ROCKS

Southern California
Indian Land
Tenure
1769–1986

Florence Connolly Shipek

University of Nebraska Press
Lincoln and London

Designed by Kim Nabity
in the Art Department,
University of Nebraska–Lincoln
Typeface: Baskerville
Typesetter: Michael Jensen
Printer: Edwards Brothers

Library of Congress Cataloging-in-Publication Data
Shipek, Florence Connolly, 1918–
    Pushed into the rocks.
    Bibliography: p.
    Includes index.
    1. Indians of North America – California –
Land tenure. 2. Indians of North America –
California – Reservations. I. Title.
E78.C15S54   1987   333.3'08997   87-5916
ISBN 0-8032-4178-X (alk. paper)

This work is dedicated to those who would learn from history.

CONTENTS

LIST OF MAPS

PREFACE

YEARS OF RESEARCH and work in applied anthropology in Southern California have made it apparent that
one of the most important needs of the Indian people is a
comprehensive analysis and presentation of land use practices
and concepts, reservation land tenure, and their associated
rights and obligations. There has been much misunderstanding of California Indian concepts of land tenure and land use
among government officials, lawyers, "advocates," community
development workers, land planners, and some scientific researchers, and by some Indians themselves, who have adopted the colonial stereotypes of the larger society.[1]

One common misconception is that all North American Indian
groups had the same system of land tenure. This was the
stereotyped "traditional North American Indian" concept of
tribal ownership-in-common for all territory, with the individual, family, or lineage having only use rights, which lapsed
with nonuse. The acceptance of this stereotype leaves unex-
amined the complex relationship between ownership concepts and the factors of use patterns, local ecology, and population density (Steward 1955; Boserup 1965).

Another major misconception has been that the "traditional Indian use of land" left the land in its "natural wild state" without
any effect on, or human manipulation of, the land and its
plant or animal biota. A careful reading of early European
explorers' descriptions, combined with a knowledge of ecolo-

gy and climax vegetation, reveals that human beings managed the entire continent and manipulated it to produce plants and animals for use as food, shelter, clothing, tools, and equipment.

These two stereotyped misconceptions have caused and continue to cause complications for California Indians (and Indians in other states) who try to use and develop the reservation lands. In this book I will therefore focus on (1) the principal problems, and (2) the intricacies of reservation land tenure types, which complicate decision making regarding modern reservation land use and economic development. This book has been written primarily for use by Indians and by those who work with and for them in California, as well as for scholars interested in United States Indian policy and Indian law. A person working with the people of any one reservation should seek further details about its unique history and conditions (see Appendix F for sources of data and methods of research). Many aspects of Southern California Indian reservation tenure and problems will also apply to reservations in northern California and in other states.

Many bands do not want their nonpublic discussions, problems, and plans identified in a general work such as this. Therefore I have not always named the reservation or individuals involved in a particular problem. When examples are given, the identity of the groups named is already public knowledge and these groups are not necessarily the only reservations that have that specific problem. I have frequently been in a privileged position with many of the bands; consequently, I respect their desire to keep certain information confidential.

The major portion of the data on which this monograph is based has been acquired from my own fieldwork, interviews, observations, and research in various archives. I began working for the Southern California Indians in 1954. Some months earlier, in 1953, Congress had passed Public Law 280, which placed the Indians of several states and their reservations under state law except for the maintenance of the trust status of the land by the Bureau of Indian Affairs, or the BIA.[2] California was one of the states named in P.L. 280. Under the impact of this drastic legal change, some Southern California Indians foresaw the need for independent, unbiased sources of information and mediation. For example, Indian leaders perceived the possibility of the discriminatory administration of state laws on welfare and health care delivery. The Indians had not, for example, had the opportunity to learn the conditions under which other citizens were eligible for treatment in county hospitals. They therefore sought knowledgeable, unbiased citizens who knew or could discover these conditions and who could recognize the difference between a misunderstanding or a failure to meet legal requirements and discrimination, if it occurred. These farsighted Indians arranged a meeting with interested non-Indians through the services of the American Friends Service Committee.[3]

A non-Indian friend of mine thought that I, as an anthropologist, would be interested in the meeting and took me with her. By the conclusion of the meeting, and at the request of the Indians, I had agreed to be available if needed. This began a total involvement of my life and the lives of my husband and two sons with the Indians of Southern California. From 1954 until his death in 1969, my husband, Carl, a marine geologist, supported much of my research. He assisted me, not only financially, but also by rearranging our lives around my irregular schedule and by going with me and aiding me when possible. My sons were also drafted to assist me from time to time.

One of the first major requests to which I responded came from the enrollment committee of the San Pasqual Band. Since the loss of their original village (both as band territory and as a Mexican Indian pueblo) to settlers in 1871, they were dispersed throughout Southern California. Although the bureau trust patented reservation land to them in 1910, this land was not within their aboriginal territory, nor was it large enough to support more than one family using the farming techniques of the period. No San Pasqual members went on the land, and finally the Bureau placed a non-Indian caretaker on the land. In 1954 the descendants of the San Pasqual Band realized that this small, mislocated reservation was their only inheritance and that they would lose even that if they did not identify themselves and organize a reservation government. The bureau told them that it would be up to them to prove their Indian and band identity. The enrollment committee, composed of band elders, turned to me for help. Thus my first band-level assignment was to prepare a history of the band and complete genealogies of all the members. It proved to be possible to trace them from the present generation through church and other records back to the San Diego mission records of the 1820s. I was impressed with the knowledge possessed by the elders of the enrollment committee, which I was able to verify with records.

While I worked for the San Pasqual Enrollment Committee, I attended its meetings and also met with all the people who thought they could prove their band affiliation. At the same time I also received requests for various other types of information from officials and members of other bands. I attended other band meetings, committee meetings, intertribal meetings, and Mission Indian Federation meetings. I came to know tribal officials and members from many Southern California bands, not only at tribal meetings, but also through informal visits at their homes and at mine. During these early years, the American Friends Service Committee also had a worker in the area, first Richard Thomas (now a sociology professor at Southern Illinois University) and then Norman Illsley. Much of their work was with the more northerly reservations, but we shared problems and information regularly and helped each other in many ways. Lowell J. Bean began his doctoral research at about this time, and we also shared information and cooperated in many ways.

Due to my involvement, in 1959 the attorneys for the Mission Indian Land Claims Case (United States Indian Claims Commission Docket 80) asked me to research the problem of the identity of the "Kamia" and their relationship to the "Diegueño" (Kroeber 1925). They also requested that I start a complete land-use study for the Diegueño-Kamia (Kumeyaay). This work was not quite finished when in 1964 the government offered an out-of-court settlement to the Mission

Indians (Docket 80), the Indians of California (Dockets 31–37), and the Pitt River Indians (this is also spelled Pit River; Docket 347). The Indians voted to accept the offer (see Heizer and Kroeber 1976, and Shipek 1980). This ended that phase of my research.

The attorneys for the Mission Indians immediately had me begin research on the water-loss aspect of the claims case (U.S. Indian Claims Commission Docket 80A). This was a claim against the government for dereliction in its trusteeship duty to protect the water rights belonging to Indian reservation lands. At that time the case named only the Soboba, Pala, Pauma, Rincon, and La Jolla reservations. Soboba's water sources had been destroyed when the aqueduct of the Los Angeles Metropolitan Water District had been tunneled through the mountain behind Soboba. The other reservations lost their water due to direct diversion of the riparian streams above reservation lands. In 1965, I presented the requested testimony at the first hearings on the case before the Indian Claims Commission.

While continuing my direct research for the Indians, and because of my accumulated knowledge of detailed changes in general land use and tenure from the Spanish to the modern period, I was asked to conduct research on the technical legal problem involving the settlement of specific San Diego Bay towns by American settlers in the period from 1868 to 1871. This began a search into San Diego County archives beyond those in which I expected to find information about Indians. However, these archives had information about Indians thinly scattered throughout, although this was peripheral to the primary object of the archives. This accumulating information resulted in an increased understanding on my part of the actual conditions and relationships between settlers and Indian land tenure and land use in Southern California.

In 1969 new attorneys took over the San Luis Rey River Reservation section (specifically, Rincon and La Jolla) of the water case (Docket 80A). The nature of the case was expanded to include a suit brought directly against the water company involved in the diversion of the river water (*Rincon Band of*

Mission Indians and La Jolla Band of Mission Indians v. *Escondido Mutual Water Company and Vista Irrigation District*). I continued as the anthropologist and ethnohistorical researcher for this new aspect of the case (Shipek 1969). The basic written testimony was presented in April 1972 (Shipek 1972). Additional written testimony for Docket 80A was submitted in July 1980 (Shipek 1980a). Further written testimony in the suit against the water company was submitted in July 1984 (Shipek 1984).

In 1970 the University of San Diego's College for Women, together with the Coordinating Council for Higher Education for California funded a program of continuing education for community development for the San Diego County reservations. This program was designed to teach the Indians local government administration, constitution and ordinance writing, community planning, tribal accounting, and such related subjects as requested by the various reservations. I was asked to direct the program and did so from July 1970 to June 1972. In the meantime, the way opened for me to attend the University of Hawaii as a doctoral degree candidate. A portion of the material on which this monograph is based was used in my doctoral dissertation on San Luiseño cultural change and cultural retention.

Most of my research was conducted in response to direct requests from various bands and individuals, and the results were communicated directly to them. I had, therefore, a rather unique relationship with many communities. Because some questions involved disputes between Indians, I made it clear that I would not take sides in such disputes but was willing to search for records and information that could be used to solve the dispute, and that in each case I would be as neutral and accurate as humanly possible. I also pointed out that because my results were being used as evidence in both judicial and administrative cases before various other agencies of the government, I could not be an advocate but could only be an impartial witness. Consequently, I made it clear that I had to be as accurate as possible and could not suppress records that a group did not like in favor of those presenting its position but must account for both the favorable and unfavorable documents. All the reservations and individuals understood and accepted this position.

Upon beginning my work in 1954, I immediately became aware of the ability of the older tribal leaders and officials to quote accurately and in detail many of the laws that had governed and affected them. I also became aware that there were at least two major opposite interpretations of the laws and their meanings and effects on Indians. These two opposite viewpoints were being expressed at that time by the Mission Indian Federation, which opposed the bureau, and by those who tried to work with the bureau, the reservation spokesmen elected under bureau auspices, who formed the California Inter-Tribal Council. Feelings ran high between adherents of the two viewpoints. Both sides made efforts to influence my views and to guide or control my work and findings. Between them, they educated me.

To describe my experiences and training by the Indians, or even to name all those who have contributed to my training and understanding of their cultures, would take a book in itself. Yet mention must be made and thanks expressed to those who made special contributions to my knowledge and understanding (those whose names are followed by an asterisk are now deceased): Mrs. Rosalie P. Robertson,* Mr. Antonio Pinto, Mr. Cristobal Pinto, Mrs. Lily Couro, Mr. Theodore (Ted) Couro,* Mr. Sosten Alto,* Mrs. Pauline Alto, Mrs. Thelma Terry,* Mrs. Juliana Calac,* Mrs. Ramona Scott,* Mrs. Josephine Jackson, Mr. Robert Lavato, Mr. Stephen Ponchetti,* Mrs. Florence Ponchetti, Mr. Winslow Curo,* Mr. James Martinez, Mrs. Jane Penn,* Mrs. Patricia Duro, Mrs. Mary Matteson, Mr. Banning Taylor, Mrs. Angelina Omish, Mr. Max Mazzetti, Mrs. Lorena Dixon, Mr. Robert Lofton, Mrs. Florence Lofton, and so many, many more.

Thanks must also be given for the unfailing aid and cheerful assistance of all the archivists of the area: in San Diego County the recorders, county clerks, tax assessors, the Delinquent Tax Office and the County Engineer's Office; the California Room of the San Diego Public Library; the Junípero Serra Library of the San Diego Historical Association; the Title In-

---

surance Company's photographic department; the National City Library; the Museum of Man; the Roman Catholic Diocesan Archives; the A. K. Smiley Library of the Redlands; the Federal Records Center and the Federal Archives for Southern California; the National Archives; the Malki Museum Library on the Morongo Reservation; the Huntington Library at San Marino; and the Bancroft Library at Berkeley. I must also express gratitude to the personnel of the Riverside Field Office of the Bureau of Indian Affairs for their cheerful cooperation and assistance in the use of records for the bands, even though we did not see eye to eye.

Acknowledgment must also be made of the influence of Dr. Emil W. Haury and Dr. Edward H. Spicer for my early training in anthropology and in the approaches I brought to both basic research and applied work. Through the years, my work has benefited from discussions with Drs. Margaret Langdon and Lowell J. Bean. More recently, discussions with Drs. Katharine Luomala, Alice G. Dewey, Richard A. Gould, and Stephen T. Boggs have given me new perspectives on my experiences. Special thanks must also go to Dr. Dewey, Dr. Bean, Dr. Langdon, Dr. Darrell Posey, Dr. Henry F. Dobyns, Dr. Richard Stoffle, and Mr. David Shipek, who have critically read and commented upon this manuscript, and to David Halmo, who helped with the editing.

I am presenting here the information and understanding I have acquired through the years. Any errors are strictly my own, but the longer I work under the constantly changing external conditions and legal situations, the more new information comes to light to improve my understanding of past events.

CHAPTER 1
Introduction

LAND TENURE ON Southern California Indian reservations is one of the least understood aspects of the entire United States reservation system (see, for example, Sutton 1965, 1967). It is also one of the least understood aspects of the history of Southern California Indian cultures. Several different types of land tenure presently exist on the reservations. Each type has its own history and its own set of rights, limitations, and socioeconomic implications.

Some thirty-three reservations and many public domain allotments (Indian homesteads) exist in Southern California. Neither the reservations nor the allotments are public lands or government lands. Reservation lands are owned by the various Indian bands, for whom title is held in trust by the United States of America through the Bureau of Indian Affairs. Allotments are owned by individual Indians, for whom the title is also held in trust by the United States. Since the passage of Public Law 280 by Congress in 1953, these lands have been subject to the laws of the state of California in every way except for the trust title, probate, property-tax-exempt status, and the "traditional" or "tribal custom" ownership and use status of unallotted lands. The exact meaning of Public Law 280 (see Appendix E) and the rights of state and local government agencies to control the use of reservation land through zoning controls, building codes, sales tax laws, and other laws are questions that have been and continue to be tested in the courts. Some of the test cases are discussed later. At least part of the interpretations has depended, and will continue to depend, on the meaning of the term "tribal custom" and what it was and is in Southern California.

One must realize that Southern California Indian history differs from the experience of Indian tribes elsewhere in the United States (Haas 1957:15). Generally, granting Indians in the United States individual legal tenure rights to land resulted in the alienation of more than two-thirds of that land and the destruction of numerous tribal governments. This did not occur in Southern California. Here less than 25 percent of the allotted acreage has been taken out of trust. Moreover, some of this out-of-trust land, or fee-patented land, is still in the hands of Indian owners. This raises the question: Why were the results so different?

To answer this question, and also to understand the present pattern of land ownership on Southern California reservations, it is necessary to understand several things: first, the original legal tenure patterns of the particular Indian groups; second, the Indians' adaptation of traditional tenure and use to the legal definitions of land tenure in United States as a whole and in California specifically; and third, the modern legal aspects of reservation land tenure. One must look at the history of the development and continual economic adaptation of the Indian peoples of Southern California to understand how, historically, the traditional Southern California Indian tenure-use system was gradually adjusted to handle each new economic and political development.

Due to local conditions, an individual has never had to reside on or use either allotted or unallotted (assigned) land in order to maintain ownership, inheritance rights, or band membership. Social, religious, and political activities, as well as tribal government, continue regardless of the location of the residence of the members, most of whom live within a two-hundred-mile radius. Both personal and telephone contacts are maintained. From the inception of the reservations, residence or nonresidence upon a reservation has been related to several interacting factors:

1. the quality and amount of land for farming
2. the availability of irrigation water
3. the accessibility of the reservation to off-reservation jobs as governed by distance and the presence of good roads
4. most recently, the presence or absence of domestic water

Problems have been created for Indians through the misunderstanding of their traditional system by the sources of governmental power and by "advocates," and also through various deliberate external pressures. These pressures presently take the form of state or county governments and zoning commissions aided by "environmentalists" demanding retention of reservation land in its "natural, traditional state," or in "rural family agriculture," or for outdoor recreation. This has happened just as Indians have begun to be in a position to participate in economic development and are in the process of investigating future economic possibilities for their reservations.

Both theoretically and practically, therefore, it would be useful to understand how a relatively successful adaptation from traditional legal tenure-use to modern legal tenure-use was achieved. In order to understand what "tribal custom" actually was and is, and what the complexities of some of the problems facing reservation governments today are, one must examine the original band tenure system.

In this book, I use the term "band" to designate the sociopolitical landowning entity regardless of how it may now be constituted or how it may have been constituted in the past. In this sense, the term "band" is equivalent to the term "tribelet" as used by anthropologists such as A. L. Kroeber (1962; 1925:3, 160–163, 228–230, 234–235, 474–475, 723–725, 830–832) and Robert Heizer (1966:2–9), who have discussed their understanding of the nature of tribelets in California. However, in spite of their superficial similarity (Shipek 1983a), a number of sociopolitical variations existed between the Southern California ethnic groups.

For all four ethnic groups, the primary territorial unit was controlled by a social, political, economic and religious hierarchical organization of shamans led by a *nuut* (also *net* or *noot*)

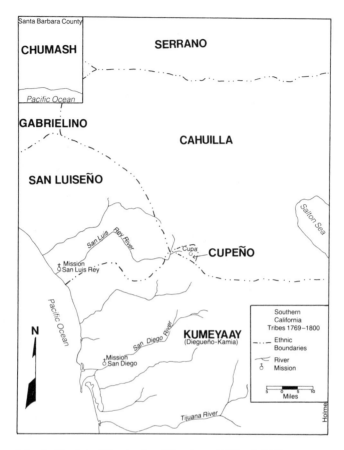

Map 1. Aboriginal Territories of Southern California Tribes

(San Luiseño, Cupeño, and Cahuilla) or by a *kwaaypaay* (Kumeyaay). These leaders were called "capitáns" by the Spanish and "captains" by the Americans. Similar religious beliefs and concepts maintained and validated these structures for all groups (Shipek 1977), but differences existed between them in the forms of kinship structures and in the power and authority of the leadership.

Although the evidence for it is controversial, a national level of organization appears to have functioned above the band territorial unit until its gradual, deliberate destruction under Spanish, Mexican, and American political controls (Shipek 1977, 1983). The Shoshonean-speaking Cupeño probably formed one national group, and one or possibly two larger national-level federations existed among each of the other ethnic groups: the Shoshonean-speaking San Luiseño and Cahuilla, and the Yuman-speaking Kumeyaay (Diegueño-Kamia or Ipai-Tipai in the earlier literature).

The nature of the aboriginal sociopolitical structure of the Shoshonean-speaking nationalities in Southern California has been discussed, and much evidence has been presented, by Kroeber (1925:685–688, 690–691, 705–706), Strong ([1929] 1972) and Gifford (1918:177–214). Bean (1972) analyzed the Cahuilla social structure in detail, relating it to the local ecology and land use. White (1963) discussed San Luiseño social structure, but his postulated reconstruction leaves many questions unanswered and contradictory lines of evidence unresolved. The historic changes in the San Luiseño political, economic, and religious structure in relation to changing the ecology and land use are discussed in Shipek 1977. For the Yuman-speaking Kumeyaay, some evidence has been presented by Kroeber (1925: 710–720, 723–724), Gifford (1918:156–173; 1931:1–3, 10–18), Spier (1923:297–311), and Luomala (1963:282–301).[4] Two of my earlier works (1982, 1982b) draw together all the evidence from mission records, other historical records, and lengthy ethnographic research to resolve the problems of Kumeyaay sociopolitical structure. A great deal of evidence for some Shoshonean-speaking sociopolitical structures and their relationship to national structures remains to be presented. However, in this book I shall summarize the results of the above combined with my own research in order to show the similarities and emphasize the differences that existed at the band level.

Among the San Luiseño, the territorial bands were composed of one or more patrilineages, with each patrilineage owning land arranged vertically from a valley bottom up to the drainage divide (White 1963). The size of the band and the number of patrilineages varied with the size and richness of each valley, but generally a band territory extended from ten to thirty miles along a drainage and up to the drainage divides and occasionally included small isolated valleys. Each band also had acorn and pine-nut territories in the mountains and shellfish and fishing territories at the coast.

The *noot,* or captain, of each band managed the religious, political, and economic life of the band as well as the military, diplomatic, and trade relations with other bands (Boscana 1933). Under the *noot* was an assistant, or "speaker," who relayed instructions to band members. Next under the *noot* was a council of *puplum* (*pul* singular), or specialists (shamans), each of whom was charged with maintaining knowledge about an environmental resource, or a religious ritual necessary for birth, naming, puberty initiation, curing, marriage, death, and mourning ceremonies. With the *noot* and his speaker, this council formed the governing body that decided when to go to the mountains for acorns or to the ocean, when to do fire maintenance work on the fields, when to have a fiesta or a religious ceremony, and when to trade or make war on the band's neighbors. Once the *noot* and *puplum* made a decision, the entire band followed their orders. These leadership positions were inherited, with the chosen heir being trained for his role. The members of the ruling body were paid for this management with produce from each family's harvest or hunt, or with shell money or other such valuables.

Cahuilla bands, as described by Bean (1972), were organized as territorial patrilineages. However, in the larger valleys they may, like the San Luiseño, have had bands composed of several lineages. Each Cahuilla lineage had vertical territory with mountain, foothill, and desert land resources and with access to fish, shellfish, and waterfowl on the Salton Sea (Lake Cahuilla or the Blake Sea) whenever the inland sea existed. Ocean resources could only be obtained through intermarriage, ritual, or trade relationships, primarily with the Kumeyaay. Like the San Luiseño, each Cahuilla band was governed by the *net* (captain) with his assistant or speaker and a council of shamans, specialists in managing resources or life crisis rituals. While these positions were normally inherited, an extremely able person could achieve upward mobility more easily than among the San Luiseño. Unlike the San Luiseño, the *net* did not issue orders but had decisions announced, and the people followed because they recognized the greater ability and access to information of the *net* and his council. The leadership was paid with food and valuables for their managerial services.

The Kumeyaay territorial bands crosscut the *shiimull* (a sib organization; Luomala 1963) or named descent groups (Shipek 1968, 1982, 1982b). Each sib was composed of a number of patrilineages, and only within a patrilineage could their ancestry be traced. The patrilineages were connected by untraceable or mythical links. In 1769, between fifty and seventy-five *shiimull* existed, and each territorial band had lineages of between five and fifteen *shiimull* present, depending on the size and richness of the valley and the availability of water. Band loyalty was crosscut by sib (*shiimull*) loyalty, and flexibility of band membership existed (Luomala 1963); that is, the ability to shift from a coastal to a mountain or desert band.

Like the *net*, or *noot*, the *kwaaypaay* (captain) had an assistant (speaker) and a council of *kusteyay* (shamans), who were specialists in resource and ritual management. After consultation with this council, the *kwaaypaay* had the speaker announce his decision to go to the mountains, or the coast or to have a ceremony, and each family was free to follow or not as it pleased. Generally most followed, because, as with the *noot*, they recognized the *kwaaypaay*'s greater ability and access to essential knowledge of resource conditions. Again, this hierarchy was paid with produce and valuables for their management.

Unlike the Cahuilla or San Luiseño, where the *net* (*noot*) was the head of the largest lineage in the band, among the Kumeyaay, with the exception of an occasional brother, the *kwaaypaay* was the only adult male of his *shiimull* in the band. Although a *kwaaypaay* role was inherited, and a son was trained by his father for the position, at the death of a *kwaaypaay* his successor would be chosen from among the sons of all *kwaaypaay* at a meeting of all Kumeyaay *kwaaypaay*. The choice also required the approval of the band. Unlike the Shoshonean-speaking band leaders, one of the primary duties of a *kwaaypaay* was to maintain harmony and arbitrate disputes within the band. According to Kumeyaay elders, "He could be more fair to all without *shiimull* mates within the band."

A named territorial band normally consisted of a large village in which the *kwaaypaay* lived. The territory extended from ten to thirty miles along a stream and its tributaries up to the drainage divides. Dispersed *shiimull* homesteads belonging to that band would be scattered along the drainage and in side valleys wherever small springs existed. Kumeyaay territory extended from the coast to the Colorado River and for about fifty miles on each side of the present Mexican border.

The Cupeño occupied Cupa, the territory that formed a triangle where the other three ethnic nationalities met: the Kumeyaay across the south, the San Luiseño to the west and northwest, and the Cahuilla to the east and northeast. The people were intermarried with, and showed cultural similarities to, all three nationalities. Cupa was the hub of major mountain passes leading east, southeast, south, southwest, west, and northwest and contained a large hot spring (Warner's Hot Springs) and numerous cold springs. The location was also at the edge of a large inland valley with a small lake and marsh, the remains of a large Pleistocene lake. Ethnographic data (Strong [1929] 1972) reveal a visible social, political, economic, and religious structure similar to those of the other ethnic nationalities. However, to hold this large, rich, pivotal valley containing permanent water (particularly in times of drought), the Cupeño would have needed a tight authoritarian organization comparable to that of their San Luiseño neighbors. Further, the necessity for such a tight organization in order to manage the people in relation to the resources is indicated by the 1795 Spanish population estimate of 2,000 persons (Mariner MS, Bancroft Library) after the Spanish had occupied the coast for twenty-six years, during which several three- to five-year droughts and at least one major smallpox epidemic had occurred, reducing the regional population. Thus, I estimate the 1769 population of Cupa to have been about 5,000 persons.

The original differences in the degree of authoritarian versus nonauthoritarian band structure and lineage as compared to sib structure have affected the postcontact changes, and they continue to affect the reservation political structures and decision-making processes. (Such differences must, however, be left to another work.) The present composition of a "band" may vary from portions of the original band in that territory to that band plus freely accepted refugees or people imposed on it by Bureau of Indian Affairs fiat (as in the case of San Pasqual) or those who were shifted for the convenience of the bureau in the past (as in the case of Campo). It may also be composed of portions of several bands of the same ethnic nationality and parts of their respective territories (as in La Jolla) or several bands of different ethnic nationalities (as in Morongo [Bean 1978] or Pala). Presently the term "band" is used by the Indians to designate the entity that owns a reservation, and it is the legal term to designate the entity that owns the trust patent title to reservation land.

This book focuses on land tenure and land use as each has developed and changed from the aboriginal to the present pattern. The main emphasis is on present conditions and problems, yet the complex contemporary situation has resulted from an historic process of Southern California Indians adjusting their traditional behavior to changing circumstances. In order to provide the reader with the background of present problems, Chapter 2 summarizes the aboriginal tenure-use pattern that existed throughout Southern California. Although many writers have mentioned aspects of land tenure in the context of their work, detained analyses have been presented only by Strong ([1929] 1972), White (1963), Bean (1972), and Shipek (1972, 1977). These sources and my own fieldwork are the primary sources for the present summary. Chapter 3 summarizes the historical events, changes, and continuities that occurred prior to and following the 1891 Act for the Relief of the Mission Indians in the State of California (see Appendix C). By this act, the United States Congress authorized the granting to each Indian band of the legal title in trust to the lands determined to be occupied by them at that time (with certain exceptions, which will be described). Chapters 4 and 5 list the various existing modern legal forms of tenure, describing the rights and duties attached to each form and its interaction with the traditional legal tenure. Finally, Chapters 6 and 7 discuss some of the problems and implications for the future that derive from this interaction of traditional and modern forms.

CHAPTER 2

Aboriginal Tenure and Use

A NUMBER OF EARLIER studies of southern California
Indian aboriginal land tenure and use explicitly or im-
plicitly took the basic view that these people were "advanced
hunter-gatherers." Strong ([1929] 1972:224–249) mapped
Cupeño ownership and use of land from this perspective.
White (1963:122–128) discussed San Luiseño concepts in detail, and Spier (1923:297–308) described a portion of the
southern Diegueño (Kumeyaay) territorial concepts in this
framework. Bean (1972:48) discussed Cahuilla tenure concepts and related them directly to Cahuilla adaptation to tribal territory, but he also suggested some agricultural considerations.

Several recent studies have described aboriginal management of
vegetational and faunal resources beyond merely passive
gathering and hunting. Bean and Lawton (1973) expanded
upon Bean's initial ideas of agricultural considerations. Lewis
(1973) hypothesized "fire swidden" as a method for Indian
management and production of native-plant food crops and
maintenance of wild animal stocks in northern and central
California, and with some modifications, this hypothesis can
explain the data available concerning land use in Southern
California. My own research (Shipek 1963, 1965, 1972, 1977),
including testimony for the San Luis Rey Water Case (Docket
80A), detailed intensive modifications of the natural environment, or plant husbandry (Higgs and Jarman 1972), and re-

late them to population densities. I described San Luiseño and Kumeyaay land ownership concepts based on this intensive land use. This massive exploitation of resources necessitated using a variety of agricultural techniques to maintain and increase supplies of native food plants as well as planting corn, beans, and squash in selected locations. These techniques included, in addition to fire swidden, a number of types of plant husbandry:

1. broadcasting grain-grass seed in freshly fired fields;
2. transplanting wild onions and other bulbs or tubers;
3. planting cuttings of cactus (Opuntia and other species) near villages;
4. clearing land for planting seeds of "wild" greens (such as chenopodium), shrubs (such as manzanita or elderberry), or tree crops (such as oak, mesquite, or wild plum);
5. clearing fields for domestic crops, such as maize, in selected locations.

This type of land use also included repeated care and labor expended on specific crop areas, specific trees, or stands of cactus and other plants, and deliberate pruning and debris removal around shrubs and trees with fire as well as by hand clearing or "grubbing." This labor also included guiding water by various techniques to specific crop stands. Repeated labor on specific plots had apparently developed into long-term, recognized concepts of rights to these plots (Steward 1938:253). This intensive land use was a function of erratic climatic conditions combined with relatively high population densities (Boserup 1965) that have been estimated for these people. These densities range from three or four persons per square mile among the desert and mountain Cahuilla (Bean 1972 and personal communication) and among the desert Kumeyaay (Kamia) to five to seven persons per square mile among the mountain and coastal Kumeyaay (Diegueño) (Shipek 1963, 1977) and to six to seven per square mile among the San Luiseño (White 1963:111–119; Shipek 1977).

There are minor variations between groups as to which types of land or food crop belonged in each category of rights. The major outlines of each concept and the categories of the concepts, however, seem to have existed for all the groups studied. These concepts, or categories of concepts, follow.

1. The most inclusive native concept was that of the "national" or "ethnic" territory, that is, San Luiseño as opposed to Kumeyaay. Within the ethnic entity, people were aware that they spoke related dialects of one language, shared some resources, maintained trails between groups, and for the most part had some variety of closer social, economic, religious, and political ties than they had with groups outside the ethnic territory. Kroeber (1962) designated this level of identification the "ethnic nationality," and Bean (1972:85) termed it the "cultural nationality." Evidence that an "ethnic nation" existed has survived, at least for the Cupeño and Kumeyaay, in the recorded military defense of their territory and for the Kumeyaay in the existence of a leader above the band level and of a national courier or information system for transmitting information from one end of their territory to the other. Further, among the Kumeyaay certain wild resource areas, in contrast to band territories, were open to any Kumeyaay.

2. A number of bands held territory within each ethnic group. The "band" territory distinguished among the various rancherias (a Spanish term used for Indian villages consisting of scattered dwellings), with rocks marking well-defined group boundaries defended by sorcery and arms. This is the largest inclusive social category that still controls land use. Therefore the band has become equivalent to a reservation tenure group. The band territory included such things as trails within the unit open to use by all members, general hunting territory, religious and ceremonial areas, the band gathering areas, and family or individual tenures. Within the rancheria, family or individual tenures were normally exclusive but could overlap or intermingle (Strong [1929] 1972:244–249, 284). For example, some trees, small groves, or small plant clumps could be retained by one family even when it allowed another family to share some of its land.

3. Most important was the concept of sacred lands, which existed at both the ethnic national level and the band level. Each

tribe or national group lived within the territory encompassed by their "bible," or creation and prophetic stories. This was their Holy Land just as Jerusalem is the Holy Land for Hebrews, Christians, and Moslems. Often, specific locations and features are described in these stories, and some are connected to specific aspects of God or his prophets. One such Kumeyaay holy place is Kuuchamaa, or Tecate Peak (Shipek 1985), another is Wee'ishpa, or Signal Mountain (Gifford 1931). Other holy places were, as in Jerusalem, associated with specific aspects of their religion, such as healing at Table Mountain (Welch 1984; Shipek 1984, 1984a). In addition to the tribal- or national-level holy spots, each band also had specific holy locations, such as a "sun watcher" mountain, used by the "sun" shaman as the place to mark for the timing and observance of solstice and equinox ceremonies. Only the band leaders and shamans, and the equivalent personnel invited from other tribes or nationalities, or in some cases invited initiated persons, could enter such locations or go to the tops of such mountains. In most instances, the general membership could gather at the base of the mountain when called for a ceremony or for special healing rites. All bands had some central brush- or pole-enclosed location as an altar or worship area that only the shamans and leaders might enter. Each band also had a cemetery or cremation area that was used for sacred disposal of the dead and that was maintained as a restricted sacred area.

In regard to this category of land, mention must be made of the fact that only during the past decade have American Indians been accorded the right that most American citizens take for granted, the right to freedom of religion. From the earliest European contact until 1934, the Indians were consistently forced to adopt some form of Christianity, first by the colonial governments and then by the United States government. Their own religion and religious ceremonies were forbidden by the Bureau of Indian Affairs in spite of the fact that in California and all other territories acquired under the Treaty of Guadalupe Hidalgo the existing population was guaranteed the right to practice its own religion. Only since the advent of the Environmental Protection Act of 1969 and the American Indian Religious Freedom Act of 1978 have Indians been able to have access to and to attempt to protect their sacred places outside of the reservation boundaries. They are still fighting for the right to protect ancestral cemeteries from both pothunters and archaeological exploitation.

4. The band gathering areas were specific sections within the band territory, and they belonged collectively to the group as a whole and were used by the entire population of the rancheria. These areas and their produce were generally under the management and control of the captain, who supervised the gathering and distribution or use of the supplies from these areas.

5. Areas owned by families or individuals within the band territory were the primary family source of subsistence. These included fields of grain-grass or other annuals, perennials, various shrubs, oak and other trees, cactus patches, cornfields, and other resources, such as clay beds, basket-grass clumps, quarries, and hot and cold springs. That is, the primary family food resources and some material resources belonged in this individually owned and individually held category. These were generally inherited patrilineally and used by wives and daughters. The individual ownership of a food resource area normally meant that the individual and his family had put labor into the development and maintenance of the resource. An individual usually owned several fields of the same type of crop in different localities and fields of different types of crops adjoining each other or in several different localities. Ownership of several types of fields and of fields in several localities, both of domesticated and "wild" (or husbanded) plants, was advantageous inasmuch as the erratic weather and water supply in Southern California might make any one locality or crop type unproductive in a given year (Shipek 1977).

Another important point is that status and power were differentially distributed within the societies (Boscana 1933:34, 44, 56; Rudkin 1956:28, 38; White 1963:175; Bean 1972; Shipek 1977, 1982). Concomitantly, those with more power and status seem also to have had more land than lesser folk. The band chief or lineage head, who was responsible for entertaining and feasting band guests and for being "generous" and feeding his ill and needy band members, generally had more and much larger family fields in order to meet such obligations. This leader also had the labor of slaves or subservient landless persons, according to Spanish colonial missionaries who observed such leaders functioning (Boscana 1933:56, 70; Rudkin 1956:28). The positions of status and power were inherited, as was the ownership of widely varying amounts of land. Also, there was some specialization of occupations and crafts, which would contribute to the need for varying types and quantities of land in individual ownership.

6. Individuals engaged in shamanism and the control of supernatural powers sometimes had special ownership rights to medicinal plants, rock crystals, and other nonfood resources. These could overlap, coincide, or be contained within any other recognized ownership area. These special areas could pass out of existence or be inherited by the individual trained by the shaman in his special arts (White 1963:124).

7. Individuals owned movable property that had been made by that person or acquired by trade or as a gift. Individually manufactured articles could be given or traded away by the living maker, but after death all personal property, including crops not yet harvested, had to be destroyed by burning. Intangibles such as songs, dances, stories, legends, and curing rituals were privately owned, and their performance ceased with the death of the originator unless they were given to a young relative trained as an apprentice.

8. I obtained details of the aboriginal inheritance pattern from the Kumeyaay and do not know whether this pattern applied in detail to the other ethnic nationalities. It seems probable that it did, inasmuch as they were making similar ecological adaptations and had developed closely related categories of use and tenure. A Kumeyaay field belonged to the individual or family who had cleared or developed it. By the time the owner died, his older children would often have married and cleared or acquired their own fields, so the father's fields

might be inherited by the youngest child or by whichever son or daughter (and spouse) or grandchild had remained with the parents in their old age. Lacking direct heirs, fields could be assigned by the lineage to the nearest lineage relative in need of them. If there were no lineage relatives, then the sib (*shiimull*) could assign the land. If a sib became extinct, the band could reassign the land. In the event that direct heirs did not have an immediate need for the fields, the family would keep the land for future use. It could remain unused or the family could lend or rent the land (for a share of the crop or other valuables) to a member of another family until it was needed by the owning family.

The term "field" is used here in its broadest, rather than its narrowest, English meaning. That is, a "field" inherited as described above was in the Southern California Indian perception any privately—individually—owned area with a food, medicinal, technical, or water resource, whether managed by (a) fire or manual clearing, (b) maintaining native growth using a fire swidden method, (c) transplanting, (d) sowing seeds of "wild" or domesticated crops using a digging stick or broadcast method, (e) relying on natural rainfall, (f) relying on ground water availability, or (g) constructing a water gravity-flow guidance system.

To summarize, at the time of Spanish contact the native peoples of Southern California had land tenure concepts that included (1) the nonpolitical, or in some cases loosely political, ethnic or national territory, (2) rancherias, or bands, which were the primary political units, each defending a separate territory, (3) sacred lands, which belonged jointly to the ethnic or national group or to an individual band, (4) specific areas within the boundaries of each band that belonged to the band as a collective whole, (5) fields, including garden areas, that belonged to family units or individuals for their subsistence, (6) special individually owned areas, (7) individually owned articles and intangible properties such a songs, myths, and legends, and (8) inherited tenure rights by families and individuals in categories (5), (6), and (7).

Briefly, at the time of Spanish contact the population of this region appears to have achieved densities of from more than three to seven persons per square mile. To support such population densities with the available material technology, the so-called "hunting-gathering" peoples of Southern California must have utilized each type of land at its highest potential economic value (Boserup 1965). The high yields necessary to maintain these densities necessitated very intensive land use and sophisticated native food crop practices, including plant husbandry and the planting of domesticates. This led to the development of land tenure concepts that appear closely related to those of permanent-field intensive agriculturalists. These tenure-use concepts are totally different from those of people who subsisted by more widely ranging hunting-gathering practices or by a combination of hunting with swidden (shifting field) corn farming and who remained at population densities well below the levels achieved in California.

CHAPTER 3
Postcontact History

E DWARD SPICER (1962) presented an excellent general discussion of the history of Spanish, Mexican, and Anglo-American colonial institutions and policies dealing with Indians throughout northern Mexico and the southwestern United States, and he has described the effects and results of these policies. However, as each government dealt with Southern California, modifications of these general policies occurred, and these are discussed here.

In 1769 the Spanish imperial government sent a colonizing force into Upper California expressly for the purpose of securing its northwest frontier against encroachment by the Russian movement south from Siberia and Alaska and against the British approach to the Pacific Coast through western Canada. Spanish army units were to establish presidios (army posts) at Monterey Bay and at San Diego Bay, which had been explored by Cabrillo in 1542 and Vizcaíno in 1602.

The Franciscan missionary order was chosen to accompany the military expedition and was charged with "reducing" the natives to Catholic Christianity and teaching them "civilized" pursuits in order to turn them into working-class citizens of the Spanish empire. The standard colonial mission policy was to bring entire villages into a mission and turn them into a self-supporting and self-sufficient community by teaching them Catholicism and European-style agriculture, crafts, and animal husbandry. The missions were expected to supply the army with food and to supply laborers for the settlers in the pueblos and for the private ranchos (landholdings) granted by the government to retired soldiers and settlers, thus taking land needed by the Indians for their own subsistence. After ten years spent in the communal life of the mission, the Indian was supposed to be ready for working-class citizenship and a small family subsistence plot of land. This seldom occurred.

Relatively few of the Franciscans in Upper California or the Dominicans in northern Baja California bothered to learn anything about the local beliefs, languages, or customs of the people. Father Geronimo Boscana (1933) is unique in writing about the Indians of San Luis Rey and San Juan Capistrano, and the Dominican friar Luis Sales (Rudkin 1956) in writing about the Kumeyaay of northern Baja California. The rest simply attempted to impose their rule without understanding the local people. Some were harsher than others, but force was the rule, and severe floggings were common. Mission San Luis Rey was unique in having only one father superior, Antonio Peyri, throughout its active period, and he seems to have been far better than most in his management and treatment of the Indians.

The general mission policy could not be followed at Missions San Diego and San Luis Rey, because the amount of arable land and the requisite irrigation water were not available close to the missions. Thus these two simply brought in a group of Indians, taught them the rudiments of the Catholic rituals, baptized them, and then released them to return to their own villages. These "converted" Indians were required to attend the mission for special feast days and ceremonies and to provide a rotating labor force for the mission. Only the unmarried girls and women, the sick, the elderly, and some craft specialists were fed at these two missions. The rest rotated as labor was needed.

The only presidio in Southern California was near Mission San Diego. Therefore the Indians of this area had more contact with, and harassment by, soldiers. Each of the other Southern California missions had only a squad of between eight and fifteen soldiers "to protect" the friars. However, all the Fran-

ciscan friars constantly complained about the morals of the
soldiers and about their vile treatment of Indian women.
Constant conflict also existed between the military comman-
dants and the friars over the quantity of food, other supplies,
and livestock requisitioned by the army. The friars believed
that they could convert more Indians if they had more food
for distribution to them, especially during the extreme
droughts that occurred between 1777 and 1830.

The first Spanish pueblo in Southern California, Los Angeles,
was founded in 1781 by settlers recruited in Mexico City and
brought overland through Sonora and Yuma to the coast. For
laborers these settlers used unconverted Indians of the region
and neophytes (baptized Indians) from Missions San Gabriel
and San Juan Capistrano. The other pueblo, San Diego, was
formed later by retired soldiers from the San Diego Presidio.
Following the Mexican Revolution and the founding of re-
publican Mexico, the official policy was to secularize the missions—that is, to convert the missions into parish churches
and to found Indian pueblos for the baptized Indians, con-
ferring Mexican citizenship and a small individual plot on
each. Due to its distance from the seat of government, in California secularization was an excuse for the settlers and retired soldiers and their families to strip the missions of livestock, supplies, and lands, and to turn the Indians into peon
villagers on the ranchos,[5] which had formerly been mission
properties supporting the Indians of each mission. Only a
few Indian pueblos were founded and a few hispanicized Indians given land grants. The village at Mission San Juan Capistrano was turned into a pueblo composed of both Indians
and Mexican settlers from San Diego and Los Angeles. Mexican records indicate that most of the inland Southern California Indians were involved in relatively successful revolts
against the Mexicans during the decade of the 1830s, a period also of good rainfall.

Anglo-American policies in Southern California also were modified from those that had become the standard elsewhere and
constantly wavered between two opposing positions. After allowing the Indians to be pushed off most of their good agri-

cultural lands, one end of the policy spectrum consisted of attempts to isolate them and have them support themselves by subsistence farming on farms that were too small and on land that was too poor or from which the water was being stolen. The other end of the spectrum was to encourage Indians to leave the reservations and to obtain laboring jobs to support themselves, because it was recognized that Indians were needed as cheap labor for the non-Indian farmers, ranchers, and orchardists of the region.

Further, when Congress passed the 1891 act creating trust patent reservations, it also placed a twenty-five-year limit on the trust status and authorized individual allotments to all Indians. The limit has been regularly extended and is now indefinite. Since 1930, repeated plans for the termination of trust status throughout California have been considered and prepared by the bureau or by Congress. The latest proposal was withdrawn in 1956 due to the concerted opposition of most California Indians. (However, Congress did pass the Rancheria Act, which terminated the small one to ten-acre rancheria homesites throughout central and northern California.)

Due to the wide scattering of reservations in the Southern California mountains, over the years only a few have had regular contact with bureau personnel. The Mission Agency has variously had an office in the towns of either Colton or Riverside (on no reservation), and from none to four or five suboffices scattered around the larger reservations in each section. Rather than boarding schools, one-room day schools were the norm except for orphans and the better students. The orphans were sent to a Catholic boarding school. The better students who were selected to advance to the next level were sent to Perris (around the turn of the century only) and after Perris was closed, to Sherman, where again the better students were selected for Phoenix or Carlisle. The majority of Southern California Indians had more contact with non-Indian ranchers, storekeepers, and ordinary laboring-class or foreman-class personnel than they did with Indian agency personnel. Many worked in the cities or towns for many years.

The Spanish Mission Period

As mentioned earlier, at neither Mission San Diego (Kume-yaay-Diegueño) nor Mission San Luis Rey (San Luiseño) were the Franciscan missionaries able to follow the standard coloni-al policy of bringing entire villages into the mission. Instead, due to the scattered and restricted nature of irrigable agricul-tural lands, they brought small groups and individuals from each village. The missionaries trained them and supervised them while Indian labor parties worked on the nearby agri-cultural fields seized for each mission. After this initial train-ing, the baptized Indians were returned to their villages and a new group was brought in. Overseers went out regularly to supervise and instruct the Indians in the use of the new plants, trees, and vines, and the new techniques and animals, as well as in the tenets of the new religion. Few Spanish were ever stationed at San Luis Rey, and the midlevel overseers there seem to have been members of the San Luiseño hier-archy. Consequently, the native population was not uprooted from its land base, nor was the economy destroyed while the new crops, animals, and religion were added and integrated into the existing pattern (Shipek 1977). Drought and intro-duced disease drastically reduced the native populations but did not destroy them.

In contrast, at San Juan Capistrano, which contained people of the San Luiseño ethnic nationality (White 1963:91), the Fran-ciscan missionaries followed the standard policy of bringing entire villages into the mission. This policy, combined with the more coastal, open, and less rugged character of the terri-tory, resulted in greater disruption of the semicultivated field resources by the practice of taking Indians out of their local environment and substituting the Spanish practice of manag-ing land for livestock rather than for food crops. The Span-ish colonial congregation policy resulted in greater concentra-tions in the mission and more exposure to contagious disease, plus a lack of sanitation, and this resulted in higher death rates (Shipek 1977).

Some Cupeño entered Mission San Diego in the early years, but only after 1821 were any significant number baptized at San

---

Luis Rey, and the major valley was used for the sheep pasture of the mission. Some Cahuilla were brought in and baptized in all three of the missions. The westerly portion of Cahuilla territory was within the sphere of Mission San Gabriel (the next mission north of San Juan Capistrano), but the colonial institutions did not disrupt the aboriginal patterns in the mountains and desert (Bean 1972:17). Major portions of Kumeyaay and Cahuilla territory were practically untouched by the Spaniards. Further, unconverted Indians—actually, those not controlled by the Spanish—were always in residence in scattered locations throughout the supposedly "controlled" portions of Kumeyaay, San Luiseño, Cupeño, and Cahuilla territory. Most reservation members are the descendants of these relatively uncontrolled, undisturbed people of the more interior mountainous regions plus survivors and refugees from the coastal missions.

Another contrast between the northerly California mission and the two southern missions comes from the fact that most of the San Luiseño and Kumeyaay were not fed at the missions (Shipek 1977). Only the sick, some elderly, the unmarried girls, and those trained and kept at the missions for craft specialties (leatherworkers, carpenters, and blacksmiths, for example) were fed directly from mission food supplies. The rest of the converted Indians were fed only during the relatively short time they were in the mission for religious training, for special religious services, and during their turn to provide labor for mission crop production, livestock maintenance, or construction projects. During most of the year they were expected to provide themselves with food. Consequently, they maintained their own land use, management, and tenure practices, adding a few appropriate European crops—including fruit trees, vines, wheat, and melons—and domestic animals. Colonial Spaniards disrupted Indian land use and tenure only in the actual mission-use areas, military posts, and early rancho (Euro-American) colonization areas near the coast.

In addition to feeding the Indians during the time they were at the missions, missionaries traded a part of the produce from mission agricultural fields and livestock to obtain the clothing rationed to converts. Most of the mission food production was used to feed the missionaries, the soldiers and their families, and visitors to the missions (Tac 1958). The two missions, San Diego and San Luis Rey, were in effect imposing a labor tax upon their neophytes. It was a periodic personal service tax that took Indians away from the labor of providing their own subsistence and that required that a part of their time be spent in communal labor on mission land for the communal purposes of the missions. The missions were not teaching individual land tenure or individual subsistence practices to these Indians. We cannot, therefore, look to the presence or teachings of the missions as the source of the individual tenure ideas held by the Southern California Indians. Instead, what little evidence exists concerning the Indian's use of his or her own time indicates that such time was spent in labor for his or her own subsistence (Tac 1958:21) and that when the Spanish arrived the Indians already had concepts of both individual tenure and the inheritance of such a right (Boscana 1933:78, 79; Shipek 1977), which they continued to practice.

The Mexican Period

Mexican independence from Spain and its declared intent to secularize the California missions initiated a period of increasing disruption of the Indian population after 1826. Full secularization, the transfer of the responsibility for congregations from the Franciscan missions to diocesan clerics supported by parishioners, finally occurred in 1834. It was followed by the almost complete dissipation of mission properties (Englehardt 1912, 1920, 1921, 1922). First, the missions and *asistencias* (subsidiary chapels) were placed under the control of secular *mayordomos*, who required salaries, subsistences, and services for their large families and relatives. This remuneration and service came from the forced labor of the Indians. Gradually, the Mexican governors granted the better, more productive mission lands to Mexican individuals as ranchos, and frequently these rancho grants enclosed Indian villages and fields within their boundaries. The grants included a statement that the grantee received all the bounded land described except for that occupied and used by the Indians. Actually, Mexican rancho grantees, some of whom included hispanicized Indians, used the people of the enclaved rancherias as forced peon labor and restricted them in many ways. For example, the Indians' water rights might be limited (Unclassified Expediente No. 163, California State Papers) or non-Indian cattle might be turned loose in their fields. Unless the Indians left the land, though, the rancho owners technically could not dispossess them of it (Englehardt 1920:243–268; Englehardt 1921:73–144; Englehardt 1922:80–94.

For any minor infraction of provincial regulations governing the Indians, they were sentenced to labor with leg-irons for public purposes, or for a private landowner (California State Papers, 1835–1839). Such infractions included going to town without a pass from the *mayordomo,* stealing a jug of *aguardiente* (liquor), or killing a calf. Depending on the offense and the opinion of the particular judge, sentences ran from two months to two years. The Mexican records also show that various Southern California Indian bands officially protested to the Mexican governor of California about intrusions upon their land and water rights, and about the other abuses of Indians committed by the appointed Mexican *mayordomos* and rancho grantees. Englehardt has discussed some of these abuses (1920:226–237; 1921:104–136). These same records also show repeated and numerous uprisings and revolts against the Mexicans. Attacks were generally organized by the inland bands and occurred most frequently between 1836 and 1841. At San Diego, for example, the Mexicans seldom left the presidio-pueblo area unless accompanied by a military guard.

In the process of secularizing and dismantling the missions, some Indian pueblos were established, and rancho grants were made to a few individual Indians. Existing records name four San Luiseño and Diegueño (Kumeyaay) pueblos and also indicate that several others may have existed. Those named are

Las Flores, Pala, San Pasqual, and San Dieguito (Shipek 1972:19; Englehardt 1920:234, 236, 240, 254; Englehardt 1921:100–114; Annual Report, Commissioner of Indian Affairs 1871:691; hereafter cited as ARCIA). By 1842, however, many of the Las Flores Indians had been driven from their land by the harassment and legal machinations of Pio Pico. In contrast, San Juan Capistrano was made into an ordinary pueblo, with both Indians and Mexicans receiving land within its boundaries (Englehardt 1922:140–148).

Within each Indian pueblo, every family received a house lot and agricultural fields for sustenance (Englehardt 1912:639). In common, they received the water and irrigation system or any other improvements the Indians had made under the missions. Further, each pueblo was to have "entrances and exits . . . and a commons, one league in length . . . [and] the league for the commons must be understood as meaning in every direction; hence that every commons must be four leagues square" (quoted in Englehardt 1922:92–93). Each pueblo was to have no more than 400 Indians. Thus by Mexican law the Indians of San Juan Capistrano should have been granted at least two pueblos, while those of San Diego and San Luis Rey should have been granted at least three or four pueblos each. Of the approximately twenty rancho grants made to Indians in Upper California, at least seven were made to San Luiseño Indians (Basic Records of Land Grants, Bancroft Library). A portion of one such grant, Cuca, still belongs to the heirs of the individual to whom it was granted.

One extant document indicates that the basic rancheria tenure-use system continued and incorporated new crops and animals into the preexisting pattern. The 1843 *expediente* written by Father Zalvidea of San Luis Rey to the Mexican governor (Shipek 1977:181, 182) transmitted a request from the Christian Indians of Cuca and Paome (Pauma) for a legal grant of the lands upon which they had their livestock, fruit trees, and vines. They stated that their stock and trees were maintained by their unconverted fathers while they labored at Mission San Luis Rey. They also requested the same protection for the unconverted Indians of those places, because they might later be converted or have children who would be. They stated that they had cultivated the land from some time past and considered it theirs by inheritance from their fathers. Individuals are listed along with an enumeration of their livestock, vines, and trees. The varying numbers of each item listed as belonging to each individual indicate that land quantities and uses were differentiated within the community at that time. It is also interesting to note that most of the lineage names listed for Cuca and Paome in 1843 are still present and represented by descendants on the reservations of that area—Rincon, Pauma, and La Jolla.

The American Period: Prereservation

Under the 1848 Treaty of Guadalupe Hidalgo, citizens of Mexico within the territory of California became citizens of the United States, with all the rights and immunities thereof. The treaty stipulated that their property rights would be respected and affirmed by title under the laws of the United States. Inasmuch as Mexican law considered settled Mission Indians as citizens, technically they were entitled to all the rights and immunities of the citizens of the United States (ARCIA 1883:xiv). In addition, the descendants of the people of the San Pasqual Indian Pueblo relate that when their ancestors gave aid to General Stephen Watts Kearny during and after the Battle of San Pasqual in December 1846, Kearny promised that the Americans would protect their land rights. Nonetheless, through a complex series of overlapping, confusing, and misunderstood events, deliberate misrepresentation, and inadequate instructions to local officials, the United States government failed to confirm legal title to the lands occupied and used by the Indians, with the exception of a few rancho grants to individual Indians. The scattered individual lots and small grants were ignored in the same fashion (Letter Book No. 1, Los Angeles District Land Office, Federal Records Center, Laguna Niguel, California).

Prior to the development of a state government, the majority of communications received by federal authorities in California seem to have been related to raids by Indians from the Colorado River and San Bernardino Mountain region (Ellison 1919:85). In many of these, the writer also remarked that, in contrast, most Southern California Indians were friendly to Americans. Several army officers were appointed as Indian subagents in Southern California, and the federal government instructed them to see that the peaceful settled Indians were not molested and to prevent Indians from "leading an idle and thriftless life" and "from encroaching upon the peaceable inhabitants of the land" (Ellison 1919:86). The federal officials were uncertain of the legal status of church real property and Indian rights therein, so they also instructed the subagents to protect the property of the missions. The correspondence also indicates that some agents doubted the validity of some non-Indian claims and felt that some Mexican rancho grants and sales of mission property were illegal. These letters indicated that title needed to be determined by a properly constituted authority, but that they (the Indian agents) were not that authority (Ellison 1919:91).

As a point of interest, it must be noted that some of the local agents, such as J. D. Hunter, did their best to protect the Indians. Others, including Cave Couts, Justin McKinstry, and H. S. Burton, acquired title to land that had been legally owned and occupied by Indians under Mexican law (San Diego County Recorder Files). At least one of them, Cave Couts, also remained in control of a considerable Indian labor force for a number of years (San Diego Union newspaper files, 1869–1875, and San Diego County Court Records). These men were merely following the example of many Mexican secular *mayordomos,* who had previously been entrusted with the care and protection of mission properties and Indian villages and who had proceeded to acquire the entrusted lands as rancho grants.

In 1849 the Department of the Interior was created, and it was given the supervisory powers over Indian affairs previously exercised by the War Department (Ellison 1919:111). That year the new secretary of the interior, together with the secretary of state, sent a special agent, William Carey Jones, to California to obtain information about land titles—that is, the land rights of the missions, the Indians, and the Mexican settlers and rancho grantees—under the laws of Spain and Mexico. During the course of his investigation Jones speculated in California mission land. From the Mexican claimant he purchased the land of Mission San Luis Rey, including the valleys of Pala (containing an Indian pueblo) and San Juan, and he resold this claim at a large profit (San Diego County Recorder Files). His Washington superiors received his report in 1849, and it may have been the source of information upon which Congress based the law determining procedures to validate private claims to land in the newly acquired territory (An Act to Ascertain and Settle the Private Land Claims in the State of California, 9 *United States States Statutes* 632, 634).

In 1850 the federal government also sent special commissioners to deal with Indians throughout California (9 *United States Statutes* 544, Sept. 30, 1850). During the negotiations in northern California, the Garra uprising focused attention on Indian problems in Southern California, particularly the problem of Cupa with J. J. Warner, a Mexican rancho grantee. In 1852 the commissioners brought treaties to be signed by the Indian leaders of the southern region. The draft treaties provided a very large reservation in the mountains, and they would have allowed the majority of villages to remain on their own lands and provided sufficient land for the existing coastal remnants to move into the mountains. But when the California draft treaties were sent to the Senate for ratification, the new Anglo-American settlers and the Mexican rancho owners objected to the proposed treaties. The California legislature sent a report to Washington opposing the treaties and recommending the removal of all Indians to Indian Territory (the present Oklahoma). The minority report, written by J. J. Warner, the Mexican rancho grantee, opposed the treaties but recommended that the Mission Indians be allowed to remain on small homesites because they supplied an excellent, indeed the only, source of labor in Southern California (Warner, Minority Report 1852). As a result of the legislative opposition and a newspaper outcry from the settlers, the Senate shelved the treaties. But no one informed the Indians that the treaties had not been ratified and that they therefore had no title to their land.[6]

During the same years, the California state government was formed and the state constitution written. On April 22, 1850, the legislature passed an Act for the Government and Protection of the Indians. This act instructed local authorities to determine the lands occupied and used by Indians, mark their boundaries, and prevent settlers from entering upon such lands and disturbing the Indians (Shipek 1969a). There is some evidence to show that local sheriffs throughout Southern California did this, and that for a short time, until 1865, some effort was made to protect Indian land use rights, at least in San Diego County (Shipek 1969a; Jackson 1885; ARCIA 1871:343; Huntington Library MS. HM:CT 2564). The amount of land so protected was not based on legal rights but on what the local official considered to be sufficient for the Indians. As the non-Indian population increased, this act and its protection were apparently forgotten by federal, state, and local governments, even though it was mentioned in the 1891 Act for the Relief of the Mission Indians (Appendix C).

On March 3, 1851, Congress passed an Act to Ascertain and Settle the Private Land Claims in the State of California (9 *United States Statutes* 631). This act appointed a federal land commission to hear evidence presented by those who claimed valid Mexican titles, and to issue valid title under United States law to all those who had been determined to have valid title under Mexican law. This act also required the federal land commissioners to determine the lands held, used, and occupied by Indians. Thus the act specifically required the commission to determine Indian claims but did not require the Indians to present their claims.

Examination of the records demonstrates that the commissioners did not fulfill their duty to determine Indian land rights; instead, they ignored all the evidence that once existed. Thus, Indian villages within rancho range boundaries that had specified rights and that could not be dispossessed under

Mexican law lost those rights because they were ignored by the federal land commissioners. The Indian pueblos, and the San Juan Capistrano Indians in the pueblo of San Juan Capistrano (who under Mexican law had documented rights to communal areas as well as individual land rights within the pueblos), had those rights ignored, even though evidence exists that the data on Indian pueblo rights was in the hands of the land commission.[7] The commission also ignored the Mexican laws concerning basic legal use rights of other settled villages, those that were neither pueblos nor on rancho grants.

All the land within California that did not have title confirmed to individuals or to former Mexican pueblos by the federal land commission (San Diego and Los Angeles, for example) became part of the public lands of the United States and as such was open to preemption and homestead filing by settlers under a variety of laws relating to the settling of public lands.

For legal purposes, such as the Indian Claims Case (Dockets 31, 37, and 80 before the Indian Claims Commission), the land was lost in 1851. In actual fact, until 1865 most villages in the interior of Southern California and a few near the coast continued in relatively undisturbed use of their lands (Shipek 1969, 1972, 1977, 1980) even though they did not acquire legal title, due to the improper inaction of the federal land commission. Although a few were dispossessed before 1865, most Indians remained in their villages, farming their lands and keeping some stock.

An examination of local records—such as tax records,[8] settler's diaries, agricultural records, news items, preemption records, and the 1860 federal census of agriculture—indicates that the majority of Southern California Indians continued as food-producing, settled village people. During this period, much of the correspondence between local officials, citizens, and the federal government was not about the settled Indians but rather the "idle and dissolute Indians wandering about and abandoning their lands." The attention of the American government, just like that of the Mexican government before it, was focused on the "troublesome" portion of the Indian population, not on the hardworking farming Indians. Further, in

Southern California those Indians who were "wandering" seem to have been (1) those already pushed out of their productive lands (near the major towns and in some cases along the major emigrant routes), (2) those being subjected to forced labor for the rancheros and settlers and attempting to evade such labor, (3) those not really wandering but going temporarily to one of their traditional distant food resource areas (the locations of pine nuts, acorns, agave, or seafood) with the full intention of returning to their crops and adobe homes, (4) those searching for native emergency plant foods during the droughts and crop failures rather than sitting and starving in their houses, (5) those without family responsibilities, and (6) those who were irresponsible, just as there were irresponsible people among the Mexicans and the Anglo-American settlers (Bell 1927).

Local records indicate that the majority of Indians formed the labor base for all agricultural and stock-raising activity as well as for whaling, fishing, stevedoring, various industries, and road and railroad building, in addition to their food-producing activities on their own farms and the sale of some of that produce. These records indicate that in spite of some land loss, Indians continued to support themselves by the farming, stock raising, and food gathering patterns that had developed during the Spanish and Mexican periods (1860 Federal Census of Agriculture; Annual Reports of the Commissioner of Indian Affairs; San Diego County Court and Tax Records) and that they received practically no rations or aid of any kind from any source. These records also indicate that within each village or rancheria each man cultivated and was considered the owner of his own fields, with the rights of inheritance and sale, and that the grazing areas were considered commons for the use of the entire membership. To supplement their income from farming and ranching operations, the men also sheared sheep and performed various types of ranch labor for nearby American and Mexican ranchers. Entrepreneurs among the Indians had developed larger fields, orchards, vineyards, or herds of livestock to obtain a cash income. Thus the differential landownership pattern related to

different land uses that had existed in the previous period
continued in relation to both the amount and types of land
needed for the different purposes.

To conclude, by 1865 many Indians living in the mountains of
Southern California still occupied ancestral lands. They believed that they had been protected in their use of the rancheria and ethnic territorial lands by General Kearny and by
the subagents, in spite of their having lost some coastal rancheria lands to a few of the agents. Second, they also believed
that their lands had been affirmed to them by the treaties
they had signed. They were unaware of the treaties' need for
ratification by the Senate. Third, many had papers given
them by county sheriffs that delineated their land boundaries
and declared their right to use that land unmolested. They
were unaware that the California law regarding their land
right would not be enforced after 1865. Further, through the
years a number of special commissions sent out by the Office
of Indian Affairs to investigate Indian rights, some of the Indian agents and subagents in Southern California, and various "friends" trying to protect Indians had assured them of
their land rights. However, none of these "friends" or agents
told them that the various papers they had been given lacked
legal standing and that the one commission that had the power to confirm legal title was ignoring them, in spite of specific
instructions ordering it to determine the Indians' title to the
lands they were using.

The American Period: Reservations

After 1865, increasing numbers of settlers entered Southern
California looking for farmland. Inasmuch as Indian-occupied lands were technically public lands open to preemption
and homestead settlement, settlers began taking the best,
well-watered Indian farmland and dispossessing the Indians,
even taking their adobe homes. Through the efforts of
friends and sympathizers who publicized this shoddy treatment of farming Indians, the president was persuaded to establish, by executive order, reservations at San Pasqual and

Pala that were intended for all the Southern California Indians and some Indians from northern California (41st Cong., 2d sess., House Ex. Doc. 296). The reservation included Townships 12 and 13 South, Ranges 1 East and 1 West, and Township 9 South, Ranges 1 and 2 West of the San Bernardino Meridian, a total of six townships, excluding the portions of Mexican rancho grants within them, which totaled about one township. Much of this reserved land was rocky and rugged, not particularly good even for grazing, much less as farmland for *all* the Indians of Southern California. The lands were adequate only for the villages already in these locations—Pala, San Pasqual, and parts of Rincon and Mesa Grande.

Many Southern California Indians opposed this reservation scheme because they did not want to leave their own homes and farms. Those at San Pasqual and Pala objected to being overwhelmed by the large numbers of other Indians who would be pushed into their small farming villages and valleys.[9] All objected to northern California Indians being moved to Southern California. The reservation plan was promoted by the rancho grant owners, who wanted to get Indian villages off the grants but who wanted Indians nearby as a labor force when needed. It was promoted by settlers who wanted the land of non–rancho grant Indian villages that were not included in this reservation. It was also promoted by people with a genuine sympathy for, and a desire to ameliorate the plight of, Indian farmers being evicted from the isolated villages. These sympathizers felt that a combined reservation would provide a safe haven for Indians. Most Indians and other sympathizers were, however, convinced that the few Indians, such as Manuel Cota, who favored this reservation scheme were henchmen of the rancho grant owners seeking to dispossess the Indians of their land use but to retain them as laborers. The executive order was canceled in 1871 due to the combined protests of the Indians, these knowledgeable sympathizers, other settlers (who wanted the executive order lands), and newspapers. The latter claimed that in Southern California "only peaceful Christian citizens" existed, farming their own lands, and that "no Indians" lived in these two valleys.[10]

As increasing numbers of settlers entered Southern California, the eviction of Indians from their farms proceeded at a more rapid pace. Indians petitioned the General Land Office for land rights, but according to this office the laws providing for the settlement of public lands through preemption and homestead claims contained no provision allowing Indians to file claims (Los Angeles District Land Office, Letter Book No. 1, pp. 308, 428–430, 444–445, 448, 458) thus Indian claims could not be validated or recognized.

By 1875 conditions for farming and ranching Indians had deteriorated, and they had lost so much land that continuing publicity about the treatment of Indians resulted in another presidential executive order withdrawing a number of small reservations from the public domain. Many of the Indians at first favored this reservation scheme, but they later came to oppose it. They followed the leadership of the traditional San Luiseño leader, General Oligario Calac. He stated that the reservations being surveyed were not preserving Indian homes and farms but were removing Indians to poor land beside their farms, that is, to lands that could not possibly provide a living, or even homes, for all of them (correspondence of M. Wheeler with General Land Office, 1875–1876, Letter Book 1, Federal District Land Office, Los Angeles). Poor as they were, however, some reservations came into existence at this time (see Appendix B).

By this time, however, the Indians were beginning to learn that an executive order could be canceled and did not confer a secure title to the land. The settlers were also aware of this insecurity and continued to file homestead claims on, and to move onto, these reserved lands. Some claimed their move predated the executive order. Some moved onto reservation lands and claimed the Indian improvements as their own, not necessarily for the purpose of acquiring the land, but rather to be able to file for payment from the government for the "loss of their improvements" when the land was finally secured to the Indians (ARCIA 1870–1885).

Land for many lesser-known rancherias was not included in the 1875 executive order, and the loss of Indian farms and grazing lands continued. Congress, prodded by the Indian Rights Association, continued to investigate the condition of the Mission Indians (Jackson and Kinney 1885; Painter 1886) but delayed taking legislative action to secure Indians in "the peaceable possession of the land they occupy or which may be selected for and assigned to them" (49th Cong., 1st sess., Senate Ex. Doc. 15).

When the Indian Homestead Act of 1883 and the later Public Domain Allotment Act of 1887 were passed, a number of Southern California Indians began filing for their individual lands under the provisions of these acts. Some filings were completed, and many individual homesteads still exist. For some Indians, one impediment to filing for a homestead was the requirement to separate from a tribal group. This had already happened for many Southern California Indians. When some bands lost all their farmlands, and others lost portions of theirs, the dispossessed families had scattered, some taking refuge with more isolated bands where they had close relatives, others finding scattered small holdings where they built shelters and continued to subsist. Whichever life they chose, they continued to follow long-established patterns of individual family subsistence. Each family had always provided the major portion of its own subsistence from its own lands, and when the repeated extensive droughts of this region had brought disaster, the families, and sometimes the Indians as individuals (Kenneally 1965:344), had scattered far and wide, seeking to survive. Thus, taking a homestead was merely validating title to their places of refuge.

Some well-meaning non-Indian individuals and organizations (as well as those who desired these scattered lands) and some Indian leaders branded the Indians who took homesteads as traitors to the bands and continued to press for the establishment of reservations that would separate and isolate Indians from other settlers. Some of the homesteads were scattered and interspersed with settlers. Friends of Indians were aware that it would be difficult to protect the individual Indian homestead lands from encroachment and felt that a distinctly separate grouping of Indians on reservations could be more easily protected. In addition, some Indian leaders were aware that individual homestead titles would destroy the economic and political control they had over the Indian labor gangs for sheep shearing, harvesting, and other purposes. An employer used a captain to hire, manage, and pay the labor gang. Further, a reservation captain could not punish an Indian by taking homestead land when he was not obeyed (Calac Journal 1887), as some captains had apparently done under aboriginal tenure. Finally, other Indians saw no reason to file papers on lands they already considered to be rightfully their own.

The publicity about the treatment of Southern California Indians, combined with the 1885 Jackson and Kinney report to Congress, finally resulted in 1891 in the passage of the Act for the Relief of the Mission Indians (see Appendix C). Under this act, a commission was appointed to investigate and determine the actual extent of the lands used and occupied by each band of Mission Indians. Such lands were then to be withdrawn from public land status, and trust patents were to be issued to each band. If the lands the Indians occupied were already in the legal possession of ranchos and settlers, then alternate lands were to be found or purchased for them.

Some of the Indian homesteads upon which the final papers had not yet been filed were absorbed into, and became part of, the reservations. In addition, some Indians were persuaded to leave homestead lands and enter the reservations, and others were simply pushed off the homesteads by white settlers and told to go to the reservations. But the Indians also had friends who were opposed to pushing all Indians onto reservations and who recognized that the proposed reservations would be inadequate to provide farms for all of them. These friends advocated homesteads for Indians. Other people posed as friends and advocated homesteads for all Indians in order to acquire some of the Indian lands that had previously been reserved by executive order. There remains the distinct possibility that more land would have remained in Indian hands had there been no pressures against Indians taking homesteads and had those truly interested in Indian welfare supported both reservations and homestead lands for Indians.

Thus, between 1850 and 1891 both well-meaning and self-serving individuals demanded reservations for Indians, and some individuals of both types opposed reservation schemes. Some saw reservations as a means of protecting Indian landownership, and others saw reservations as a means of taking the remaining farmland from Indians while keeping Indians handy as a cheap labor force. Each position had its Indian advocates.[11] Some members of each group were convinced that they were advocating the solution that would provide the best protection for Indians as a whole, while other advocates of each position were self-serving, as were some of the Indians. The net result of these confusing pressures, presentations, and misrepresentations was that less land remained in Indian ownership.

The commission established by the 1891 Act for the Relief of the Mission Indians is known as the Smiley Commission. It was composed of Albert K. Smiley, the chairman and a businessman of Redlands, California, and Lake Mohonk, New York; Judge Joseph B. Morse of Lapeer, Michigan; and Professor C. C. Painter of Washington, D.C. All three were active in the Indian Rights Association of Philadelphia, and the Lake Mohonk Conference of Friends of the Indians. Their correspondence and reports in the National Archives and in the Smiley papers in Redlands show that all three men made a sincere effort to investigate the situation and to determine and reserve the proper lands, that they were concerned with preserving individual Indians rights fairly and justly within the reservations, and that they were concerned with obtaining and preserving the water rights necessary for farming on the reservations. Funding and time limitations, however, reduced the accuracy and effectiveness of their work, and they were unable to visit all the villages, especially those in the rugged parts of Kumeyaay territory. Also, their effectiveness was reduced by the existence of deliberately or accidentally confused earlier survey lines, an unsympathetic General Land

Office, and also less competent, or some possible less-than-honest, employees and surveyors who were necessarily entrusted with carrying out the work of actually locating lands and boundaries.[12] Considering these obstacles and the scattered nature of Indian lands, the commission accomplished a great deal in the limited time and within the limited budget available to it.

Between 1892 and 1910, officials of the Office of Indian Affairs (later the Bureau of Indian Affairs) gradually surveyed the lands reserved by the Smiley Commission and then issued trust patents for the reservations to the respective bands. In the establishment of the trust patent reservations, only a few bands were moved entirely out of their aboriginal territory. For example, due to clerical or surveyor error, the San Pasqual reservation was located in the wrong township. Land was reserved where no San Pasqual Indians lived and that was one township north of the land on which band members sought refuge after losing the San Pasqual Pueblo land. Another reservation, Cosmit, was located within band territory, but it was on an uninhabited and uninhabitable waterless, rocky hilltop rather than in the diagonally adjacent section, where the people were living near a spring. Other types of errors were also made, such as trust patenting the land of one band to a different nearby band.

Some of the scattered, small southern Kumeyaay groups did not have lands reserved for them specifically. Smiley's intention was that they would move onto nearby large reservations, and some effort was apparently made to convince them to do so, but it was unsuccessful (Smiley Report, Capitan Grande section, National Archives). In this category were Indian people near Mission San Diego, in Jamul, El Cajon Valley, Spring Valley, and in many small valleys of southern San Diego County.

Some Indian groups, although known to the Mission Indian agents, had no provisions made for them, and no evidence exists that the Smiley Commission members visited such groups. For example, while the San Juan Capistrano Indians had ceased being mentioned by Indian agents after 1880, the

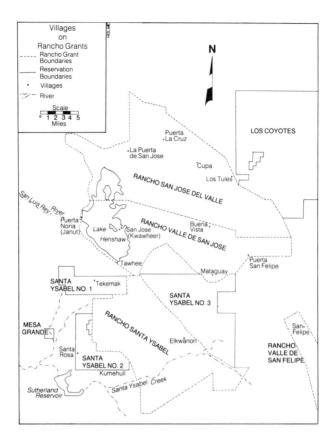

Map 2. Indian Villages on the Rancho Grants of Valle de San Jose, San Jose del Valle, San Felipe, and Santa Ysabel

Mission San Luis Rey group were still listed by agents until 1905. As of 1986, both groups were attempting to achieve federal recognition.

Villages on Rancho Grants

The preceding discussion focused primarily on those bands whose homes and farmlands were on the public lands of the United States. Those bands that were on rancho grants lost title to their lands through a slightly different but related

---

sequence. Under Spanish and Mexican land laws, grants of rancho lands always had a clause that excluded the land in the use and occupancy of Indians (ARCIA 1873:37). The grantee could not legally dispossess Indians of their lands within the rancho's boundaries. The information concerning this exclusion was apparently not presented to the land commission. Neither did the federal land commission fulfill its instructions to ascertain Indian land rights. Titles to rancho grants were confirmed without the exclusion of Indian lands, and therefore grant owners began to institute ejection proceedings against the Indians (ARCIA 1881:13).

Some countersuits were filed on behalf of the Indians, including one for the Pauma Band. The case for San Jacinto was carried to the California Supreme Court, where the Indians won (*Byrne* v. *Alas et al.,* January 31, 1888). The San Diego superior court specifically rejected that case as a precedent in the case of the Cupeño against the owners of Warner's Rancho and decided for the grant owners. The Cupa Indians appealed this adverse decision to the United States Supreme Court, which in 1901 decided in favor of the grantees (*Barker* v. *Harvey,* 181 U.S. 481). The Supreme Court based its decision against the Indians on the grounds that they had not presented their claims to the federal land commission, as required of all persons claiming title from Mexico according to the act that created that commission. However, it was not the Indians but the land commission that had not carried out the requirements of the law. The Supreme Court made a decision (which at a later date it called a "political" decision) and refused to allow the *Barker* v. *Harvey* decision to be used as a precedent in other cases (*United States* v. *Santa Fe Pacific Railroad Company,* 314 U.S. 399, 350). In other words, the Supreme Court also set a precedent that stated, in effect, that it is acceptable to break the law and to steal land if it is done against American Indian populations and the lands stolen are Indian lands (see the discussion of Pechanga in Chapter 4 and boundary questions in Chapter 6). All of the grant owners who had previously agreed to abide by the decision in the Warner's Rancho case were now able to evict the remaining Indian villages—Santa Ysabel, Cupa, Mataguay, San Felipe,

Puerta La Cruz, San Jose, Tawhee, Puerta Noria, and Cuca.
Many Indians of the villages in the Santa Ysabel and San Jacinto
ranchos, while still living in their homes, had not been allowed to plant crops or graze their stock on their former
lands. Instead they planted crops and grazed their livestock
on hill lands bordering the ranchos wherever they had been
able to find a little water. These were the lands that had been
reserved by the 1875 executive order and that were now trust
patented to the bands.

Even though the original grantee of Cuca Rancho was an Indian
of that village, one of her heirs evicted the other families
from the village between 1879 and 1889 and sold a portion
of the grant to a non-Indian. Most of the evicted people had
found land near relatives on Rincon or La Jolla reservations,
which together surrounded the Cuca grant. Some of the
grantee descendants still own the unsold portion of the grant.

Although the Smiley Commission was empowered to purchase
land occupied by Indians in cases where non-Indians had a
legal claim to the land, generally the grant owners or settlers
(as in San Pasqual Valley) asked highly inflated prices for the
lands and improvements. As mentioned earlier, in many cases
the improvements for which these persons asked recompense
had actually been made by the Indians and had been forcibly
taken by the settlers or grant owners. The Smiley Commission was certain that Congress would not approve purchases
at the outrageous prices and sought land elsewhere. The only
lands the commission purchased at this time were those occupied by the Indians on Pauma Rancho. Here, a small amount
of land was purchased from the Catholic bishop of the diocese, the owner of the rancho grant. This purchase included
three plots of land and water rights. The largest, known as
Pauma, contained 250 acres, with the right to thirty inches of
water from Pauma Creek. The second piece, Yuima, was the
home of one family and contained 3.5 acres, with 3.5 inches
of water. The third small plot was merely the right to lifetime
occupancy for one elderly childless couple.

In the case of villages on Warner's Rancho (Cupeño, San
Luiseño, and Kumeyaay), Mataguay Rancho (Kumeyaay),

---

and San Felipe Rancho (Kumeyaay), the owners were asking an equally inflated price for the entire ranchos and refused to sell only the portions used and occupied by the Indians. (This presents a case of the basic difference in the value of land with and without surface water, because the Indian villages occupied the portions having surface water). Therefore a special commission was appointed to examine lands offered to the government and charged with the selection of the best location for the government to purchase the lands for the Indians about to be evicted from these two ranchos. The government appointed as chairman of this commission Charles F. Lummis, the founder of the Southwest Museum in Los Angeles and the publisher of *Out West* and *Land of Sunshine* magazines. Lummis had also founded the Sequoya League, whose primary activity had been to investigate and publicize the plight of Southern California Indians and to bring welfare aid to the Indian villages. He knew that the Indians did not want to leave their own villages. Unable to arrange their purchase, however, he conscientiously found the best land that was available for purchase, recommending the purchase of 3,438 acres in the valley of Pala and the reserving of approximately 8,000 acres of adjoining public lands (Preliminary Report of the Warner's Ranch Indian Advisory Commission 1902). The purchase would incorporate the small San Luiseño reservation that already existed at Pala. The reserved adjoining public lands were primarily brush and woodlands that could be used for grazing and firewood and that would also provide a source for some of the native food and medicinal plants still used by the Indians.

The land at Pala was purchased, and in 1903 the army came and moved the people from the villages on the Warner's and San Felipe ranchos to the newly purchased reservation of Pala. The villages moved included Cupa, San Jose, Puerta La Cruz, Puerta Ignoria (Noria), Tawhee, Mataguay, Puerta de San Felipe, and San Felipe. While the army took a majority of these people to Pala with what they could carry on their backs and in their wagons, a few elderly people hid in the hills to die there. Some people fled over the hills and went to various cities in Southern California, and some fled to other reservations, requested refuge, and were accepted by these bands. Santa Ysabel, Mesa Grande, La Jolla, Los Coyotes, and Morongo are known to have accepted such refugees. The newly enlarged reservation of Pala now contained the original San Luiseño members and some Kumeyaay, but the majority were Cupeño, that is, the people from Cupa or Warner's Hot Springs. During the next few years, several pieces of land were removed from the newly created Pala Reservation because tourmaline gem crystals were discovered there. Bureau correspondence (Federal Records Center, Laguna Niguel) indicates that it was not bureau policy to include lands containing minerals, but only farm and grazing lands. Thus the mining properties, which could have provided a good income to the Indians, were removed from the reservation. The uninsulated temporary housing placed on Pala for the relocatees was totally inadequate compared to the adobe houses in their original villages. It was not designed for the dampness and chill of Southern California mountains in the winter. In addition, relocating the people from a more dispersed residence pattern and crowding them into a small village that lacked sanitation resulted in increased illness and death, especially among the children and elders.

The purchase of Pala and the forced migration of various villages essentially closed the period during which the federal government imposed its system of restricted land ownership on the Southern California Indians. The only exceptions were the purchases of some small pieces of slightly better agricultural land on the fringe of some reservations and the purchase of more adequate farmland for the Campo Band in about 1910 and small pieces at other dates for a few other reservations.[13]

Proposed Additions to the Reservations

More recently, in the fall of 1985, after examining the public lands of Southern California, the Bureau of Land Management proposed the transfer of some lands to the U.S. Forest Service and of others, which adjoin Indian reservations, to the nearby reservation. Congressman Duncan Hunter intro-

duced a bill into the House of Representatives to effect that
change. If passed by Congress, the proposed transfer would
add over 8,000 acres to thirteen reservations, divided as follows:

Barona Reservation	857.13 acres
Cahuilla Reservation	611.88
Campo Reservation	3,189.64
Jamul Reservation	80.00
La Jolla Reservation	355.51
La Posta Reservation	85.00
Mesa Grande Reservation	800.00
Morongo Reservation	150.00
Pala Reservation	385.00
Pechanga Reservation	302.64
Rincon Reservation	320.00
Santa Ysabel Reservation	21.52
Soboba Reservation	960.00

A few persons holding valid existing grazing permits will have
the opportunity to purchase such acreage if they desire, and
existing rights-of-way will be preserved under the transfer of
title in trust to the above-named bands. The bands concerned
are hoping that the bill will pass and that the first major addition to their inadequate reservation lands will occur.

The Allotment Program

The trust patents issued for each reservation gave each band
member of the named band an undivided interest in the reservation as a whole. The Smiley Commission had indicated,
as had Helen Hunt Jackson (Jackson and Painter 1885), that
everywhere in Southern California the Indians were ready
for individual allotments, or individual title to their homes
and farmland. Both had recommended that surveying for individual allotments begin immediately after title to the whole
had been secured. Most Indian groups also requested the immediate division of the lands to individuals in order to secure
title to their existing personal or inherited improvements, or
they desire to place new improvements upon the land having
secure title.

Grazing lands were not allotted, because most reservations lacked enough such land to allot each family the legal minimum 160-acre grazing unit. Depending on the amount of farmland available, the head of each family was to be allotted up to twenty acres of approximately equal quality land for a homesite and irrigated and/or dry farmland. Unmarried adults were to be allowed ten acres. The allotments were to be laid out in an equal-sized rectangular pattern that would fit into the artificial section, township, and range (cadastral) public land survey of the United States. A few reservations (Sycuan and Pechanga, for example) were immediately mapped on this basis, and the allotments were approved by the Bureau of Indian Affairs and the General Land Office.

This idealized, equalized, rectangular, bureaucratic allotment system did not conform, however, to the varying types of land use and amount of improvements that already existed, or to the irregular shapes of arable valley land. Nor did it conform to the remnants of the pre-Spanish landownership pattern that still existed in some places (DuBois 1908:159). It must be remembered that most reservations were within traditional rancheria territories and that long-term family and individual rights to land had accrued. The Indians wanted title to the improved lands they already held and used individually, so they objected to the way in which the allotting and surveying were being done.

In 1892 one of the first allotting agents, Kate Foote, pointed out the irregular nature of the land and of the existing improvements. She sought permission to make irregularly bounded allotments. She received such permission from the office of the commissioner of Indian affairs and proceeded with surveying and allotting in this metes-and-bounds fashion (Letters of the Commissioner of Indian Affairs, National Archives). Rincon, at least, was surveyed in this way, and the Indian owners received preliminary title papers. But the General Land Office refused to accept the surveys made in this fashion, and they were never approved. In the furor over this survey, Miss Foote resigned and the surveyor working under her was fired by her successor (Smiley Papers, National Archives, Record Group 75). By 1895, Cave Couts, Jr. (whose opposition to Indian land rights and pro-settler bias was well known [Odell 1939]) was hired to finish the survey of reservation boundaries and allotment divisions (Smiley Papers, National Archives; Couts Papers, Huntington Library). According to the Indians who witnessed the process, he resolved all boundary disputes in favor of the non-Indian settlers.

Pechanga, where the majority of people were refugees evicted by the sheriff from the Temecula rancho grants in 1875, was allotted in 1892 at the request of the people. According to Jackson (Jackson and Painter 1885:29) these people had originally planned to make individual claims to the land under the provisions of the 1883 Indian Homestead Act but had been prevailed upon to accept an executive order reservation. However, they expressed their disappointment when they discovered they did not have individual title to their lands within this reservation. Their request to the Smiley Commission was that immediate allotment follow trust patenting of the reservation. Miss Foote also surveyed the Capitan Grande Reservation for allotment at this time. Although as late as 1960 some members were still under the impression that they had allotments, the map was never approved, and the land remained in undivided title. Sycuan, a very small southern Kumeyaay reservation, was mapped and allotted using the rectangular survey system in 1894, but the allotments did not conform to the member's preexisting ownership and use of the land. The people were dissatisfied, and the majority ignored the allotments and for many years continued to use the land as they always had. Only in the present generation has there been an effort to conform house locations to the inherited federal land allotments.

Other groups, such as the group from Santa Ysabel, which still had cases in court over its eviction from the land grants, refused to accept allotments on the poor, hilly lands of the reservation. They felt that by accepting such allotments they would be prejudicing their case and giving up claim for recovery of their farmland from the grant owners.

At other villages, Indians were aware that the quantity of land specified as an allotment for each Indian under the General

Allotment Act of 1887 and also in the 1891 Act for the Relief of the Mission Indians was 20 acres arable or 160 grazing. When their entire reservation obviously could not supply that amount of land to each family, they opposed accepting smaller allotments. They wanted their previously owned and held lands, which had been taken by settlers, or at least the full amount of land the law allowed.

Many Indians, even those without active court cases, concluded that they would be prejudicing their claims to previously held lands by accepting these minuscule allotments. For example, at Mesa Grande a prolonged controversy erupted between the settlers and the Indians over the external boundaries of the reservation lands (trust patented as Santa Ysabel Nos. 1 and 2; see discussion in Chapter 4). Here a series of repeated boundary surveys progressively reduced the lands of the Indians and crowded several Indian families onto the remaining lands.

Finally, bands that had accepted refugees and had allowed them to live on the poorer lands in a subordinate position objected to the loss of their individually held and improved lands to these refugees. The Indians were well aware of the differing qualities and quantities of land and water needed for even a bare subsistence farm. In some cases, even without a refugee problem, the members of a band held differing amounts of land and had various improvements upon the land and objected to the equalization, which led to the loss of their aboriginally owned land and improvements to other members. In other words, contrary to the United States ideal concerning an individual's ownership rights with respect to improvements, the government was still confiscating the private property of some Indian families and imposing "communal" and "equal" rights to insufficient farmland—which meant, potentially, equal poverty—on all Indians.

Organized Opposition

In 1892 a new interband and interreservation organization began to develop. The organization of "troublemakers" (as the bureau called them) was based on opposition to the external boundary surveys, which allowed formerly Indian-used lands to be turned over to settlers. Interestingly, the leader of this organization had visited the Paiute Ghost Dance and used this form to develop the core of his oppositional organization (Bean, personal communication). This organization also opposed the individual allotment surveys, which would drastically reduce the amount of land held by each Indian and/or result in the loss of some improvements to other Indians. The Indians' opposition was not to individual ownership per se but to the limiting effects of the surveys, the loss of individual improvements, and the overall loss to white settlers. This early organized opposition to the allotment program centered at Morongo, Santa Ysabel, Mesa Grande, and the other mountain Kumeyaay reservations, and it caused the entire allotment program to halt between 1896 and 1920, except on the purchased lands of Pala from 1903–1905.

After 1917 the Indian Bureau reactivated the allotment program for Southern California Indians based on two additional acts of Congress (Section 17 of the act of June 25, 1910, 36 Stat. L., 859, and the act of March 2, 1917, 39 Stat. L., 969–76) which authorized "the allotment of irrigable lands to Mission Indians of California in such acres as may be in their best interest" (Letter of Franklin Lane to Julio A. Norte and others, Sept. 24, 1919, Bureau of Indian Affairs Records, National Archives). Throughout the years since 1891 some San Luiseño reservations had regularly petitioned for allotment title (Mission Indian Agency Records, 1900–1915, National Archives), expecting the title to be based on the earlier surveys. However, the allotting agent and surveyors began the process on Morongo and by July 1919 had approved an allotment schedule for that reservation over the protest of Indians who had lost improvements they had developed based on the 1891 assignments. Here, as on the San Luiseño reservations, the allotting agents ignored irregularly shaped individual improvements based on land configurations and mapped equal-sized rectangular plots of five acres, except on some Coachella Valley reservations, where more land was available per member. The size of the allotment depended on the amount

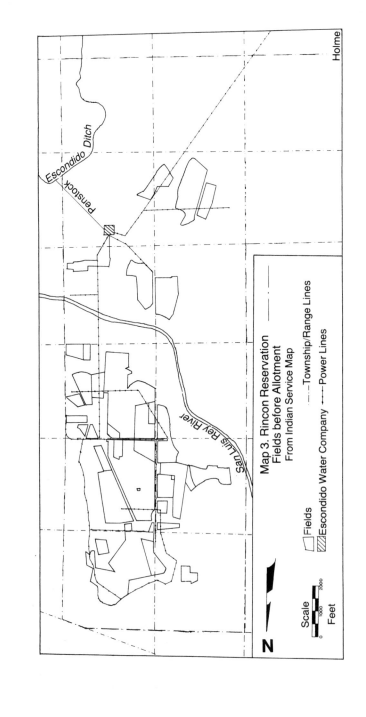

Map 3. Rincon Reservation Fields before Allotment

From Indian Service Map

Fields

Escondido Water Company

Township/Range Lines

Power Lines

Escondido Ditch

Penstock

San Luis Rey River

Holme

Scale

Feet

0   1000   2000

N

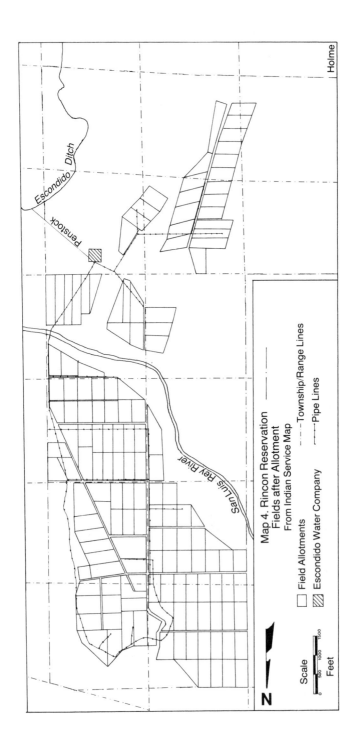

Map 4. Rincon Reservation Fields after Allotment
From Indian Service Map

Field Allotments

Escondido Water Company

Township/Range Lines

Pipe Lines

Scale

Feet

N

Escondido Ditch

Penstock

San Luis Rey River

Holme

of dry and irrigable farmland and the number of band members per reservation. For example, on Rincon each person was allotted five acres instead of the original twenty acres to heads of families and ten acres to single persons as planned, surveyed, and "assigned" in 1892. Large families benefited and small families were penalized. Furthermore, five acres was not a viable farm size for an individual. Even families with four or more children realized that in the next generation each family would be limited to five or fewer acres. Many families lost improvements that had been developed based on their 1892 papers from Kate Foote and on some assignments made between 1893 and 1910 by bureau surveyors. Some families refused allotments and lived on tribal land; others left the reservation (Shipek field notes). Court cases were filed in opposition to the allotments both in Riverside County (Morongo) and San Diego County (La Jolla and Rincon). The government won both cases in the late 1920s and proceeded with the allotment program based on five acres per person, again confiscating private improvements. The bureau appraised the improvements and paid for them, but according to many elders, the bureau appraisal did not meet the value of the actual long-term loss to each family. Southern California Indians felt a great deal of bitterness toward the government, and factionalism within the bands increased. The oppositional organization, now called the Mission Indian Federation, gained new members. Indian antagonism to allotment was now so great that the bureau started no additional mapping, and the allotment program was not extended to other reservations. Also, the disastrous effects of allotment on the midwestern reservations had become apparent (Haas 1957), and the program officially ceased unless allotments were requested by the members of a reservation. Since 1930 the Coachella Valley reservations have had a somewhat different history and will be discussed separately from the other reservations (see Chapter 4).

The unique history of Pala provides a special situation. In 1903 some 3,438 acres were purchased for the Cupeño, San Luiseño, and Kumeyaay evicted from the Warner's and San Felipe rancho grants. These lands and people were joined to the original San Luiseño reservation of Pala and were thereafter administered as a unit. A very small group of San Luiseño were the only Indians with accrued land rights and surveyed, confirmed allotments. All the rest, new residents, were given newly surveyed and confirmed allotments within a relatively few years. A centralized village was planned, and the new occupants received a town lot and farm plots of irrigable and dry lands. Pala was the only reservation planned with a central village surrounded by its farm and grazing land. Elsewhere on allotted reservations, each home was located on the allotted farmland.

Reservation Land Use

Available records indicate that at least two patterns of the economic exploitation of trust patent reservation lands emerged very quickly after 1891. The reservations were the homesites and the locus of subsistence farming for some people, but most Indians engaged in the production of such cash crops as fruit and honey and in the raising of poultry, cattle, and horses. While much of their production was on a relatively small scale, due to the limited size of the individual land base, some Indians were soon farming as much as sixty acres of reservation land (part of which was rented from other members) and more than five hundred acres of rented land outside the reservation. Other Indian entrepreneurs quickly planted what developed into highly productive orchards. Some individuals received considerable income from farming and hired other Indians as laborers (Bureau of Indian Affairs Records; Shipek 1977). Indians rented, bought, and sold land rights to each other within the reservation (Omish Journal). Even at Pechanga, which had little irrigation water, dry farming provided a portion of the income for many members during most years.

After 1891, Indians tried new crops on reservation fields. Market-garden crops—tomatoes, yams, onions, chili peppers, squash, and watermelons—replaced the extensively farmed wheat, beans, and corn as the primary cash crops. New orchards of apricots, lemons, oranges, walnuts replaced the traditional olives, peaches, and grapes. Combined with the production of crops for sale was a certain amount of wage labor for other ranchers and farmers in Southern California. Other Indians went into towns and acquired new labor skills (Shipek 1977, 1978). Rations were issued only to a few disabled or aged Indians (ARCIA 1880–1930).

Throughout the years there were occasional droughts, and the effects of droughts were compounded by an increasing lack of sufficient irrigation water from streams as non-Indian ranchers and agriculturalists developed the surrounding lands and took control of existing water supplies formerly used exclusively by the Indians. In some regions, supplemental native food gathering still existed, but in others it did not, and for all the Indians most of the former emergency food sources were no longer available. The primary source of replacement income in drought years became wage labor. Members with allotments could use their land only for a hay crop or pasturage, working in town and returning to harvest their hay. They could also rent their houses and lands to other Indians. Indians without allotments, while technically unable to follow the same practice, sometimes rented or sold their land and house rights to other Indians. In some cases, they simply had to abandon their improvements, though not their membership rights in the reservation. Even though some members left the land at each new crisis—for example, because of a drought, because an allotment procedure was seen as unjust, or because the water had been taken by non-Indians—annual farm production statistics show a fluctuating but gradual increase in crop and livestock production prior to World War II. In many cases, those remaining on the reservations increased production and changed crops to maintain yields and income in spite of water and crop losses (Bean, personal communication; Shipek 1972).

Following World War II, farm activity began to increase. The young men returning from military duty intended to develop and expand previous family farming ventures. Through the years, the Indian farmers had been finding ways to compete

in modern agriculture in spite of disabilities pertaining to the
various types of Indian tenure rights under Bureau of Indian
Affairs trusteeship and to the loss of irrigation water. They
had managed larger acreages by renting from, or sharecrop-
ping with, relatives or neighbors who were not farming the
land themselves. They found private financing for mecha-
nized equipment, new seed, orchard stock, and some fertil-
izers. They learned to hold back crops for better prices and
to organize cooperatives to purchase supplies and market
their crops (Bean 1978; Shipek field notes). But water was the
stumbling block, and a lack of it ended this increased farm
activity.

Drought conditions again developed during the late 1940s and
1950s in Southern California. Reservations that were riparian
to rivers and streams or had running springs (Morongo, Rincon, Pala, Pauma, La Jolla, Campo, and others) seldom received the share of water to which they were legally entitled.
Water was being removed from the river basins above the reservations, the lack of basin replenishment and intensive
pumping of underground water by adjoining ranchers lowered local water tables everywhere, and there were many other types of actions by local government agencies or private
parties that removed water from reservations. BIA personnel
often wrote letters of protest, but the bureau took no other
action. Dry farming was no longer possible; irrigation was now
necessary even on lands that had never needed it before.
Springs and wells went dry, orchards and crops were lost,
and some homes were without domestic water. It was necessary for Indians to search elsewhere for jobs and income.
Whether an Indian remained as a resident on the reservation
came to be determined by the distance and condition of the
road that would be used to commute to a job and the presence of domestic water. Many reservations became the homes
of the retired, the unemployed, or those with local jobs (Shipek 1978).

In 1951, as a result of the illegal taking of water and a lack of
protection by their trustee, the United States, some reservation bands instituted claims cases against the United States

government for dereliction of its duty. Specifically named in Docket 80A of the Mission Indians Claims Case were the San Luis Rey River reservations and Soboba. In 1971, San Pasqual Reservation, which was also on a tributary of the San Luis Rey River and was crossed by the flume of the private company that was taking the river water, was added as a plaintiff in the case.

There were also other instances where bureaucratic delays and a lack of any action had frustrated the Indians' redress of the illegal taking of reservation water, as at Campo, Capitan Grande, and other reservations. As a result, since 1971 many more (although not all) reservations have filed claims against the federal government for a dereliction of its duty as a trustee to protect their water supplies (Docket 80A-2 before the court of claims).

The Soboba case was unique. During the 1930s, when the Metropolitan Water District of Los Angeles was constructing its aqueduct through the mountains near Soboba, aqueduct construction interrupted and destroyed the entire subsurface flow of water to reservation springs. There had always been sufficient flow into these springs for crops, even during extreme drought years, so the loss of the Soboba springs was a major water loss. The surrounding non-Indian farmers were rapidly recompensed for their water loss, but not the reservation. Thus this loss was included in the Mission Indian Claims Case filed in 1951. In 1976 the Indian Claims Commission decided this case in favor of Soboba and also further delineated the government's duty to protect and maintain reservation water supplies.

Additional water use problems were caused by Bureau of Indian Affairs procedures and mismanagement. After 1910, the bureau's irrigation division began studies of the existing available water in order to develop irrigation systems and small dams for the reservations, but the engineers were not acquainted with local conditions. Diversion ditches, canals, flumes, small dams, wells, and pumps were planned, dug, or built on each reservation, whichever seemed practical to the Indian Irrigation Service. During the early years of these systems, the inadequate design regularly resulted in floods, washouts, and continual delays in replacement, because most "improvements" had been planned without consideration for local conditions—torrential rains alternating with droughts. The wells, for example, had been dug without taking into account the droughts, lack of basin replenishment, and deeper non-Indian wells that continually lowered groundwater levels. Repairs and improvements always took several years due to bureaucratic red tape, which required many reports and investigations that passed through numerous hands before reaching Congress for appropriations and then back through the bureaucracy for implementation. Each time this happened, the Indians' crops were lost.

Further, the work had been done on a "reimbursable basis" without any request by the Indians or input from them concerning the appropriateness of the engineers' planning. While the bureau supplied the materials and engineers, the Indians were required to labor on the systems with no pay. Finally, they were required to pay water charges for the water received. The Indians, however, concluded that the systems were their own. After all, in most villages they had always managed their own systems without outside help. They could not see why they had to pay for their own water. The result of the combination of this conclusion with the system's failures was that water liens (charges) piled up against many allotments, and if an allotment was sold, the lien had to be satisfied before the Indian received any cash. Not until the early 1960s did Congress finally cancel all remaining water liens. The Indians had convinced it that the liens were assessed for totally substandard systems that had been inadequate even when new.

The domestic water situation has been improved during the last decade. For two reservations, Rincon and La Jolla, the federal district court ordered that, pending final settlement of their case against the water company, a specified amount of water must be delivered to the reservations. On another, San Pasqual, residents paid the cost of connection to the local water district. Until recently, because they were on untaxed land, they were required to pay double the amount that a person on taxed, nontrust land paid for domestic water. In the last decade, too, responsibility for domestic water supplies on California reservations was handed to the United States Public Health Service's Indian Division, which has been the process of digging deeper wells on many reservations (see the discussion in Chapter 6).[14]

Combined with these new water facilities, new programs have been developed to finance home building on the reservations, and the highways have been improved. Improvements in these three areas have enabled many families to return to the reservation as a place of residence. Morongo, Pala, Pauma, Sycuan, San Pasqual, and Rincon are examples. Further, where water supplies and the location of the reservation have permitted it, some income-producing enterprises have been reinstituted—as at La Jolla, Rincon, Los Coyotes, Viejas, Pala, and Barona—and many other commercial enterprises are in various stages of planning.

Most recently, some of the reservations have contracted with Bingo companies and have used tribal halls or built Bingo halls for the games. Indians are hired to run the games and the food concessions, thus providing individual employment as well as tribal income. They advertise in the local newspapers and many have developed a sizeable following and produced an excellent income. A few reservations may be losing income, as they are not requiring adequate accounting from the Bingo concession and are undoubtedly being cheated. However, many are using it beneficially. Some have instituted per capita payments from the tribal income, and others are using it to develop other tribal businesses and services.

CHAPTER 4

The Present Status of Reservation Tenure

As the people today reactivate and increase the use of the reservation lands with new expectations of home or income development, they are faced with a variety of modern and traditional forms of tenure that affect their lands. There are complex decisions to be made. The Southern California of the 1980s is a totally different environment from that of less than twenty years ago, and the bands will control, expand, or dissipate their future depending upon their decisions within the next decade. This chapter will describe the various forms of tenure that now exist and point out some of the problems involved in living with multiple land tenure systems.

Executive Order Reserves

Executive order reserves were lands withdrawn from the public lands of the United States by an executive order of the president. Many of the present reservations were originally preserved for Indian use by such action. Most were withdrawn from the public lands for the use of a specifically named band and have since been trust patented to that band. One of the reserves in this executive order status, known as the Mission Reserve, was the only land in Southern California withdrawn for unspecified "landless" Indians "if needed." An analysis of documents leading to its withdrawal (Shipek 1958) indicated that it was intended to be an addition to the lands

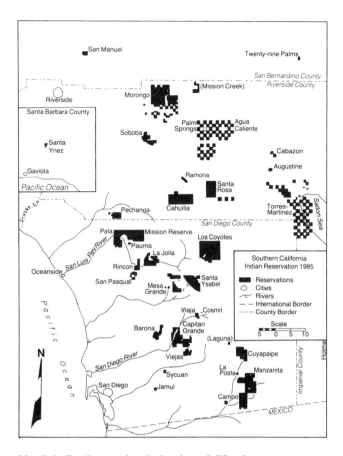

Map 5. Indian Reservations in Southern California

purchased at Pala for the use of the Indians moved from the Warner's and San Felipe rancho grants in 1903. The documents indicate that portions of the area were already being used as grazing lands by Pauma Band members. Several attempts by the Forest Service to have it returned to the public domain were defeated by Pala and Pauma assisted by numerous non-Indian organizations. Both reservations then joined in requesting Congress to officially transfer title to them, basing their request on the 1958 analysis and documentation.

This has now been completed, and the land has been trust patented and divided between Pala and Pauma.

During the 1960s, while the Mission Reserve was still in executive order status, the adjoining Agua Tibia Wild Area was created. During the hearings, attempts were made by "environmental" organizations to include the Mission Reserve in the wild area. They claimed that, historically, Indians did not disturb or affect nature and thus this land should be included in the "Wild Area" designation. An Indian designated by the reservations had spoken early in the public hearings, not expecting this type of argument. I was one of the last speakers, and the reservation members present asked me to respond to this allegation of nonuse. After the hearing, the "environmental" people came up and apologized and claimed that they did not intend to restrict Indian economic development.

The other land still in executive order status—that is, not trust patented to a specific named band—is known as the Kelsey Tract. It is somewhat farther down the valley from Pechanga and does not adjoin the trust patented part of the reservation. All documents concerning its status indicate that it was purchased in 1912 to provide the members of Pechanga with a small acreage of moderate-quality farmland and with a slightly better supply of water than the Pechanga Reservation then had. The tract's name derives from the name of the Indian Office inspector who investigated the condition of the Mission Indians during the preceding few years and who recommended that this tract be purchased for the Pechanga Band because they did not have adequate farmland to survive. Somehow the Bureau of Indian Affairs never got around to trust patenting it to Pechanga, in spite of sending Pechanga members to farm it during the years after its purchase. In recent years, as the tract has become more valuable due to surrounding non-Indian development, the Bureau has refused to allow Pechanga to develop the tract, due to its executive order reserve status. Apparently, to acquire this tract, which had been purchased for its use, Pechanga must institute the same congressional process used by Pala and Pauma to acquire the Mission Reserve as part of their reservations. In contrast, other small pieces of land purchased for the same purpose for other reservations, but which adjoined the reservation, were added to the trust patent at the time of purchase.

Trust Patent Reservations

Trust patents, or trust titles, to reservation land have been issued to the named occupying band under the authority of the 1891 Act for the Relief of the Mission Indians or one of several subsequent acts of Congress authorizing withdrawals or land purchases. An undivided interest in the tribal land is confirmed to members of the named band. Two basic types of trust patent reservations exist: (1) those that have not had individual allotment programs, and (2) those that have. I shall discuss the general tenure rights and problems first, then focus on unallotted reservations, and finally upon allotted reservations.

MEMBERSHIP REGULATION

Membership in a band is determined by that band, subject to the approval of the secretary of the interior. Due to their opposition to being required to obtain the approval of the secretary, some bands have never developed formal rolls. They have watched the first bands (San Pasqual, for example) go through enrollment procedures and be forced by the Bureau of Indian Affairs to accept individuals whom band members knew did not really belong. In spite of these difficulties, within the past twenty years some bands have developed formal membership rolls, and others are still working on enrollment procedures. Each band supposedly has the right to develop its own set of membership enrollment procedures, regulations, and requirements. Generally, the adoption of enrollment regulations that specify the qualifications for membership precedes the development of a constitution, and the regulations are then incorporated into the constitution or articles of association. Membership is limited to some degree of direct bloodline descent, generally with some provision for band adoption.[15] The trustee, however, through the Bureau of Indian Affairs, must approve the constitution, enrollment regulations, and enrollment and has often insisted upon specific rules or has administratively added substantive changes that negate the intent of the tribe.

The formal basis for membership is the presence of an individual or an ancestor on a specified early list of residents of that reservation as compiled by the Bureau of Indian Affairs.[16] The year of the census list used is determined by the band, subject to the approval of the bureau.

Most bands have 1/8 degree blood limitations, though a few have 1/16. A 1/8 degree of blood means that out of eight great-grandparents, one was on the specified census list. The limitation may be expressed as "blood of the band" or "Indian blood," terms that have different implications. For example, a band that requires 1/8 degree of "blood of the band" may have members who are 1/4 to full "Indian blood" or tribal blood (San Luiseño, Kumeyaay, or Cahuilla) but who are only 1/8 "blood of the band," that is, one great-grandparent was a full-blood member of that band.

The children of members having the minimum fraction will not be eligible for membership unless that member marries another band member. One band, under its existing membership rules (1/8 blood of the band), has more than one-third of its members who are such "terminal" members—that is, the children of these members would be 1/16 and thus not eligible for membership unless the 1/8 member marries another member of the band. Some terminal members are full-blood Indians.

Current marriage and kinship practices prohibit marriage to anyone with whom there is any traceable relationship or who is presumed to be a kinsman of any degree, and some bands trace back to beyond the fifth generation. These rules operate to prevent most young reservation members from marrying within the band or with most other Southern California band members. In order to maintain membership and inheritance rights for their children, many reservations face changing either their membership rules or their marriage rules.[17]

The Bureau of Indian Affairs census upon which band membership is based was not a membership list for a reservation but a
census of residents. In many cases individuals or families
were residents upon reservations of which they were not
band members.[18] Many errors exist in the bureau determination and recording of degree of blood in old census lists, as
well as in the more recent lists. Under the existing need for
bureau approval of membership enrollments (and thus effective control over the Indians regardless of statements to the
contrary), unless the census taker noted on that particular
census the nonmember's origin, the bureau has not accepted
any proof that such a resident or his or her descendants
should not have membership rights (see the San Pasqual discussion in this chapter). Some persons in this category and
their descendants have never developed close kinship and social ties with the band members, and following the granting
of individual allotments they have been one source of the fee
patenting and sale of allotments. Yet after such a sale the descendants continue to claim membership rights to the unallotted portion of such reservations and to the distribution of any
per capita membership benefits. Inherited homestead lands,
even those inherited by direct descendants, do not bar one
from also claiming membership on a reservation and availing
oneself of all reservation benefits.

Marriage does not change band membership. If a husband and
wife hold membership in different bands, they may live on
either reservation or on neither. Each retains full rights in his
or her own reservation but acquires no rights in the spouse's
reservation. Children may all be registered with either reservation or split between them. Siblings may thus be members
of different reservations, and a child raised on one reservation may hold membership in a different reservation.
One cannot inherit tribal rights on two reservations, so the
child must make a choice between the father's and the mother's reservation if the parents have not already made such a
choice for him or her.

Many reservations, even those with official enrollments, have
never updated their rolls since the last bureau census or their

original enrollment procedure. Thus they do not actually have records indicating the number of existing children and grandchildren or the degree of blood of such descendants. In other words, except in a few places, reservation population figures are primarily estimates based on the last official BIA census in 1940. This is discussed again under housing.

Membership rights and duties generally include the right to live on the reservation, graze cattle on it, plant crops, cut firewood, gather native plant foods or materials, hunt (regardless of season), attend band meetings, vote in band decisions, hold office, hold religious rites of passage in the band chapel or church and in the "wake" house, and be buried in the band cemetery. They also include a right to an equal share of any membership distribution of band assets. One may not as an individual legally sell or lease any portion of tribal land or any reservation asset (for example, firewood or leaf mold) and may not contract to graze livestock owned by a nonmember on tribal land. One may legally sell only crops and livestock he or she has raised.

One does not have to reside on the reservation or be present and active in order to retain such rights and to pass them on to children of the proper degree of blood. An individual may formally relinquish such rights by so stating in writing to the tribe and the Bureau of Indian Affairs. Also, an individual may simply leave and sever all connections with the band.[19]

These general rights for all members are subject to varying limitations by resolution of the band. For example, a band may vote to limit the number of cattle a member may graze on tribal land; it may vote to limit the gathering of firewood to dead trees and branches (a pre-Spanish practice); it may vote a range improvement program and restrict all livestock for a year or two; or it may formally lease to a nonmember use of a portion of the reservation for the duration of the lease. Except for the formal lease use, which must be approved by the Bureau of Indian Affairs and is enforced by it, the band has, however, no means to enforce any voted limitations on its own members. Thus such limitations tend to be meaningless (as discussed later in this chapter and also in Chapter 7).

In general, equal rights for all reservation members are assured
by the Bureau of Indian Affairs. They may not be abrogated
by the band under any provocation, but some individuals
have been extralegally restrained from exercising all their
rights by tacit consent of the majority. In some cases a particularly strong family has restrained, also extra-legally, a majority of the members from exercising many of their rights.

UNALLOTTED TRUST PATENT RESERVATIONS
Legally, all band members have an undivided interest in the
whole reservation. Individuals may acquire use-rights to a
portion, known as an assignment, through formal application
to the band, band approval, and registration with the Bureau
of Indian Affairs. By bureau regulations, use-rights are supposed to lapse with nonuse and are not inheritable. According to bureau regulations, upon the death of the assignee an
heir has ninety days to remove personal property. After ninety days, everything remaining reverts to band ownership unless the band votes to reassign the property to the heirs.
Most bands in Southern California have not followed these bureau regulations, however, and have not registered band assignments. Instead, they have followed "tribal custom," which
allowed inheritance of land by the nearest direct kin. The
Omish journal suggests that the tribal trust status of legal title
to reservation land may actually have restricted a previously
developed right to sell or trade lands in individual tenure to
other non–band member Indians. The "tribal custom" tenure
rights modified by the trust status, which have actually been
in operation since the beginning of the reservation period,
were spelled out in 1963 by the United States District Court,
Southern District: Central District, in the case of *United States
of America, Plaintiff* v. *Osevio J. Salgado, et al., Defendants.* Inasmuch as the Findings of Fact in this case may be relevant for
all Southern California reservations, they are quoted in full:

1. That assignments of the several and exclusive rights to use, occupy, improve and segregate by fencing or otherwise, designated portions of the Soboba Indian Reservation became

vested in various members of the Soboba band.

2. Such assignments carried with them the right to the assignee to voluntarily transfer his or her assignment rights providing the transferee was also a member of the Band.

3. Such assignment rights were inheritable by will of the deceased assignee or by descent providing that the divisee or the heir-at-law was a member of the Band, except that a non-member surviving spouse could inherit a life interest and, upon the death of such surviving spouse, the assignment would devolve upon the next of kin who was a member of the Band.

4. All or part of the rights to use and possession under any assignment could be leased or permitted to another occupant, or occupants, regardless of whether such lessee or permittee is or is not a member of the Soboba band, or is or is not an Indian.

5. Such lease or permit cannot extend beyond the time the assignee holds such assignment and will terminate with (a) the death of the assignee or (b) the transfer of the assignment of such assignee or (c) the sooner termination of the lease or (d) the revocation of the permit or license by the assignee.

6. Such assignments could be reassigned to another member of the Band if there was no living surviving spouse or surviving descendant who was a member of the Band to inherit it from a deceased assignee. Otherwise such assignments could not be reassigned to another member.

7. There was no fixed limit to the number of assignments which could be held by one assignee. Some held more than one and an assignee did not have to reside upon an assignment to maintain his continuing rights therein.

The rights of an assignee delineated in the above findings for Soboba can be applied to most reservations in Southern California, with some minor variations. Some reservations allowed the rent or lease only of a building and its immediate grounds. They reserved the productive economic use of the land to the members individually or as a whole.

Recently, practices have been changing, and in most bands a member now goes to the band at an official band meeting and requests an assignment of tribal land. Some bands apportioned out the land to various families when the band first went to the reservation, and a member goes to the head of his family or lineage to receive an assignment within the family bounds.

By traditional tenure-use, tribal land upon an unallotted reservation is all that land that has not been assigned. This includes land that could in the future be assigned to an individual as well as the land used for tribal purposes, such as the church, fiesta, and ceremonial grounds; the tribal meeting hall; the cemetery; rights-of-way, grazing ground, and land used to produce tribal income. Grazing ground is generally used by those who have cattle, with no fees paid to the tribe for such individual income-producing usage of tribal assets. Tribal land may be leased wholly or in part by the band to produce tribal income. Recently, bands have been developing their own income-producing businesses on selected portions of tribal land. Depending on the vote of the band members, such tribal income may be held for use for capital improvements and enlargement of the business or for additional ventures, or it may be disbursed to band members on a per capita basis.

Several problems exist on the unallotted, or assigned, reservations. The traditional tenure rights go back to the earliest period on the reservation and are sometimes prereservation in origin, but in practice tenure rights and boundaries are dependent upon human memories, which can be fallible and lost at death. Also, children who have been raised in a rented house may not realize the rental status (and consequent ownership by another Indian family) and argue that the house belongs to their family. For most bands, minutes of tribal meetings have only recently been consistently maintained, and none of the reservations have consistently mapped and recorded the assignments. Arguments and lawsuits have been caused by fallible human memory and an incomplete knowledge of past boundaries, yet only a few bands have begun a systematic recording and mapping of all known past assignments in an attempt to avoid problems in the future.

A second problem derives from the practice of renting houses to nonmembers, which began at an early date and which has been one cause for the inclusion of nonmembers on various reservation census rolls. As already noted, this inclusion has caused complex membership determination problems because the bureau insists that anyone on the older census rolls is a member unless designated on the roll as a nonmember.

Third, the lack of recognition by the Bureau of Indian Affairs of the existing traditional tenure rights and its consequent lack of support for efforts to obtain a secure legal title to individual assignment holders has been one of the reasons for the apparent partial abandonment of some reservations. Bear in mind that the original basic subsistence unit was not the band but the family. The reservation system, along with the changing economic and political environment, brought independence from the need for any form of general band support and cohesion economically, politically, or militarily. Combined with this lack of external pressure requiring band cohesion, the dominant external society has removed many economic, judicial, and political functions of the traditional internal band government and has removed the traditional positive rewards and prestige that existed in the pre-Spanish society. Further, most of the traditional sanctions used for enforcing internal band government—whipping, ostracism, banishment, and execution (Bean 1972:121; Shipek field notes)— have long been forbidden by the current external legal system, and the development of new types of sanctions has not been permitted (see Chapter 7). The Bureau of Indian Affairs personnel were always inadequate in numbers and in duration of stay among the numerous scattered reservations to acquire any understanding of the local conditions, but they would not necessarily have been able to effect any legal or de facto changes in bureau procedures even if they had tried. The result has been the lack of any form of civil law among the Indians.[20]

On a few reservations this lack of law enforcement has allowed a physically stronger and numerically larger family to push smaller families, one by one, off the reservation entirely or to limit their use of the reservation to a few small homesites. Such strong families have sometimes been able to expand and to place some of their members upon other nearby reservations. They begin to acquire "rights" on them, which eventually are recognized by the bureau as if such persons were legitimate members of that reservation band. Control by such strong families may change with generations.

Not all reservations with single-family use or very small bands are the result of this extralegal condition. There are cases where the lack of residents and small membership numbers are the result of the small size of the band at the time of trust patenting. Then, through the vagaries of births and the registry of children on a spouse's reservation, band membership has been reduced to one or two members. Such reservations have legitimately become the property of one family. Because the land is "tribal" property and not individual property, such lone members must be certain that they have direct lineal heirs who are eligible as band members, or they must write band adoption ordinances and adopt their chosen heirs as band members. This procedure has already been accomplished for two such reservations, Cuyapaipe and La Posta. In both cases, close direct relatives who were also direct lineal descendants of original band members were adopted.

Before leaving the subject of unallotted reservations, one special case must be described. The Capitan Grande Reservation was reserved for two bands, Capitan Grande and Los Conejos, and part of a third, Mission San Diego Band. Some other remnant band members were also placed there at an early date by the Indian agent. Later, the city of San Diego negotiated to purchase the central valley of the reservation as a dam site. The purchase was authorized by Congress (Act of February 28, 1919, 40 *United States Statutes* 12206, as amended May 4, 1932), and other lands were purchased in 1932 and 1933 for the Indians. The two primary bands chose two separate locations, Barona Ranch and Baron Long Ranch (Viejas). Each ranch purchased was in a valley that adjoined the Capitan Grande, Barona to the west and Baron Long to the south. The others chose individual land, either rural land or urban land within the city of San Diego, which was purchased for them and placed in trust. Some of these individual sites remain in trust. All the lands, both group and individual, were bought, and per-capita-value homes were built and furnished for each family based on the individual membership shares of the purchase price of the Capitan Grande land.

Originally, the Capitan Grande Band irrigated its agricultural lands directly from the San Diego River. As the city of San Diego developed, the San Diego Flume Company was formed to bring water from the dam built at the headwaters of the San Diego River, thus cutting the river flow through the reservation. The company agreed to provide water to the reservation in return for a flume right-of-way through the reservation, but the terms of this agreement were not enforced for the benefit of the Indians any more than such terms were enforced elsewhere. Crops were often lost due to lack of timely and sufficient irrigation water. When the central valley of Capitan Grande was sold to the city of San Diego as a dam site and the lands of Barona and Baron Long were purchased for the bands, no provision was made for supplying any irrigation water to these purchased lands. Nonreservation neighbors had deep wells tapping the underground water of these valleys, lowering the water table. In addition, drought conditions and the loss of the Capitan Grande accrued water rights reduced economic land use of the formerly rich, productive lands to a limited amount of grazing. Nonetheless, proximity and ease of transportation to the city have resulted in high residential use in both places.

The houses on these reservations are the private property of each family because they were built with each family's share of the purchase fund. The houses are inherited either through the will of the deceased owner or by standard state probate laws. For these reservations, the question of the inheritance of a house by a nonmember spouse, either Indian or non-Indian, has not yet been tested. Although the land is in undivided trust ownership to the band, it was purchased by the pooling of what were individual shares of money, and the houses were built on the basis of individual shares. These special conditions of private ownership under an undivided trust may cause new legal problems to develop.

The remainder of the original reservation land still belongs jointly to all three groups—Barona, Baron Long, and those who took individual holdings. Some members also feel that their families still retain individual tenure rights in the portions they had used previously, and some are under the impression that they had received valid allotments from surveys made between 1890 and 1910. These were, however, among the allotments that were never confirmed by the bureau, and this issue remains to be resolved.

ALLOTTED TRUST PATENT RESERVATIONS

Trust patent reservations that have been allotted contain four basic types of land tenure, and each type may include several subtypes. The four primary types are: allotments, assignments, tribal lands, and rights-of-way.

Allotments   The term "allotment" in this context derives from the individual private land ownership that was instituted for Indian reservations throughout the United States by the General Allotment Act of 1887, commonly called the Dawes Act. This act authorized the dividing of reservation lands into individually owned plots where sufficient lands were suitable for agriculture and grazing. The purpose of the Dawes Act was to teach the Indians to become individually self-sufficient farmers, to instill pride in private ownership and accomplishment in tribal Indians. But the program resulted in the loss of more than two-thirds of the land in Indian ownership, the destruction of the tribal government, and the return to a much-reduced tribal land base for many tribes (Haas 1957:15).

In contrast, by 1980 less than 30 percent of all allotted acreage in Southern California had been taken out of trust and converted into fee patent land, and some of this fee patent land is still in the hands of Indian owners. Also, if the Coachella Valley reservations, which were subjected to special external pressures, are excluded from the figures, less than 9 percent of the rest of the allotted acreage had been fee patented.

Thus, the effects of allotment upon Indian ownership of land in Southern California cannot be equated with the effects among other American Indian tribes in the United States. Southern California Indians lost most of their lands before any land was reserved for them by the federal government. These people now preserve their reservations as ethnic symbols. Recognizing the likelihood that they would somehow lose fee patented lands, most Southern California allottees have kept their allotted lands in trust status so that they cannot be alienated. Families are motivated to retain lands and band membership to keep their children eligible to receive future benefits, assignments, and income distributions, and most important, to be certain that their children inherit their rights as Indians, along with the traditional family lands.

The 1891 Act for the Relief of the Mission Indians contained its own allotting provisions, which included a twenty-five-year period of trust after which the allottee might apply for the title in fee patent. Some have done so. When the fee patent was granted, the trust status was to be removed, the grantee was considered competent, became a citizen, and technically ceased to be a tribal member. The land became subject to local laws and property taxes, and it could be mortgaged, become security for a loan, leased, or sold without supervision of the federal trustee. Inheritance rights, both in trust and in fee patent, were individual and subject to the laws of the particular state. However, Congress has repeatedly extended the twenty-five-year trust period, and the trust status has been maintained, except in certain cases to be discussed later.

Allotments may include a town lot, irrigated farmland, or dry farmland. Trust title to these lands is vested in the individual. Therefore, decisions concerning land use are made by the individual, and neither band consultation nor approval is necessary. Allottees may live on their land, farm it, or use it for pasture. They may leave it unused, or may rent it out to whomever they please. They may put a noxious business on it, such as a fertilizer plant or junkyard, or build a trailer park. They may build a shack or a nice home and maintain their allotment in poor or excellent condition. Allottees may build several houses on their allotment and rent them to non-Indians or place a trailer camp on the allotment for the same purpose. On most reservations, informal social pressures have maintained and controlled the use of allotted land by the allottee. Only an occasional recalcitrant individual has abused the right to this unrestricted use. On the other hand, as reservation populations have increased, the potential for abuse is becoming apparent to the members, and some reservations are considering methods for preventing abuse of rights and of restricting uses to those that are acceptable to the entire membership, that is, they are adopting their own form of zoning ordinances.

Only if an allottee leases his land formally or takes it out of trust does he need formal approval of the Bureau of Indian Affairs. In 1971 it became possible, with trustee approval, to mortgage a homesite portion of an allotment to obtain a home-building loan. In the past, while it was theoretically possible to mortgage it or to arrange for existing bureau development loan money, in practice no one was able to do so. It was necessary to take land out of trust for an individual to obtain a development loan from private sources. At least one individual did this and successfully developed his property. Taking an allotment out of trust gives the owner full right to sell, mortgage, or otherwise encumber the property and also the obligation to pay property taxes to the local government. Indians are already subject to income tax, sales tax, and gasoline tax. Sales to Indians from Indian-owned stores on reservations are not subject to state, county, or city sales taxes, but sales to non-Indians are. Only trust property is exempt from local property taxes, and income derived from trust property by the Indian owner is not subject to income tax.

To continue with allottee rights, an allottee may will his property to an heir or heirs, to a non–band member, to an organization, or to the band. Some allotments on Pala were willed to Pala Mission, whereupon they were removed from trust and reservation status and became church property. (Resentment exists against the church for accepting such land rather than returning it to tribal ownership.) If an allottee dies intestate, state inheritance law is activated. In the absence of children, all relatives of varying degrees of relationship and collaterality receive shares commensurate with their degree of relationship. Lands that have passed through probate more than once may have been divided into 1/64 or lesser fractional shares. Some persons have inherited shares in several allotments and also upon different reservations where they are not members.

Technically, shares may be traded or sold between heirs, but in practice this is difficult to accomplish through the bureau's probate division. If all the heirs agree, the trust may be removed and the land sold by the Bureau of Indian Affairs in order to effect a cash division of inheritance rights. This has been the favorite bureau solution to fractional heirship problems even when heirs have desired to trade rights among themselves.

If an allottee or heir has a non-Indian spouse, upon the death of the Indian owner the share of the non-Indian spouse passes out of trust. To avoid this, an allottee may will a life estate to the non-Indian spouse, with the final disposition of the property to the allottee's chosen Indian heir or heirs occurring after the death of the spouse.

Another heirship problem exists that may cause internal family friction. During the original period of allotment, each adult member and each child born prior to the allotting date received an allotment in his or her own name. Children born after that date did not receive individual allotments. Unless the parents made provision in a will, all the children (those with and those without allotments of their own) would receive an equal inheritance share from their parents. This would result in an unequal land ownership position among the members of a family.

As stated above, a person may inherit shares in allotments and also may inherit shares in allotments on different reservations. An Indian may become a reservation resident on an inherited allotment and yet not be a member of that reservation. Such a person will have no vote in community or band affairs unless the band should choose to adopt that person and, if adopted, that person relinquishes membership in any other reservation. A person may not retain tribal membership rights in two reservations. Also, if one inherits an assignment on one reservation and an allotment on another, advantage would be gained only if membership rights were held in the reservation of the assignment. Otherwise, the assignment could not legally be inherited.

One factor that has confused probate procedures and caused wider division of inherited property than necessary is the use of kinship terms by most Southern California Indian groups in a way that differs from the standard American legal usage. The Indians use the same term for "brother" and "sister" as for parallel cousins (that is, children of siblings of the same sex; see note 17). In at least one tribe, this usage is carried to the fourth generation of descendants of siblings of the same sex. Other terms—for example, those translated as "uncle" and "aunt"—had similarly extended meanings. This has allowed some persons not in the relationship position intended in the American legal sense to share in an inheritance division of property under the management of the bureau's probate division. Through time, as the Bureau of Indian Affairs began keeping more marriage, birth, and death records and as the Indians began to use English terms in their more restricted sense, this type of confusion (for the bureau probate procedures, not to the Indians) has occurred less often.[21]

As pointed out, some allotted lands have been sold, which brings up the subject of out-of-trust allotments and sales. Land has gone out of trust by being inherited by a non-Indian spouse, by being willed to a non-Indian individual or organization (as at Pala to the Catholic church), or by being taken in fee simple title (the kind of title any non-Indian holds) by the allottee or heirs and then sold.[22] While the percentage of such sales has been relatively small, complications have resulted for the bands. Some allottees, desiring cash for themselves or desiring to move into town and needing cash for a down payment on a house there, have sold their allotment. At a later date, they may move back onto unassigned tribal land. While they cannot demand a second allotment for themselves, they often demand allotments for their children in order to acquire tax-free trust land again for them. They may at the same time be liable to inherit shares in one or several allotments of their parents or other older relatives. It is not that such people do not understand the concept of private land ownership; frequently they own or have owned one or more pieces of property off the reservation that they have purchased and on which they have paid taxes. Rather, such persons are attempting to acquire from the band more than the normal share of band assets for themselves and their children.

The other aspect of such sales is that most of the bands do not like "foreigners," or non-Indians, living in the heart of their communities and using such tribal assets as water and rights-of-way. For example, the bureau has on occasion given priority of water rights to such out-of-trust lands by constructing irrigation pipes to these lands before doing irrigation or domestic water construction to Indian-held trust lands.[23] As a result of this type of inequity, most bands would like to buy back out-of-trust lands and return them to tribal status.

Assignments   On reservations that have had allotment programs, assigned lands are those lands to which individuals who lack allotments may acquire use rights through application to the band, band approval, and registration with the Bureau of Indian Affairs. Assignments made by bands prior to 1950 have generally not been formalized and recorded with the bureau, so in order to avoid future controversy, some bands have begun a process of researching, mapping, and recording old assignments, thus clearing their land records prior to any new developments or allotments.

As on unallotted reservations, assignments are technically use rights, which should lapse with nonuse or the death of the assignee and which are not inheritable. In practice, most bands have followed past customs and allowed inheritance and continuation of rights regardless of nonuse. Legal title, however, remained in the hands of the band, and the land could not be alienated, as could an allotted land title. Some reservations have handled each case of potential assignment inheritance on an individual basis so that each heir must request the continued use right from the tribe.

Some allotted reservations that still have tribal land available are under pressure to provide allotments to those members who have never received an allotment. One reservation had decided to grant such allotments, but upon examining their land and potential allottees, they realized that their membership had grown and that they would be unable to distribute to each eligible member the same acreage as earlier and have any tribal land left for tribal purposes. Because they desire to have lands for community purposes and tribal income, they are debating the granting of one- and two-acre homesite assignments instead of allotments.

LAND CATEGORIES IN BOTH TYPES OF RESERVATION

The retention of some land for the use of the community as a whole and for access to the various parts of the reservation is characteristic of both allotted and unallotted reservations. Nevertheless, these tribal lands and rights-of-way do have distinctive histories and problems arising out of local conditions.

Tribal Lands   Tribal lands are all those lands in the reservation that are not allotted, assigned, or designated as rights-of-way. Generally the bands have formally or informally designated specific areas that are to be used jointly for such purposes as meeting halls, churches, cemeteries, fiesta grounds, ballparks, recreation lands, and economic development areas. Recently, clinics (at Morongo and Rincon), museums, and cultural centers (at Morongo, Pala, Torres-Martinez, and Rincon) have been added to this category. Most children attend public or parochial school (at Pala on church-owned ground), and therefore school lands are not needed, but preschool childcare facilities have recently been built on some reservations.

Most bands have joint grazing lands upon which any member may turn his stock. No grazing fees are charged against members who use this resource, nor have the number of animals per member or the overall number of animals been limited. Frequent periods of overgrazing (some of which was due to non-Indian cattle and sheep illegally trespassing on reservation land) have resulted in an as yet unknown expense to the band as a whole. Erosion control, range restoration, and adequate range management practices have yet to be generally instituted. Only in the last few years have the reservations been permitted to reinstitute the essential prereservation control-burning land management practices.

The use of tribal land for grazing has seemingly been equated with the use of band hunting territory on the basis of animal use. An individual band member was allowed to hunt freely over the entire band territory, and there was no control over his act of hunting, though controls existed on the "income" side through some form of required distribution of the meat killed by each hunter. Now, the income from grazing cattle accrues to the individual, with no provision for any return to the band. Under modern economic circumstances, it might be more appropriate if the bands were to equate grazing lands with joint gathering territories, which were under the control and management of the chief, with sanctions against any misuse. Based on this different equation of concepts, and through the administration of the tribal council, the bands might then institute fees on a per-animal basis, limit the overall number of animals or the number of animals per family, and institute proper range restoration and management practices. Effective control of tribal-land use would require that the bands have the power to impose sanctions against misuse. The bands would also need to have the desire and will to develop a political structure for handling such authority and the will to abide by such decisions regardless of personal and family ties.

Rights-of-Way   Roadways that existed before reservation lands were withdrawn from the public domain belong to the appropriate highway division—county, state, or federal. Some portions of the major paved highways through reservations belong in this category. To widen or straighten such a road, however, or to put in a new road, the highway division must negotiate with the band and pay for the value of the land taken. This is a right-of-way easement, not an outright sale. The land may only be put to highway purposes; any abandonment of the road, or any portion thereof, will cause the land to revert to the band. Years ago, the counties widened or straightened some of the highways through reservations without such negotiations, but when the California Indian Legal Service investigated the rights-of-way for the bands involved, the counties admitted their error, began to negotiate, and settled the matter out of court, as in the case of Mesa Grande and San Pasqual.

Within the reservation, the road system is maintained by the Bureau of Indian Affairs with public highway money. Therefore, the roads the bureau maintains are considered public roads available for public use. Some reservations have refused bureau road maintenance over certain roads for this reason. They prefer to be able to close some roads to public use upon occasion. Therefore, some of the poor roads exist by design, but not all poorly maintained roads are in this category. The bureau has never kept sufficient equipment for maintaining roads throughout the widely scattered reservations; thus, repairs and maintenance have been inadequate even on the roads desired by the Indians.

For many years, the bureau has stated its desire to turn road maintenance over to the counties, which have more adequate maintenance equipment immediately at hand, but the counties are willing to accept the road system only if the roads are first brought to county standards, which include a width of sixty feet. To meet county standards, almost every road within the reservation would have to be widened at the expense of reservation acreage, either tribal or allotment or both. It seems doubtful that any band will ever voluntarily vote for such a program.

A right-of-way over any public or private land in California (except federal land) may be acquired by an individual or the public by the unopposed free passage over the path, drive, or whatever for a certain period of years. A gate across a private road must be closed occasionally to maintain the "private" status. Such a right-of-way cannot, however, be acquired in this fashion across Indian trust land by anyone, including another Indian. Anyone having or buying property locked by reservation land (that is, the only entrance is by way of reservation land) must negotiate with the band and meet any restrictions the band cares to impose. The bands have been reasonable in their negotiations unless they have reason to distrust the requesting party. However, they object to giving unrestricted, permanent right-of-way easements. They regard this as the equivalent of an outright sale of land. Because passage is through their home lands, where children play and livestock roam, they prefer to restrict passage to the owner's family and to specified quantities and types of vehicles or to a limited period of years. They realize that changing the land use changes the land value, and they do not intend to have an easement that was negotiated for one purpose subverted to another that should be charged at a higher rate because it brings heavier traffic across the reservation.

Rights-of-way across allotted land must be negotiated with each allottee individually. Even a band member cannot cross another's allotment without permission. This has resulted in difficulties unforeseen by the bureau when it was laying out and distributing allotments. Allotments to several members of a family were generally clustered, and some of the allotments were located without specific access except informally across the allotment of a close relative. In cases of later family quarrels, the interior owner has occasionally been cut off from access into and out of his home.

Electric power line and telephone line rights-of-way must also be negotiated with the various bands. Under the supervision of the trustee, through the Bureau of Indian Affairs, some of the early easements were granted at very much lower rates than would have been paid to a non-Indian owner. Also, the right-of-way did not include the requirement that service be made available to the resident Indian population at reasonable rates. Recently, most such contracts have been renegotiated at reasonable rates and also have required the service to be brought to the reservation residents formerly ignored.

Following the passage of the Environmental Protection Act and its amendments, any development that uses federal money or affects federal lands must have an environmental assessment, and if the development has the potential to have an impact on the environment, a detailed EIR, or Environmental Impact Report, must be prepared. The act also has some special provisions that mandate a study of the potential effects of the development on American Indian reservations and former tribal territories and that require a consideration of the Indians' religious rights. Some of the early EIR studies (for example, that done for the Sun Desert Power and Transmission Line Project) ignored this mandate and barely mentioned the affected reservations even though transmission lines and other rights-of-way, such as access roads to the lines, were involved. The Indians objected and brought suit (along with non-Indian groups who were opposed to nuclear power) to stop such development. The Indians demanded an accurate study of the potential effects of the rights-of-way on the reservations.

California has its own state environmental protection act modeled upon the federal law, and studies are mandated if any state money or land is involved. In addition, some counties have their own laws and requirements, which may also require studies of the potential effects on the environment and on historic or prehistoric sites on private lands. Thus environmental assessments and environmental impact reports that ignore important Indian village sites or sacred sites will also be opposed. An example is the Cupeño opposition to the 1976 environmental assessment that stated that nothing of archaeological or environmental importance existed at Warner's Springs, the major village from which the army forcibly removed the Cupeño in 1903. Basically, the various reservations and tribes are stating that they may no longer be ignored and that they will demand their rights under the law. In each case, when the affected Indians have been properly consulted, they have been reasonable in negotiating with the government agency or developer. However, they also object, as do private non-Indian landowners, to having a noxious or disruptive business (like a garbage dump or a sand and gravel pit) placed adjacent to their reservation. They are concerned about the effect of increased traffic, especially heavy trucks—

air pollution and noise—on the quality of life due to such developments.

Provision was made in the 1891 Act for the Relief of the Mission Indians for the granting of rights-of-way for irrigation canals and ditches across reservation lands and allotments. This provision has been carried out in that such rights-of-way have been granted to irrigation companies and districts, but the negotiations for rights-of-way have not always provided for the delivery of water to the Indians. When they did provide for such delivery, the provisions did not always assure an adequate amount of water for current or possible future needs. Nor has the Bureau of Indian Affairs enforced the few water delivery provisions that it did negotiate for the Indian reservations.

A number of cases presently before the United States Court of Claims and the federal district courts concern the protection of Indian water rights, as in the case of the Pechanga, Cuyapaipe, La Posta, Morongo, and other reservations. The San Luis Rey case (covering the Rincon, La Jolla, Pauma, Pala, and San Pasqual reservations) was settled in 1985. In addition to those reservations that have cases presently before the courts, other reservations should have been advised to file for the water taken illegally from the reservations. The irrigation problems of the reservations in the Coachella Valley are a special situation and are discussed below in connection with the history of those reservations.

THE COACHELLA VALLEY RESERVATIONS

The Coachella Valley reservations are in a different ecological environment, have had a different history, and have been subject to more intense economic pressures than the reservations located in the mountains and foothills to the west. The Coachella Valley is desert land, in the rain shadow of the San Jacinto Mountains, which are over 10,000 feet in elevation. The broad and relatively flat valley slopes upward from the Salton Sea more than 200 feet below sea level northwestward to over 1,000 feet above sea level near the narrow San Gorgonio Pass, which leads through the mountains toward the coast.

In 1891 the surviving Cahuilla villages were located around the primary water sources in the desert region. Where sufficient water existed, either from a running spring or mountain run-off, the Indians planted corn, beans, and squash in addition to managing and using the native food plants. However, before any valley land was reserved for the Indian occupants, the railroads had been granted the odd-numbered sections of land (ARCIA 1881:14). The Smiley Commission was not able to reserve all the contiguous lands in actual use and occupancy of Indians. They reserved the even-numbered sections and made some land exchanges with the railroad for a few Indian-occupied sections. The resulting checkerboard pattern allowed settlers to alternate with Indian lands, and the Indians lost some of the springs and other naturally irrigated lands.

Any farming other than the previously existing Indian plantings in carefully selected runoff areas or subirrigated areas near natural springs required extensive capitalization. In the early 1900s some deep wells were drilled and pumping plants installed by the Bureau of Indian Affairs and some large-scale farming was begun on bureau demonstration farms and on some of the Indian land, within the limits of available water and the economy of the time. The non-Indians did not begin large-scale farming in the desert until the government developed major irrigation projects with massive water movement from the large dams on the Colorado River. These irrigation projects were designed to include the entire district, both reservation and nonreservation lands. In some places major canals traversed reservation lands, and in return for the rights-of-way, Indian-owned lands were to be connected to the canals and receive irrigation water. Instead, the irrigation district and the Bureau of Indian Affairs argued over which of them should pay the costs of making the connection necessary to use the water traversing Indian land—leaving the Indians without water for decades.

The extensive capitalization necessary for clearing, leveling, and preparing the land and for purchasing irrigation pipe, distribution valves, and other major equipment was not available to Indians. Their lands were in trust and could not be mortgaged as security for the capital. Therefore, the Bureau of

Indian Affairs arranged leases of land to non-Indian farmers who could get the capitalization to improve the land. The bureau considered this to be a benefit to the Indian because the improvements would be put in and the Indian would receive the lease income. The bureau leases were generally made, however, at a lower rate of return than that for which a non-Indian owner would lease equivalent land, and there was never a provision for the Indians to receive a share of the crop or profit, as would be the case with a non-Indian landowner. It is also doubtful that any lessee would install equipment or improvements of greater value than that required for the duration of the lease and would thus leave no improvement to the Indian. Also, leased lands were often overused and depleted by the lessee.

These small Indian bands did not have the manpower to substitute intensive labor for capital equipment, which is possible, in any case, only for some types of improvements. Moreover, participation in large, modern irrigation districts requires a large amount of capital per acre for the necessary technological equipment. Therefore, development was prevented for most reservation lands within irrigation projects both by the lack of available capital and by the lengthy period of disagreement between the Bureau of Indian Affairs and the irrigation district. Meanwhile, the privately held checkerboard sections were developed into high-value farmland.

Torres-Martinez The original member-to-land ratio was low for the desert reservations, so the bureau allotted forty acres to each Indian here. As elsewhere, controversy existed over the allotment program because the bureau ignored existing land uses. Some members did not accept allotments during this early allotment program. By the mid-1950s, however, all the members of the Torres-Martinez without allotments had for years been requesting that the allotting be completed, in particular the young men who had returned from World War II and who wanted to start farming. The band wanted the potentially valuable land bordering the Salton Sea retained as tribal land. Here the soil was too salty for farming, but the band planned to lease it for resort development to bring tribal income that would be used to defray the costs of farmland development elsewhere. (At that time, it cost about $600 per acre to prepare land for irrigation farming in that region.) Under bureau rules, however, any land can be allotted that the bureau considered "irrigable," and it defined "irrigable" simply as any land to which water could easily be brought, ignoring the salt content or other qualities of the land. Therefore, the first lands allotted were along the shore of the Salton Sea, and the first to receive allotments were the very elderly individuals, the disabled, orphaned minor children, and families without fathers, all persons unable to farm and to support themselves.

In the meantime, passage of Public Law 280 in 1953 had placed the California Indian, as a person, under state and county services. Indians had begun to receive old age pensions, disability aid, aid to dependent children, and county hospitalization on the same basis as any other citizens. In Riverside County a person otherwise eligible for these services was required to sell any valuable property and live on the proceeds before receiving welfare services. Because the forty-acre allotments of Coachella Valley were extremely valuable, the elderly Indians, the minor children, and the disabled persons who had received allotments under the allotting program at Torres-Martinez were required to sell the land and live on the proceeds before receiving any further aid. Because such Indians had no means for developing the land for income purposes and, due to age or other factors, were unable to support themselves, they had no choice but to sell the allotment. Both this type of allotment action and the requirements for welfare aid were protested and eventually stopped, but not before economically valuable recreation acreage was lost to the tribe. This is one of the categories of sales of allotments that has increased the percentage of sales of Coachella Valley allotments and lost the potential tribal income from land that could only be classed as "recreation development potential land," not as irrigable farmland.

Before leaving the subject of the Torres-Martinez reservation, mention must be made of its relation to the Salton Sea. On

Map 5 it can be seen that some of the land of this checkerboard reservation is under the sea. Torres-Martinez was reserved before the sudden 1906 inundation of the valley floor
resulting from the breeching of the headgates used in the
first major attempt to harness the Colorado River for irrigation in the Imperial Valley, and part of the reservation was
flooded. In recent years, the amount of irrigation water
brought into the Imperial and Coachella valleys has increased, and all water entering these valleys drains into the
Salton Sea, which has therefore continued to rise and flood
more land. A progressively increasing loss of land around the
edge of the sea by Torres-Martinez and other sea-edge owners can be expected unless some action is taken to provide
drainage from the basin or to raise the evaporation rate of
water from the sea. This situation may totally change in the
future if the Imperial Valley–Coachella Irrigation District is
required to sell "surplus" water to Southern California coastal
water districts, as proposed in 1986. Recreation uses may be
lost, because saltiness and pollution of the sea will increase
without sufficient "surplus" to maintain the present condition.
The required sale of water from the irrigation district must
be carefully balanced with the need to maintain the sea without increasing the salt or pollution levels. A solution to both
aspects of this problem—increasing land loss or its converse,
increasing saltiness and the loss of recreational uses—will require careful study of water uses, drainage, and salt accumu-
lation to develop new management techniques for irrigation
water, waste water, and salt in the entire Imperial-Coachella
drainage into the Salton Sea basin.

Palm Springs   Due to special conditions, Agua Caliente, or Palm
Springs, Reservation must also be considered separately.
Here, part of the odd-numbered checkerboard sections were
developed as a luxury resort, Palm Springs. Thus parts of the
reservation lands became quite valuable at an early date, with
the result that a separate agency office was eventually established at Palm Springs.

Controversy and court cases over the original allotment plan delayed completion until 1948. By this time the nature of the

area's development was known and the allotting plan had been modified to include a two-acre town lot, a five-acre "irrigable" plot, and forty acres of grazing land. For farm and grazing purposes in the Coachella Valley, the allotted sizes were totally unrealistic; however, the resort and town development potential made some allotments quite valuable. But inasmuch as some allotments near non-Indian resorts and in Palm Springs were more valuable than others farther away, many Indians were still dissatisfied with this allotment plan. New court cases reflected the desire for an almost total division of reservation land, with an equalization of value rather than of acreage. This aim was accomplished in 1958. Some strategically located and some sacred lands were retained in tribal status. Even though the lawsuits eventually benefited all the band members, the individuals who brought the cases had to pay all the legal costs. This necessitated their selling valuable portions of their allotments, and this is one source of the allotment sales for this reservation.

The economic development of the reservation land was further delayed because the question of individual allotment and title was under dispute for so many years. Development was also hindered by federal legal restrictions on the length of leasehold time. In one sense, this had been a benefit and protection to the Indians, as the short-term lease restriction was designed to prevent long-term leases at improperly low rates. In another sense, however, this restriction hindered development, because no lessee would put a major capital-intensive development on land without an assured long-term lease. As a result, the tribal council has repeatedly requested that Congress adopt a legal change that would allow for ninety-nine-year leases, and the tribal council has, in fact, negotiated some long-term leases, allowing development to begin. For example, the Palm Springs Airport now includes reservation land.

In a related matter, the Bureau of Indian Affairs did not previously use the standard business practice of a base-rate lease plus a sliding rate stated as a percentage of the yearly income from the leasehold usage. This is still not a standard bureau

practice elsewhere, but the Agua Caliente Band has successfully demanded this type of lease in recent years.

In general, the economic development of much of the reservation trust land was delayed in relation to the development of
the alternating sections that contained the major hotels,
apartments, office buildings, stores and other such high-income-producing buildings. During the 1970s, due to concerns with the environment, the planning and zoning bodies
of Palm Springs began to think in terms of open space and
some low-density, low-use areas. They could think of no better locations to restrict to low-density use than the reservation
lands. Thus, by using zoning laws, they recently tried to restrict the economic potential of Indian land and thus benefit
the economic potential of non-Indian land.

This aspect of economic development—"environmental concerns" and the attempts to limit development on Indian
lands—is not limited to Palm Springs. Attempts to place limitations on Indian development have been occurring on all reservation lands in California and in other states. Morongo and
Rincon (and Hupa in northern California) represent only a
few of the reservations where cases were filed. In the lower
courts, the Indians have generally lost the cases. Then, with
the aid of California Indian Legal Services, the cases have
been appealed, and at the appeals level the Indians have generally won their cases. The appeals court determined that
P.L. 280 placed Indians under state, not county, laws.[24]

For the purposes of this book on Southern California Indian
land tenure as a whole, I have touched on only the high
points of the Agua Caliente cases. I have not, for example,
mentioned the problems of conservatorships for the estates
of minor children, the aged, and disabled persons. As in so
many cases where estates have extremely high values, some
conservators are more concerned with the management fees
than with the welfare of the individual or even with estate
maintenance. Anyone interested in obtaining more details on
this controversy should read Wendell Oswald's 1978 book
This Land Was Theirs and George Ringwald's 1967 series of articles entitled "The Agua Caliente Indians and Their Guardians."

To this point I have described the general circumstances and conditions common to at least several, and frequently to a majority, of the Southern California Indian reservations. Yet each reservation has its own specific conditions and history that affect the ideas and attitudes of its members toward land tenure and use, as well as their political and social institutions. A few have special problems requiring research and action by the members, and these deserve mention because each has had a major effect on the band involved, and all the other bands have watched the bureau's actions for an indication of its ability to be just, historically accurate, and fair.

San Pasqual   San Pasqual, a Kumeyaay band, had become an Indian pueblo under the Mexican government, and it had very superior farmland located within an easy transportation distance of San Diego. (Some details of its history are given in note 9.) In 1870 the San Pasqual Valley and the surrounding hills, along with the Pala Valley, were reserved for Indians by an executive order, but the order was canceled in 1871 due to the protests of California newspapers that there were no Indians there, only peaceful, settled Christian farmers (Shipek 1972, 1980). The Indians themselves protested that the valley was only large enough for their own operations. With their captain, Panto Duro (Mutewheer sib) they went to San Diego to see Judge Benjamin Hayes, who showed them the records in the county courthouse delimiting and granting them their pueblo lands. According to the San Pasqual Indians, he said he would take their captain to Washington, D.C., with him to prove the Indian title to the land (see note 9). However, Panto died within the month and the trip was not made. After the cancellation of the executive order reservation, these peaceful Christian farming Indians were evicted from their neat adobe homes and farms by the sheriff in response to homesteaders who had filed on Indian lands and who claimed the Indian improvements and adobe houses as their own.[25] A petition to the district land office in Los Angeles signed by the San Pasqual Band leaders seeking rights to their land was ignored. Following the eviction, some of the

Indians joined relatives in the nearby mountain villages of the Mesa Grande Band, whose territory had adjoined and possibly overlapped theirs. Others scattered throughout Southern California wherever they could find work; some settled in the hills surrounding the San Pasqual Valley and remained within San Pasqual Band territory. About ten families managed to find small springs and clear tiny fields to support themselves. Eventually, after 1883, they filed for Indian homesteads on these little isolated holdings. To survive, they also toiled on their former lands as laborers for the people who had evicted them.

The Smiley Commission apparently investigated their condition and intended to make the area containing these homesteads into a reservation for the band. In 1892, however, either through clerical or surveyor error (Cave Couts, Jr., was now the surveyor), the land reserved was mislocated one township north and within traditional San Luiseño—that is, enemy— territory. This reserved land was even poorer than that on which they had taken refuge, and the best areas had already been filed upon by non-Indian settlers. Only the most marginal hill land was available for the reservation—barely enough to support one family. The band members did not go to this land; indeed, many were not even aware they had a reservation for some years. They all remained wherever they had jobs or had developed some form of land rights.

Due to complex problems on other reservations that had resident Indians, the bureau did nothing more for San Pasqual until 1909. Apparently unaware at first of the mislocated reservation land, the schoolteacher on the Mesa Grande Reservation began efforts on behalf of the San Pasqual members and recommended the purchase of land in the San Pasqual Valley for the band. The land was not purchased because, according to a special agent, the price asked was exorbitant, only the most marginal land in the valley was being offered for sale, and the offer was being made by the settlers in an effort to maneuver the government into providing the entire valley with a dam and an irrigation system at no cost to the settlers (Bureau of Indian Affairs Correspondence, 1909–1910).

In the meantime, the Mesa Grande schoolteacher had listed the known members of the band in 1909. After this attempt to get land in their own valley, the mislocated reserved land (Township 11 South, Range 1 West instead of Township 12 South) was patented to the band in 1910. Most band members were already supporting themselves elsewhere, so none went onto this obviously very poor quality land. Only one non-Indian settler within the reserved area had not patented his claim prior to the 1892 reservation order, and the government purchased his improvements in 1909. In 1910 the bureau hired a non-Indian caretaker to protect the purchased improvements, which included a small house. This caretaker had a part-Indian wife who was a member of the Santa Ysabel Band, and their children, two daughters, continued to live on the reservation long after he and his wife were deceased. The bureau, while originally recognizing their Santa Ysabel origin, began to list this family as residents of the San Pasqual Reservation in 1910 and neglected to write in the employee status of the father, a non-Indian.

During the many years of the San Pasqual dispersal throughout Southern California, the band members maintained a variety of social, kinship, and ritual ties. Fiestas to celebrate the patron saint's day of the original chapel at the pueblo of San Pasqual were held annually for many years, either at the chapel, at members' homesteads in the hills, or even on other reservations, such as La Jolla, where some members had married. In spite of living apart and being scattered for some eighty years, the older members had maintained sufficient contact to identify all the members and to give complete genealogies for all of them, and records were found to prove the accuracy of their memories.

In 1954 the descendants of the original band realized that they would lose even this small piece of mislocated reservation land unless they organized to reclaim the reservation. The Indians were required by the bureau to develop proof of their descent from the original San Pasqual members. The bureau required the creation of an enrollment committee composed of the oldest members (five members survived who were on the 1910 list of San Pasqual members, including the daughters of the non-Indian caretaker). This committee was to determine qualifications and examine the required proofs for membership, and it asked me to prepare genealogies and find documentary proof.

A lengthy dispute followed between the enrollment committee and the bureau over the right to use the 1909 membership list prepared by the Mesa Grande schoolteacher who knew the members, rather than the 1910 census list on which the resident non-Indian caretaker and his family had been added. The 1910 census also listed one other non–San Pasqual person, the spouse of a member, who was not identified as to origin but who was of a distant tribe. All other non-Indians (or Indians from other tribes) were identified as such. A copy of the 1909 roll was in the possession of the chairman of the enrollment committee. The bureau enrollment officials insisted that they had no 1909 roll, that the 1910 roll was the only one that had and the only one they would recognize as an official basis for membership. At that time I was not allowed access to other bureau rolls, but at a much later date I did find the 1909 roll among the records in the bureau office.

Working on the regulations, the band enrollment committee replaced the wording "1/8 degree Indian Blood" with "1/8 degree Blood of the Band" in the requirements for membership. The committee had concluded that even a person's inclusion on the 1910 roll did not prove that that person had "Blood of the Band" and that all applicants must still prove ancestral San Pasqual membership prior to 1910. The committee believed that this wording would protect the band. When I suggested that the enrollment committee needed an attorney's advice on the meaning of this compromise wording in conjunction with the other membership regulations, the bureau official interrupted and responded that the Indians did not need an attorney, that the bureau was looking out for San Pasqual's interests.

At every point throughout the process, however, the bureau officials insisted that all those who felt they had a potential right to membership should have the right to participate in the proceedings and to vote on all matters. Therefore the families in dispute who lived in the immediate area could always get their members to the meetings, but the San Pasqual members, some of whom lived two hundred miles away, could not get all their members there every time. Further, in the voting for committee members, the bureau insisted that the nominee who received the largest number of votes would be chairman of the committee and that all other nominees with any votes at all would become committee members. Thus, those persons not recognized by the band always participated in all discussions and voting and could always place one or two members on the committees to have a direct voice in band and enrollment committee decisions.

The enrollment regulations as finally published in the *Federal Register* also included an "administrative addition" to the effect that any Indian who had been attending band meetings for five years without a protest from the band would be considered a band member if he or she applied. The band members had been consistently protesting the attendance and voting of persons whom they considered nonmembers, but they had not put their protest in writing. (Remember that the bureau required that the enrollment committee consist of persons who had been on the 1910 roll, and the band members who fulfilled this requirement were all past seventy and had little education, whereas the non–band members on the 1910 roll had been infants at that time and had received more education.) Had I been an Indian, in fact, this administrative addition would have made me eligible for membership, because I had attended all the meetings without a protest from the band.

The committee carefully examined the claims and proof submitted by each member and compared the material to my copies of various types of records, including records that proved the nonband origin of the disputed persons. The committee did not approve the applications of those persons who did not fit their concept of 1/8 degree of "Blood of the Band." However, the bureau reversed the enrollment committee vote, and the band was forced to accept all those listed on the 1910 census as "Blood of the Band," regardless of the individual's origin. The enrollment committee recognized slightly more than two hundred persons based on full genealogies extending back over a hundred years into records that preceded those of the bureau. In addition, they were forced to accept twenty-nine other individuals whom the bureau said were qualified based on the 1910 roll even though these people did not have the required degree of "Blood of the Band" based on the enrollment committee's interpretation of those words. The bureau's decision on the enrollment was appealed as far as the secretary of the interior, who merely deferred to the local official bureau interpretation and made no investigation of the matter. This dispute lasted fifteen years, and only as the older band members died or became inactive and the younger members realized the futility of fighting the bureau did the band begin to organize on the bureau's terms. But intense factionalism based on this membership identity problem remains and affects all band attempts at economic development and all other actions.

The details of this dispute have been described because many other bands foresee similar problems for themselves due to early bureau censuses that include, without identifying them as nonmembers, persons who were renting reservation houses or leasing a portion of the reservation from the band. In some cases the census rolls include individuals who used force to move onto a reservation, or in other cases nonmembers who had come to live with a relative who had married into the band. The bureau's actions in the San Pasqual case do not encourage other bands to trust the bureau's ability to be historically accurate, fair, or just in their dealings with the reservations. The development of formal membership rolls for many reservations has been delayed while bands have searched for past rolls that correctly reflected their membership before attempting any discussion with bureau officials.

On the other hand, cases have occurred in which individuals have petitioned to have their ancestor's identity changed to increase the descendants' degree of blood to make additional generations eligible for membership. In at least some cases, the bureau has made the change based on three or four internally inconsistent and unverified records. Such actions contrast with its reaction to the quantity of proof developed by the San Pasqual enrollment committee, which the bureau refused to accept.

Mesa Grande   The Mesa Grande Band also has a unique problem that has affected legal tenure and development. The government officials who originally recommended and surveyed land for the executive order reservations in 1875 had such an incomplete knowledge of the area, the band territories, and the political organization of the Indians that they designated the lands and rancherias—the villages of Mesa Grande (Tekemak), Mesa Chiquita (Kumehall), and Santa Rosa—of the Mesa Grande Band on the official survey as Santa Ysabel Numbers 1 and 2. The land reserved for the actual Santa Ysabel Band was designated as Santa Ysabel Number 3.

The original locations of the band territories adjoined each other but were in different drainages of the upper San Dieguito River. Parts of each territory were incorporated into the Santa Ysabel rancho grant, Santa Ysabel, or Elkwanon on the east side and a small portion of Mesa Grande or Pamo territory on the west. Thus their relation to the rancho grant and their position on opposite sides of the rancho may have been the cause for the confusion in the minds of a few early officials. The surviving Mesa Grande rancherias were entirely west of the rancho grant and were in a different stream drainage from the primary drainage of the rancho grant and of the Santa Ysabel Band territory. Mesa Grande was part of the mountain territory of the Pamo Band. Aboriginally, the divides between stream drainages formed band territory boundaries. The Santa Ysabel villages were fifteen miles east of the Mesa Grande villages and along the eastern edge of the rancho grant. The villages of each band were distinct and separately identified in many mission records. Tekemak (Mesa Grande) and Kumehall (Mesa Chiquita) were identified as two of the numerous rancherias belonging to Pamo, and Elkwanon was identified as an entirely separate band, with a number of smaller rancherias belonging to it.

Between the 1875 executive order and the trust patenting of the
lands in 1892, each group remained in its home villages—the
Mesa Grande villages to the west and Elkwanon (Santa Ysabel) to the east. Because they had been forbidden to plant on
the rancho grant, Elkwanon members grazed their flocks and
planted crops wherever they could find a small usable plot in
the hills and mountains immediately outside of the rancho
grant, and most of the people went to the mountains east of
the rancho grant. It was this land that was designated as Santa Ysabel Number 3. A few of the Santa Ysabel people lived
in a small rancheria near the western side of the rancho grant
but east of the divide separating Elkwanon from Pamo territory. When pushed off the grant, because some were related
to Mesa Grande (Pamo) members, a few asked for and received permission to move onto a corner of Mesa Grande territory. In contrast, the majority of Mesa Grande people were
of the Pamo Band and not originally part of Elkwanon or
Santa Ysabel. Mesa Grande was on the northwestern edge of
the grant, with most of its land west of and outside the grant's
boundaries.
While the records of the Smiley Commission and various officials,
special commissioners, and Indian agents who had visited, in-
spected, or supervised the reservations all indicated that they
recognized and dealt with the two bands, Santa Ysabel and
Mesa Grande, as separate, independent entities, the trust patents of all three pieces were issued in the name of the Santa
Ysabel Band, ignoring the Mesa Grande Band's rights to
Numbers 1 and 2. Instead, the small, isolated 120-acre Indian
homestead of one man was trust patented as the Mesa
Grande Reservation (Helen Hunt Jackson Correspondence,
National Archives).
This confusion resulted from the fact that continued incursions
by settlers after the setting of the 1875 executive order reservation boundaries had caused a number of the Mesa Grande
members to file for Indian homesteads when the law was
passed making that possible. Compounding the trust patenting error, the homestead application filed by the elderly captain of the Mesa Grande Band, Cenon Duro, on 120 acres in

the depths of Black Canyon was trust patented as the Mesa Grande Reservation in 1891. This 120 acres was never the home of anyone but Cenon Duro and his direct descendants. The homestead application was for land that had been part of the traditional lands of the Duro (the Spanish translation of Mutewheer) sib lineage of Pamo. The homesteads of other Mesa Grande members, up on the mesa, were ignored and either incorporated into Santa Ysabel Numbers 1 and 2 or taken by non-Indians when the 1891 reservations were designated and surveyed. These two portions, Santa Ysabel Number 1 and Number 2 were continually occupied in the past and continue to be occupied by members of the Mesa Grande Band, while Santa Ysabel Number 3 became the home of the members of the Santa Ysabel Band after they were evicted from the rancho grant. The only papers containing the errors were the 1875 executive order and the 1891 trust patent. More than 98 percent of the massive existing records correctly identify the separate areas and indicate that the Mesa Grande (Pamo) people have always resided on the lands now known as Santa Ysabel Numbers 1 and 2.

Modern development programs that began after 1968 were the first that required that the band be organized and also have a clear legal title to its land for participation in the programs. Bureau records indicate that its officials had been aware of the situation for many years but that they had never bothered to clear the title to the lands. Some of the Mesa Grande Band leaders were aware of the situation and occasionally asked to have the title cleared but were never able to get bureau action. In 1970 the Mesa Grande Band elected a committee that had instructions to seek a solution and attempt to get clear title to the land they had traditionally occupied. This committee acquired copies of the historical documents I had accumulated, and it then developed a statement of the problem, which it submitted to congressmen and various government officials. As a result, the Department of the Interior ordered an impartial investigation of the matter in preparation for an administrative hearing and a possible title correction.

The Bureau of Indian Affairs contracted with Dr. Lowell J. Bean to investigate the matter, and I turned over to him all the documentation I had accumulated.[26] He then went to archives I had not yet checked and acquired additional documents. He testified before an administrative judge of the Department of the Interior and presented massive documentation, which began with the very early mission records and early ethnographic interviews and included the federal government records dating from 1848. The documentation supported the separate identity and historic locations of the two bands and indicated that the only errors had been in the wording of the 1875 executive order, followed by the wording of the trust patents in 1892. The administrative judge ignored this massive documentation, refusing to study it, and said he was confused. He decided against the Mesa Grande petition, writing in his decision that 51 percent proof of the existence of an error was insufficient to correct a federal document, that he would require 75 percent proof. Quite obviously he did not study or consider the documentation, more than 98 percent of which contradicted the only two documents that had created the error. He further suggested that the two bands merge and become one, the same suggestion that the bureau had been making during recent years and that had been rejected by the bands because there was a great disparity between the two bands in the size of their membership. The Mesa Grande Band plans to continue its fight for justice and a recognition of its land rights.

Interestingly enough, the 1875 executive order also made a mistake by including Rincon, Potrero, La Jolla, and Ya Piche as one reservation called Potrero. The last three were rancherias high on a mountain shoulder, and Rincon was a rancheria down in the canyon of the San Luis Rey River. Rincon was separated from the other three by the rancho grant of Cuca. The Smiley Commission correctly identified and trust patented Rincon as a separate reservation. It also correctly identified the three mountain villages but deliberately decided to include them as one reservation, which they named La Jolla (Smiley Commission Records), particularly because the peoples of La Jolla and Ya Piche were "jealous of each other." Of further interest is the fact that at least one Indian agent of that period, Francisco Estudillo, did not know or recognize this differentiation, and as late as 1895 his records consistently confuse and misidentify the Rincon, Potrero, and La Jolla villages and reservations (Mission Indian Agency Records).

One possible cause for the original errors in the 1875 executive order was that the Indian agents and surveyors were still recognizing and dealing with the tribal officials identified as "generals," and who were able to call most of the band "captains" and members to special meetings. The San Luiseño general was Oligario Calac, a resident at Rincon who frequently dealt with Indian agents and surveyors and who represented and spoke for all the captains of the neighboring San Luiseño bands. The northern Kumeyaay or Diegueño "general" was resident at Santa Ysabel and frequently spoke for the assembled captains of the surrounding Diegueño bands, such as Mesa Grande (Tekemak and Kumehall), as well as Inyaha, Capitan Grande, San Pasqual, San Felipe, Mataguay, Tawhee, and San Jose. (The last four were villages on other rancho grants and were included in the Warner Hot Springs case and thus in the 1903 order to remove to the recently purchased lands of Pala. The people of Mataguay fled to Santa Ysabel and those of San Jose and Tawhee fled to Mesa Grande, and both groups were accepted as refugees in those places.) Thus there would be as much justification for having placed the lands of Iñaja, Capitan Grande, and San Pasqual Bands under Santa Ysabel as for having placed Mesa Grande under Santa Ysabel.

The tenure-use problems of both the Mesa Grande and San Pasqual bands have been described because they have had a serious effect on band organization, tenure rights, and land development. These problems have also taken the time and effort of the band memberships for many years, thus delaying any positive developments. These past actions by the bureau continue to be a source of internal division and occupy most efforts of the members of the bands so involved. Further, as stated earlier, most other reservations have closely watched the bureau's actions in these problems, and they are making decisions concerning their own problems based on the bureau's ability to correct the record of historical errors and to develop fair, just, and acceptable solutions. The bands have not been reassured by events.

Pechanga. In 1978 the Pechanga tribal council first acquired and examined the executive orders and the trust patenting of its reservation and discovered that a discrepancy existed for which they could not account: additional land had been reserved but not trust patented to the reservation. Upon investigating the discrepancy, the best available evidence indicated that the section in question had contained a homestead claim that had been disallowed by the General Land Office as fraudulent. However, the government had not served the defrauder with the final papers in the case, and at a later date the claimant sold the land, even though he did not have clear title. By 1978 the land had just recently been sold to a large development corporation that had ignored this original cloud on the title. The Pechanga Band brought suit to recover the land. The case was decided, not on the validity of the original title, but on the fact that modern landowners were making decisions based on the belief that they had bought clear title. In other words, the court decided, as it had in the earlier *Barker* v. *Harvey* decision, that different principles would be applied to land stolen from Indian reservations and that such land was not recoverable. The court to this day is still selectively using and applying laws relating to stolen land if Indians are involved.[27]

FORMER PATRONAGE TENURE

Two small reservations were not part of the lands reserved as a result of the investigations of the Smiley Commission. One, Santa Inez in Santa Barbara County, was delayed in its establishment because of the commission's inability to resolve the existing differences between the Indians and the landowner. The other, Jamul in southern San Diego County, was not established by the Smiley Commission because it considered the bands too small and scattered to visit and their landholdings too small to develop as reservations. Both cases resulted in the formation of trust patent reservations due to the patronage of the Catholic church and, in the case of Jamul, the original patronage of a rancho grant owner.

Santa Ynez. Santa Ynez is a small reservation located in Santa Barbara County near the former Mission Santa Ynez. It was not included in the lands visited by the Smiley Commission and was not trust patented as a result of its work. The Indians of the village were living on lands belonging to the Catholic church, that is, on the lands immediately surrounding the old Indian cemetery belonging to Mission Santa Ynez. In 1901 the Indians apparently persuaded the bishop of that region to deed the land to the United States government to be trust patented to the Indians living there. This was done, and since 1901 Santa Ynez has been a trust patented reservation under the Southern California Mission Indian Agency.

Jamul. Jamul was the only nonreservation village or band with land that survived until recently. Although the Smiley Commission planned for and reserved what they thought was sufficient land at Capitan Grande to provide homes for the small band fragments scattered through southern San Diego County, most Indians refused to go there. To the Indians, Capitan Grande contained only portions of the territory of the two bands already living there, and one band member did not go onto another band's land without a specific invitation from that band. Further, the Smiley Commission had received instructions to reserve land that the bands actually occupied and used wherever the lands were unless the land was already claimed by a non-Indian. Thus commission members did not follow their instructions, because they felt that they had neither the budget nor the time to locate the many small bands scattered throughout the southern part of the county. The history of these small remnant bands is varied. A few persons slowly assimilated; some went across the border into Baja California (Shipek 1968), some married into other reservations, and some joined Jamul.

The Jamul Band was one of the bands contacted by the Spanish missionaries within a few years of the founding of Mission San Diego. By 1900 they were no longer living in their aboriginal village but were still within their band territory. The heart of their aboriginal territory had been granted as a rancho during the Mexican period, and the band had been forced to move to the edges of their Indian cemetery on the rancho grant, thus on a minute portion within their aboriginal territory. Most of the Indians were employed on the rancho grant or on other nearby ranches. By 1912, John D. Spreckels (the president of the Spreckels Sugar Company) had become, as head of the Coronado Beach Company, the owner of the rancho grant. Spreckels deeded title to 2.5 acres that "included an Indian Cemetery and the approaches thereto" to the Catholic bishop of the Diocese of Los Angeles. Spreckels then told the Indians, who were his ranch hands, that they would always have this place to live, that they could not be evicted. Children who were present at this meeting with Spreckels were still alive in the 1950s, and they described the meeting.

The people of the Jamul Band still occupy and use this small remaining portion of their aboriginal territory. In 1971 they asked the University of San Diego Reservation Community Development Project for instruction in organizational development, constitution and ordinance writing, and community planning. They then developed a formal organization and joined the Southern California Indian Intertribal Association. Following this, they applied to the California Indian Legal Service and the Indian Rights Association for aid in obtaining federal recognition. I prepared a notarized testimony giving the history of the band and the identity and genealogy of the band members (Shipek 1972a). I was able to trace the genealogy of the Jamul Band members into the previous century and, as for San Pasqual, some families could be traced much earlier, even though a gap in the church records existed between 1900 and 1919 because the church in charge of Indian religious rites through that time had burned. Other records were found for that period of time. The Indian Rights Association carried the battle through the Bureau of Indian Affairs and Congress, and the band obtained federal recognition in 1976.

Such recognition made the Jamul village and its members eligible for all federal programs for Indians. Because part of the land they occupied was a Catholic cemetery, the bishop of San Diego was approached to determine whether the land could be divided, with the cemetery and chapel remaining as dedicated church property and the part occupied by the homes of the people being turned into a reservation. The band also asked the bureau about the possibility of having additional land purchased for them, and by 1982 additional land had been acquired, so that the reservation then encompassed 6.03 acres. During 1985 the Bureau of Land Management determined that eighty acres of public land near the Jamul village was surplus land and could be turned over to Jamul as trust reservation land if Congress passed the necessary legislation.

CHAPTER 5

Indian Lands outside Reservations

PREVIOUS CHAPTERS HAVE sketched the very complex history of Southern California Indian efforts to retain ownership of some lands within their aboriginal holy lands and have focused on the various forms of reservation tenure. In addition, many Indians achieved success outside the reservations, with the result that numerous Indians own lands that are not within reservation boundaries. Families that have achieved a degree of economic affluence working in Southern California towns and cities have even become rentiers. Like non-Indian citizens, they have saved their money, obtained Veterans Administration, bank, or savings and loan association mortgage loans and purchased homes and income properties. This type of purchase, using their own savings and their borrowing ability, is only one of the several alternative ways in which Southern California Indians can and have acquired lands outside reservations.

Public Domain Allotments

The Southern California Indians did not wait passively for the federal government to reserve and trust patent lands for them. Evidence indicates that they were aware of the General Allotment Act of 1887 as soon as it was passed. Many Indians immediately began filing for public domain allotments, which have generally been called "Indian homesteads." By 1891, when the Smiley Commission was determining the extent of

Indian land occupancy and use for reservation purposes, some Indians had already completed the homestead paperwork, and their land was in trust to them as individuals. Others had only partially completed filing on their individually occupied land, and their land was included within reservation boundaries. A number of families have expressed the dismay they felt upon finding out that what they thought was their homestead had become reservation land and thus belonged not to their family but to an entire band.

While the reservations were being trust patented, other Indians continued to file for the trust public domain allotments wherever they were using and occupying small, isolated mountain valleys not yet entered by settlers. Indians were also acquiring other homesteads by the regular entry and patenting process, not through the public domain allotment act specifically for Indians, and these homesteads were not trust lands. Some of the homesteads are still in the hands of the Indian owners or their descendants, some have been sold, and some lost, depending on the individual or the heirs. Numbers and acreages of the nontrust homesteads filed and retained, sold, or lost would be almost impossible to estimate because well before 1890 many Indians had translated their names or acquired a non-Indian surname through a non-Indian father.

In filing for Indian trust homesteads, the Indian was required to state that he had separated himself from tribal status. As a result, some Indians called the Indian homesteaders traitors to the band. They pressured homesteaders into leaving homestead lands and entering the reservations. Non-Indian settlers who desired to acquire the land occupied by Indian homesteaders participated in this name-calling and pressured Indians to leave their homesteads. None of the bands seemed to realize that because the "Indian homesteads" were in trust status, homesteading was no different from accepting an allotment within a reservation, except that in Southern California a person usually acquired larger acreage through the homestead process than was possible by reservation allotment. In terms of the federal government's attempts at forced transculturation, both processes were intended equally to terminate with fee patent title and citizenship status rather than tribal status for the individual.

Of those Indians who maintained their homesteads, many also maintained their membership in their band and participated in all band activities. Some of these people have been an asset to their bands, participating in all band activities and band deliberations, and thus they are helping to maintain the viability of the band and band assets. They participate in attempts to improve reservation conditions for the residents and other members of the group. On the other hand, there have been families that acquired homesteads and that also sought to control and acquire reservation assets in addition to the homestead. Some families have actually acquired or inherited and sold several homesteads and then moved onto a reservation, not because they did not understand land ownership, but because they also desired reservation assets. While the Bureau of Indian Affairs does not allow an Indian to share in the membership rights and assets of two reservations, it has, by ignoring it, allowed this form of access to double rights.[28]

Many of the problems that exist for homestead trust owners and heirs are the same as those faced by reservation allotment owners, such as a lack of adequate road access and a loss of the trust status in whole or in part due to inheritance by a non-Indian spouse. In the case of one public domain allotment, the direct descendants of the original owners have protected their family by drawing wills that eliminate inheritance by any but direct line-of-descent heirs and that allow the non-Indian spouse to have only a lifetime use-right.

In other cases, so many heirs exist and shares are so small that the decision has been made to sell the homestead and divide the cash. Frequently, many of the heirs have become city dwellers, and they use the inheritance money toward purchase or improvement of their city home. The recent experience of one group of heirs has shown, however, that in spite of the high value of Southern California acreage, there is little to be gained by selling unused homestead land. This sale was authorized by the heirs, all city dwellers, in the late 1960s.

The real estate division of the bureau sold the land for less than one-tenth of the going price for comparable land in that particular region of San Diego County, the avocado orchard area. The heirs, knowing land values, were shocked by the pittance each one received from this sale.

Some homesteads lack adequate right-of-way provisions and have become practically unusable. Entrance is possible only through private land across which the owner will not allow any form of road, or only a single dirt track. Other homesteads are so distant from any maintained roads that access to and from the homestead by car is practically impossible. Most of the homestead lands are extremely valuable under modern population conditions. Some are potential avocado or orchard land and need only capital and guaranteed water to be productive. Others could be homesites or recreation places for families.

Terminated Reservations

Any discussion of private landholding by Indians must emphasize that at least since 1900 Indians have been buying, using, and selling other lands outside of trust status. Some have even bought land for investment purposes, such as business property, additional houses for rental purposes, or empty land for resale at a later date.

One Indian, claiming that his family was the sole surviving family of one reservation, requested that the 320-acre reservation be fee patented to his family. Another Indian disputed this claim, but the bureau sided with the first claimant, Congress finally acceded, and the Laguna Reservation became private land. Since the early 1940s this individual used the land as a private ranch while also owning a very nice city home, and the tract was recently sold.

Another case is the Mission Creek Reservation. In the mid-1950s no residents remained. A man who had a claim through an ancestral member of the reservation searched out all the other people who had such claims. They then cooperated in every way with the bureau in developing a tribal roll, constitution, and bylaws. They also cooperated with the bureau in planning to attract some economic development. They needed wells and water first, and then bureau loans for houses and other planned economic development. After years of frustration and in spite of every attempt on their part to be completely cooperative with the bureau, they finally decided to give up and sell the reservation land. All of the people involved in this attempt were high school or college graduates, and many had had their own successful businesses outside the reservation system for years. With all their competence, they felt that the effort was taking too much out of them, and they finally decided that it would be a failure in the long run, that the Bureau simply did not want them to be successful.

Rancherias

Throughout central and northern California, in addition to some reservations, there were a number of rancherias, which were basically lands reserved for landless California Indians and generally small, relatively isolated house plots held in trust for one or more extended families. The Rancheria Act, which terminated the federal trust status, was passed by Congress in 1964 after the people of the larger reservations fought against and defeated the proposed termination bill for all California trust lands (Public Law 85–671, as amended August 11, 1964). In each case, among other promised amenities, the Bureau of Indian Affairs was supposed to bring road access, water rights, and domestic water availability up to state standards. Many members of these former rancherias have sued the federal government for lack of performance and have requested a return to trust status. Neither road access nor domestic water were developed, and the Indians have often discovered that local property tax structures had changed, making property taxes an impossible burden.

CHAPTER 6

Modern Developments

COMBINED WITH A federal policy of allowing increased self-determination and self-government under
the federal trust provisions and new laws providing for various types of federal grants to local governments, Indian reservations are seeking solutions to a number of past problems
and searching for solutions to the housing needs of their
members and the need for compatible modern economic development on the reservations. In some cases, the problems
of the past need research and solutions either before new
programs are developed or concurrently with the development.

A variety of programs and development opportunities have been
and will be offered. Selection among the opportunities requires a careful study of the potential effects of each program, the federal regulations under which each might operate, and the potential for creating a political threat to the
survival of the reservation. Even the best programs contain a
potential for damage unless the implementation is carefully
managed.

Boundary Surveys

Some of the problems concerning the surveying of reservations during the trust patenting period have already been
mentioned. Discrepancies existed between the 1875 and 1892
surveys for the reservation boundaries, as well as in township

and range line locations, as noted by the later surveyors. In 1891 the first reservation surveyor noted errors and found that in some places settlers were on lands previously reserved for Indians. He was fired when this information became public, and his survey notes for those incorrect areas are not available. In the Coachella Valley other surveyors noted that early corner stakes had often been moved or removed entirely (Office of Indian Affairs Records, National Archives, Record Group 75). In addition, according to Indians on most of the reservations, several successive surveys were made, and in each case each successive survey moved reservation boundaries inward onto the Indian side, especially if good farmland or water was involved. My own examination of township, range, and section lines on the pertinent United States Geological Survey topographic maps seems to indicate that reservation sections are consistently smaller than nearby nonreservation sections on the same map, some by more than forty acres. The number of small sections is far beyond the number that might be expected from random error.[29]

During this early period, 1891 through 1910, most reservations were fenced by the Indians, with some of the wire being supplied by the bureau and shipping costs being paid by the Indians. Some wire was purchased directly by the Indians. (The cost of the bureau-supplied wire and fencing materials was included as part of the offsets in the Indians of California Claims Case, and thus it was eventually paid for by the Indians.) Following this early fencing of the reservation by the Indians, in many cases adjoining ranch owners replaced fences and moved them inward.

The "walking fences," as they are termed, have affected both reservation and Indian homestead lands. In one homestead case, in 1956, the original Indian fence was replaced by the adjoining landowner and the fence line moved inward 20 feet. There had been no resurvey of the land; the fence was simply moved in onto the Indian homestead. Immediately after moving the fence, the ranch land was sold. The new purchaser was unaware that some of the land he was buying did not belong to the seller. The Indian homestead owner attempted to have the bureau resurvey his land and have the fences corrected. At that time the bureau official said they would be glad to resurvey the land if the family would sell the homestead, which was in the midst of valuable avocado land, and since then the family has been repeatedly told that no surveyor is available or that there are no funds for such a survey.

Another recent example is a small reservation, Cosmit, which is a part of Iñaja. It has already been mentioned that Cosmit was mislocated on a dry, rocky hill on which no Indians lived. The land was unusable except for the occasional grazing of cattle and as a source of a small amount of firewood and a few minor usable plants. Recently the mountainous valley beside the reservation became valuable as the site of mountain recreation homesites. The developers, in clearing the non-Indian land and marking lots for sale, removed the old fence surrounding the reservation and placed the new fence several yards inside the old boundary line. The protests of the Iñaja-Cosmit members and requests to the bureau for protection and for a new survey were ignored. Interestingly, on the bureau list of reservation lands the BIA has recently reduced the acreage for this reservation by approximately thirty acres.

In another case, a major dispute was developing between reservation members over the use of a road that everyone, including the bureau official, thought was within the reservation boundaries and crossed several allotments. To avoid what the bureau thought would become major violence, it finally had the road resurveyed. As a result, it was discovered that at some early date the reservation boundary markers had been shifted on two sides and that the road was outside the reservation, so the reservation gained an equal-width strip on the opposite side of the reservation.

Although several homestead owners and some of the reservation members may have sufficient individual funds to hire a surveyor independently, it is impossible for them to do so. A federal law prohibits anyone from contracting to do anything on or for Indian trust lands without the approval of the Bureau of Indian Affairs. Thus the bureau has effectively prevented any private contracting for surveying (or private digging of wells) and the bureau itself has not done it, except in the one case of threatened violence.

A complete, accurate, and honest resurvey of all reservation and homestead lands is urgently needed. In addition, justice demands that the Bureau take action to recover the trust lands from the private parties who have, in effect, bought stolen property. The course for the people who presently think they own that land should be to take legal action against those individuals from whom they bought the land, not to continue to hold the fraudulently obtained or stolen land, as has occurred in some cases, such as Pechanga and Warner's Hot Springs.

Housing

Many bands took advantage of modifications in the Housing and Urban Development laws that allowed Southern California reservations to organize and form a joint All Mission Indian Housing Authority (AMIHA) for the purpose of developing low-cost houses for band members who meet the income and other qualifications of the general housing authority laws. Joining AMIHA requires a formal band meeting, passage of a resolution to join, and passage of the necessary ordinances giving authority to formally elected delegates to represent the band on the housing authority board. The band must determine which portion of tribal land is to be used for the housing development, and the tribal land upon which the houses are to be placed must be leased to the housing authority for 50 years. For persons with individual allotments, the house-lot portion may be marked off, and it alone becomes security for the long-term house loan.

If an owner fails to meet the low payments or the house falls vacant for any reason, the housing authority must take over the unit and find a qualified person to occupy the house. From the Indian point of view, this is a drawback of the HUD housing authority program. The laws governing the housing authority forbid racial discrimination, so that if no "community member" could meet the requirements for occupancy at that time, a nonmember would be able to move in. The general requirements for original occupancy may be limited to "community members," thus, in most but not all cases, limiting the original occupancy to Indian band members. The prohibition against racial discrimination would only become a problem if a house fell vacant for any reason. On tribal land, the non-Indian occupant would have the house for the remainder of the fifty-year tribal land lease to the housing authority. However, if the house were on an allotment, inasmuch as that portion of the allotment was mortgaged, that portion would be lost to Indian ownership entirely. Most bands prefer to maintain their community identity, so some have considered ways to solve this problem before committing land to AMIHA housing. Some bands have refused to join for this reason.

Some of the bands would like to develop a tribal fund that would be able to take over the payments if for any reason a member were unable to make his payments. The house would then become a tribally owned house, and future tenants would be determined by, and pay rent to, the tribe. One band, Pala, has already developed its own tribal housing by financing the building of low-cost tribally owned houses for elderly pensioners who would not meet the minimum housing authority occupancy qualifications because of their age.

The Housing and Urban Development AMIHA program was designed to develop low-cost housing and is limited to low-income families. Many Indian families exist that do not qualify for this program, as their income is above the maximum allowed. Some families in the more affluent group have managed to build homes on the reservations, using their family income and their own labor as capital, and financing and building increments when they have the cash available. Others have bought houses in towns where they have jobs, using the normal financing channels because such city lots were not trust land. Some have bought several houses in this manner, increasing their real estate holdings to rent some of them for income purposes. Thus they have increased their capital and income and then built or improved their house on the reservation.

For Indians who do not meet the low-income AMIHA requirement but who have insufficient capital to build out of their own income, the bureau completed arrangements in 1970 with the Federal Housing Administration (FHA) so that Indians who have allotments (or private legal trust title) may mortgage only the house-lot portion of the allotment and obtain home construction financing. This does not make any provision for housing for those living on assignments on unallotted reservations or for those lacking an allotment on allotted reservations. No portion of an assignment may be mortgaged, because no legal private title to the land exists. Consequently, no financing has been arranged for Indians with assignments. These people are building as they have in the past, out of current income.

The bureau also has a housing program, known as the Housing Improvement Program (HIP). This program provides funds for the construction of low-cost homes for Indian families at no cost to the Indian and for home repairs or improvements for existing homes needing them. Sufficient funds are not available to build homes for all Indians on all the reservations, so a selection procedure must be operating, but the criteria are not obvious. Some houses have been built for families that could have managed their own financing on their allotments, and some homes have been built for families that would be eligible for other programs. In other words, the home-building program has not been limited to those who could not manage to build a house on their own or to those who could not qualify for any of the available programs.

These housing programs have been functioning for sufficient time to reveal some unforeseen problems. Many of the houses built by the housing authority or under the bureau programs were poorly located or poorly built or both. In one case, a stream flowed through the house after every rain. Almost all houses needed major repairs within a year of being built. Also, for economy in the construction and maintenance of utilities, HUD prefers to locate HUD housing together in a small neighborhood as if the houses were on small city lots. For most reservations, this is contrary to the usual method of spacing houses far enough apart so that each family has enough space surrounding it to allow for privacy. Most feel uncomfortable when crowded together on very small lots.

Other arbitrary Housing and Urban Development rules forbid fireplaces and require gas stoves for cooking in their low-cost homes, as HUD considers fireplaces and cast-iron wood stoves to be luxuries. On the reservations, however, gas, oil, or propane fuel for cooking and heat are expensive luxuries and require cash outlays. In contrast, firewood is available on the reservation merely for the effort of obtaining it, and Indian families have always used firewood. But the housing authority rules make no provisions for this. In addition, the HUD-approved house plans provide relatively small kitchens and dining alcoves. Indian homes, in contrast, were always built with a large kitchen with space for a dining table for family and guests. For this reason, many Indians have complained of feeling strange and uncomfortable in their HUD houses. Another cause for complaint is the fact that all visitors must be reported, and regulations forbid having visitors stay in the home longer than three or four days. The home occupant must report anyone staying for longer than that, because the income of such a person must then be added to that of the residents, which may place the total income above that allowed for occupants of such housing. This precludes the type of family visiting that has always been characteristic of Southern California Indian cultures, and many non-Indians are undoubtedly also upset by this nonvisiting rule. It precludes having an elderly parent or close relative permanently in the home, because even a single elder's minimum social security income will put the family over the allowed income level. Again, this has long been the preferred manner to care for the elderly members of the Indian family. To the Indians, in addition to the family caring for the elder, the elderly member contributes to the family through the cultural training and teaching that the elder provides the children. Many Indians feel that these unforeseen HUD housing regulations are destroying their family and cultural life.

The people also feel that they are constantly being watched due to these types of rules. HUD personnel, without warning and fairly often, inspect each person's house for care and cleanliness. How many of us keep our houses immaculate at all times, ready for such an inspection? Most Indian homes with which I have been acquainted, even some very old "shacks," were so scrubbed that one could have eaten off the floor. Regardless, HUD officials lecture the women on how to clean house, and they distribute to all the women a booklet detailing how to clean each part of the house and the furniture. The booklet includes several pages on how to clean and polish the family silver, as if families qualifying for low-income HUD housing had quantities of family silver.

Another problem with the income limitation on reservation HUD housing is that it tends to force young Indians either to remain in low-income jobs or to move out of their home if they have begun to acquire job skills and move up the pay scale. Yet no provisions are made for reservation housing for those who begin to develop slightly better incomes. If forced out of the HUD housing, they often must leave the Indian community.

Planning

One final modern problem must be discussed, and it relates to the present value of land and housing in Southern California and the increasing movement of the general population to the Sun Belt states. Due to the population pressure on land and housing, many people are looking to the reservations not as open space but as potential low-cost housing for themselves. At the present time, reservations with good highway access are under housing development pressure equivalent to the resource development pressures seen on reservations having coal and oil (Geisler 1982). Daily, individuals appear at the tribal offices claiming to be Indians and requesting information about reservation housing. On some reservations, ineligible children (that is, children with too low a degree of blood to qualify) have already had housing constructed for them under one of the programs described above. Compounding this problem is the fact that many reservations have not updated or analysed their membership rolls. This, of course, relates to the problems with the bureaucracy that were discussed in the preceding sections. However, it seems imperative that reservations should now carefully reexamine existing enrollment regulations in relation to their population. In other words, they should develop their own tribal roll if none exists and then analyse the number of members on the most recent official tribal enrollment by degree of blood, and carefully record all their children and grandchildren, sorting by degree of blood to determine the potential population for which housing will be needed. This relates to planning for future roads, water use, sewage and trash disposal, and other utilities and community services. Some Indians are also considering obtaining all the existing mission, church, federal census, and bureau records and attempting to determine their actual membership and remove those not truly qualified.

Tribal Income

One aspect of tribal land use has not yet been discussed: the cash income from such land and its use. Under bureau regulations, income from tribal trust lands is "trust income" and must go to the bureau, where it is placed in a trust account for the band. In the past, bands have had difficulty in obtaining an accounting from the bureau of the amounts and use of this money. Formerly, the bureau made the decision about how this money was to be used without consulting tribal members, and in the past such money was often used for bureau administrative costs without the knowledge of the tribe. The Indians have had delays and difficulty in obtaining use of the money for tribally determined projects. Also they have objected to the extremely low interest rate that trust money draws while in trust accounts; the rate was even lower than the interest paid on individual bank savings accounts. Thus, Indians have almost universally expressed their resentment of the bureau's handling of their trust accounts. They concluded that no incentive existed to develop tribal income because neither the group as a whole nor they as individuals would ever see or obtain any benefit from the trust money. For several generations, many Southern California Indians have been handling their own financial affairs outside of the reservation in a most satisfactory manner and consider that they are entirely competent to do so with reservation funds.

Under more recent bureau regulations and procedures (meaning those followed after 1960 in Southern California), a tribe may develop a budget for using tribal money to cover tribal operating expenses or to build tribal buildings, or for some other tribal purpose, or it may decide to have a per capita distribution of the money. Also, if the reservation has developed a legally responsible organization and bonded its treasurer, the reservation members may vote to take the tribal money, or portions of it, out of trust and handle it themselves. Pala is an example of a reservation that is using tribal funds for development. The people there develop a budget for their yearly tribal operating expenses and have already built a tribal office and meeting hall, a cultural center, and an industrial park, and they have started a tribal housing program. In addition, some funds are distributed to the membership yearly on a per capita basis.

As mentioned, a great deal of resentment still exists over the way in which the bureau handled trust tribal funds in the past. Many well-meaning non-Indians and non-Indian organizations are aware of this resentment, and in their attempts to aid Indians, they have sometimes succeeded in obtaining for them the right to remove the money from trust. But they, and sometimes the Indians, have not understood all the implications of doing so and have not recognized that some protection for the Indians may exist in the trust control of the money.

One example of this is protection for the elderly and for disabled people or minors receiving assistance from various programs, such as the Old-Age Pension and Aid to Dependent Children programs. A per capita distribution to persons in this category may cause them to be dropped from the assistance program, or at least cause a withholding of an equal sum from the assistance source. A per capita distribution provides no benefits to persons in such categories unless a special provision has previously been approved that exempts such per capita payments from consideration in calculating the eligibility of the person. Such a precedent exists in the regulations developed for the per capita distribution of the monies received in the Indians of California claim cases.

A second reason for not withdrawing tribal funds from trust control was discovered by some bands only after they were aided in getting the funds out of trust and into the control of the tribe in the person of a bonded treasurer. These bands have discovered that the out-of-trust funds could not be used for one of their most desired but seldom discussed purposes. Many bands would like to buy the pieces of non-Indian-owned lands that are within the boundaries of the reservation. These "holes" may be the result of several different causes. They may be land enclaved within a reservation because a settler had completed filing his homestead application prior to the order (that of 1875, 1891, or one of several other orders) for withdrawal of the land from the public domain for Indian reservation purposes. Other holes have resulted from sale by an allotment owner or by multiple heirs. Sometimes fractions of allotments have been sold or passed out of trust through inheritance by a non-Indian spouse. Band members are also concerned that through inheritance problems or individual needs in the future, other land will pass out of trust and be sold (Bean 1978 and Shipek field notes), and they would like to have the tribe be able to purchase such land as it comes on the market.

To buy any of these lands as they become available for sale, and to have such land added to the reservation (or for a member to buy out an allottee and keep the land in trust), it is necessary for the band (or the individual) to have trust money available. For land to enter trust status it must be purchased with trust money earned as income from trust land or from the sale of right-of-way easements across trust tribal or trust allotted land. This potential use of trust money should be considered before money is removed from trust for other purposes. A recent court decision in the case of *City of Tacoma*

v. *Cecil B. Andrus, The Puyallup Tribe Civ. A. 77–1423 (Federal Supp.)* may change this bureau requirement.

Economic Development

Recently, some bands have set aside certain portions of the reservations for band enterprises and for economic development purposes. Practically all the reservations are looking for some form of economic development that will function in and be compatible with their rural residential area. Their desires and planning are dependent on the amount and type of tribal land available, its proximity to their own residences, the possibility of providing highway access to the economic enterprise without disturbing the residence area, and the area's access to the fast, modern highway system of Southern California. Some of the possibilities are specialized agriculture, (including orchards), light industry, gasoline stations, restaurants, motels, lakes with resort development, leased housing, and camping, fishing, and recreation grounds. Most recently, bingo halls have been added to those reservations that are easily accessible to the non-Indian population.

Several developments have already started and have begun to produce income for the tribe. Pala, for example, already has a sand and gravel industry operating on a lease. This lease provides income to the tribe and a number of jobs for Pala members. In addition, Pala has a recreational campground and a designated industrial park, and it is looking for light industry that would employ tribal members. La Jolla, high on a winding mountain road, has the beautiful San Luis Rey River in a canyon and has developed an attractive campground with good fishing obtained by stocking the river. It was necessary for the band to obtain an assured flow of water from the Henshaw Dam, which is controlled by the Escondido Mutual Water Company, against whom the San Luis Rey River reservations had filed a water case for removing all except winter storm water from the river. In 1972, pending the hearing and settlement of the case, the federal district court ordered the release of at least six acre feet yearly and on a continual basis, after which La Jolla completed and expanded its development of the very popular and profitable fishing and camping park and store. The case was settled in 1985 with the return of water permanently to the reservations, pending approval by Congress. Los Coyotes, also isolated in the mountains east of Warner's Springs, has developed a very popular campground, and Viejas (Baron Long), just off Interstate 8, has developed a popular recreational vehicle park.

While some other reservations also have this special suitability for income production through the development of recreational facilities, others do not. The original part of Pauma reservation, for example, is prime orchard land. In the early part of the century it contained extremely profitable orange and apricot orchards, and the Indians used all the water in Pauma Creek for irrigation. When the surrounding landowners realized how profitable the fruit trees were, they replaced sheep with fruit orchards and diverted all the water, including that which belonged to Pauma according to the deed of purchase of the reservation land. Furthermore, under California water law, the United States, as their trustee, should have filed upon all the water in the stream because it should have belonged to the Indians by right of prior beneficial use.[30] Following this diversion, which began in 1916, Pauma became a dry island in the midst of lush, high-income-producing citrus and avocado orchards. Under the terms of the settlement of their part of Docket 80A, however, the Pauma will begin receiving sufficient water to replant orchards. Other reservations have land suitable for modern agribusiness truck gardens for specialty vegetable crops on a year-round basis by using plastic ground covers or hothouses. They are also close enough to population centers to market such produce profitably. Other reservations are located along major freeways and are sufficiently distant from major cities that motel, garage, and restaurant facilities should be profitable. Still others, with adequate access to transportation routes and a potential labor force, are suitably located for light industry.

The most recent development is bingo. Among others, Sycuan, Barona, and Rincon have built bingo halls and have been running very profitable bingo games for the non-Indians of

San Diego County. In Santa Barbara County, Santa Ynez is managing a profitable bingo hall. In all these cases, Indians are employed to manage the food concessions and have received training to manage and operate the games. At least one case in Southern California has already been filed and heard in an attempt to prevent the reservations from developing this new source of tribal income. Dr. Lowell J. Bean presented data on the traditional gambling practices and their modifications during the Spanish, Mexican, prereservation, and early reservation periods (personal communication). The Indians won the case and the right to continue the bingo games, though this case has now been appealed to a higher court. Following the loss of this case, however, the state of California approved a state lottery, obviously in an attempt to obtain some of the gambling profit for the state. In 1986, Congress passed a law limiting gambling on Indian reservations to bingo and "traditional games" until it has thoroughly investigated the situation. Obviously, Congress has never read any literature describing "traditional" Indian gambling for any tribe, because many forms of gambling were popular pastimes.

Many bands have been offered—and have considered, discussed, and refused—what could have been profitable proposals that the members concluded were incompatible with their own residential use of the reservations (Bean 1978; Shipek field notes). Several, including Rincon, have refused sand and gravel operations in recent years, as past observations of such a system on another reservations had demonstrated the potential problems.[31] Although on Pala the sand and gravel operation is off to one side and the trucks leaving the plant do not have to pass through residential areas, on other reservations such separation would not be possible, and the trucks would continually pass residences and children's play areas. Therefore residents have declined such offers.

Another reservation turned down what could have been a highly profitable long-term lease offer from developers who planned a moderately high density residential development. The comment heard most frequently was that in the section to be retained for band use, "our houses would be too close together and we would always be seeing our neighbors." Another reservation turned down a proposal to use its mountaintops for the wind-powered generation of electric power. The tribe felt that the power lines and numerous mountaintop windmills would be incompatible with its cultural view of mountains and land use.

All the reservation communities are investigating development proposals in detail. They are attempting to discover the hidden costs—cultural, social, economic, and ecological—as well as the benefits that the promoters emphasize. They have all had long experience with government officials and potential lessees who present a rosy picture of the glowing benefits and money the tribe will derive from accepting the proposal. Too often in the past a tribe accepted a lease proposal only to find that the inconveniences to tribal members and other disadvantages of the proposal were hidden, sometimes knowingly by the promoter and the bureau personnel. These hidden social, cultural, economic, and ecological costs only became apparent after the lease project had been instituted. Many tribes are now studying each lease proposal very carefully for such hidden costs and potential dangers. Others still need to develop such practices.

Indians are also well aware that they have received, and will continue to receive, proposals from individuals and organizations that are hoping to bypass safety, health, and other such building and use standards normally imposed by city, county, and state governments. An example is the placement of large propane gas storage tanks on Campo in the highest population use area, the area that encompasses the church, the meeting hall, the health center, and the fiesta grounds and that is near several residences. The tribal vote to approve this lease proposal was protested by the majority of the tribal members as having taken place at an improperly held meeting and as having been affected by votes cast by some nonmembers (that is, individuals below the required degree of blood). However, the bureau refused to investigate or respond to the majority's petition for a recall election. Indians have concluded that the

Bureau of Indian Affairs, as the agent for their trustee, has seldom fulfilled its duty to protect their assets but has instead approved leases on Indian land for much less than the prevailing rates and conditions for the same type of lease on non-Indian land and, as in the case of the propane tanks, on leases for relatively dangerous uses refused by non-Indian landowners. The Indians have begun to protest and do not intend to submit any longer to these types of exploitation. While many reservations have not explicitly spelled out their own restrictions as formal zoning codes and ordinances, such restrictions are implicit in their discussions of proposals. Also implicit is the extremely high value placed on personal freedom, physical space, and band independence for decision making. It may be time for the tribes to enact explicit ordinances to control future land use and potential leases.

In spite of this record of responsible behavior on the part of most reservations, several Southern California counties continue to "cry wolf" every time some new developer offers a proposal to a reservation, with the county expressing concern because it cannot "control" reservation development. Most county and city officials need to remember that such concerns work in both directions and that the reservations have much more often suffered at the hands of the county and other non-Indian governmental bodies and private developers than counties have suffered at the hands of Indians. A problem often faced by reservations is that landowners surrounding the reservation, sometimes with the approval of county planning officials, may decide to place adjacent to the reservation some unpleasant or noxious development that is unacceptable to the reservation residents. For example, Rancho California developers planned to put a garbage and waste disposal facility directly beside the Pechanga Reservation, and the reservation spent a great deal of effort for more than a year fighting that location. Other such nuisance developments are often planned beside reservations. The most recent is a proposal to establish a sand and gravel quarry on non-Indian land adjoining a reservation village. The quarry's trucks would go through the village past the school and church. The reservations are upset by such a lack of consideration for their quality of life, just as they are upset by the external attempts to prevent any economic development on reservation lands, even that which is compatible with their homes and their cultural views of the land.

Zoning

Although the bands have generally not zoned their reservations or put formal restrictions on their members in the use of allotted or assigned lands, it is apparent that they have in their minds, if not on paper, their own environmental requirements for any potential development, and the recent attempts of city and county governments to impose zoning restrictions must be examined in this light. These external governmental bodies have tried to limit reservation land to "natural habitat," rural family agriculture, or outdoor recreational purposes, which is a reversal of the local governments' previous policy.

For years, Indians had unsuccessfully requested county cooperation to prevent reservation lands from being used as convenient trash dumps for the entire region. In one instance, a car wrecker from Los Angeles was using a reservation, Pala, as the place to dump and burn old tires and car bodies. It took the reservation several years of concerted political pressure, publicity, and the aid of non-Indians to get action in this case. In other cases, Indians have found it almost impossible to persuade law enforcement agencies to cooperate to prevent the stealing of truckloads of valuable oak leaf mold (from Campo), to prevent hunters from trespassing on reservations and shooting at Indian cattle and homes (in the case of many mountain reservations), to prevent constant trespassing by hikers and campers who leave trash in the springs, which are domestic water supplies, and to prevent cars from dumping trash in the fields alongside highways. Motorcyclists and other off-road vehicles have ripped up grazing lands (at Capitan Grande) and speedsters have drag raced along Indian reservation roads, even the public roadways, unhindered by law enforcement officers. On at least one reservation the Indians themselves have found it necessary to post a guard to prevent the cemetery from being looted by pothunters. Only in rare cases, and then reluctantly, have local agencies given law enforcement cooperation. Since 1953, under Public Law 280, criminal and civil law enforcement has generally been under the local jurisdiction of county sheriffs.

An example of the problems involved with law enforcement and P.L. 280 is the Campo leaf mold case. Apparently a nonmember "sold" to an Imperial Valley firm the right to gather leaf mold from the reservation. The Campo chairman called the Bureau of Indian Affairs and was first told that it was the sheriff's responsibility. The sheriff said that because the leaf mold was on the land it was the bureau's job. Another call to the bureau brought the reply that if the reservation would give the bureau the right to sell the leaf mold, they would handle the case. Finally, the next time the truck appeared, several Indians took their rifles and told the men to leave. This type of action should not be necessary to protect the assets of a reservation.

One of the reasons that prior to 1955 many California Indians had been active in requesting termination of the trust status of the reservations was that they desired equal protection of the law for themselves and their property. In addition to the problems discussed above, at Pala the Indians were concerned about the homes, buildings, irrigation and domestic wells, and sewage systems that had been constructed for them under the trusteeship and control of the Bureau of Indian Affairs and that did not meet the standards of the existing county codes. The Indians believed that as citizens they should be entitled to the same safety and sanitation protection as any other citizens.

Over the preceding years, many Southern California Indians had been asking for a termination of federal control, and for several decades the Bureau of Indian Affairs had made various preliminary studies of Southern California Indian readiness for termination of the federal trusteeship (for example, the Indian Irrigation Office Study, April 1931, Mission Indian Agency Records, National Archives). By 1949 the Bureau had begun a serious study of the readiness of all California reservations for termination. This study continued, with a number of hearings being held by the commissioner of Indian affairs, Congress, and the state legislature. For the next ten years the attention of the California Indians was focused on the possibility of termination and an analysis of the bills that were proposed to accomplish this end. As they began to realize the ill-conceived and extremely damaging nature of the termination proposals, even those who had originally desired an end of the trusteeship united to defeat the bill then being considered. It was during this time, while the Indians' attention was focused on the proposal for termination, that Congress quietly passed Public Law 280 late in 1953 with almost no discussion by the California Indians. The Mission Indian Federation hailed the inclusion of California in P.L. 280 as freeing California Indians from the control of the Bureau of Indian Affairs and allowing them to have the protection of the law on the same basis as any other citizen. Other Indians were appalled and worried about the potential ramifications, many of which became a reality.

Some Indians immediately requested county law enforcement, building inspections, and public health inspections of sewage and domestic water systems. They were either ignored or repeatedly told that, as Indians, they were the responsibility of the federal government. The same problems existed in other areas of city, county, and state services even though California had indicated to the federal government that it would be able to handle these services to the Indians. Admission to the county hospital was refused to desperately ill Indians, even though each county received funds from the Bureau of Indian Affairs for the purpose of Indian hospitalization needs (see note 21). At best, occasional service was grudgingly given. Even criminal law enforcement officials came only when *they* saw a need, not when the Indians saw a need and desperately requested their aid. Several cases of harassment and abuse by county sheriffs occurred. More recently, under the impact of civil rights legislation, the general level of law enforcement and the provision of services to the Indian population have been improving. However, trespassing, illegal shooting, trash dumping, cemetery looting, and pothunting are still major problems and do not receive law enforcement attention even when individuals are basically caught in the act or with the evidence (see the *San Diego Union* January 30, 1986, through the spring of 1986).

In 1970, after fifteen years of this negative approach and attitude on the part of Southern California counties, and without any discussion with or notice to the Indians, county supervisors and planning agencies decided to impose building and zoning codes on the reservations. The codes were not imposed against contractors who were still constructing substandard and unsafe buildings but against Indian home owner-builders for not obtaining a county building permit (see, for example, *Ricci* v. *County of Riverside*). This sudden about-face also occurred in the matter of trying to impose city and county zoning controls (*Agua Caliente Band of Mission Indians* v. *City of Palm Springs* 347 *Federal Supp.* 42; *Rincon Band* v. *County of San Diego* 324 *Federal Supp.* and others, No. 3371). Planning and zoning procedures normally require that all landowners and residents be notified that an open public hearing will be held concerning any change in or imposition of zoning in any area. Such notifications were not sent to the reservations, nor were open public hearings held by the County of San Diego concerning the designation of Indian reservation lands as open agricultural lands on countywide planning and zoning maps. In 1975, however, the court of appeals decided that the counties did not have such zoning jurisdiction. Thus this aspect of the problem has been solved for the time being.

Another aspect of restriction exists, however. At the federal hearing held to consider the creation of the Agua Tibia Wild Area, which would adjoin the then 8,000-acre Mission Reserve (now divided between Pala and Pauma reservations) a number of conservation organizations stated that the Indian land should be included in the wild area. Most were willing to let it remain as Indian land, but only on the condition that it be left in its "natural state" according to their understanding of "Indian tradition" as never using or affecting the "natural state" of the land.[32] Thus as urban sprawl and population densities have increased in Southern California, the cities, the counties, and the "conservationists" have apparently begun to see the reservations as "open space" that could be retained at no expense to "private" landownership, income, or development and at no cost to local agencies and taxpayers, though at considerable cost to Indians.

That Indian reservation land should be maintained in its "natural state" and in "traditional use" (really "nonuse" or "without economic use") is a pervasive approach throughout the West, yet it misunderstands what Indian use of the land was at the time of Spanish contact and also what "Indian tradition" actually is. Southern California Indians did not leave the land "untouched" or in its "natural state" any more than most land in North America was unused, or in a "natural state" (see, for example, Lewis 1977 for the Northern Cree; Dobyns 1981 for the Sonoran desert; and Stoffle and Dobyns 1983 for the basin-plateau region of Nevada and Utah). This was true, at least, prior to European contact and the severe depopulation resulting from the introduction of such Euro-Asian epidemic diseases as smallpox, measles, and bubonic plague (see, for example, Dobyns 1966, 1976, 1976a, 1983). As has earlier been pointed out, the Indians of Southern California, like those elsewhere, managed their entire territory by the available technological means in order to make the land produce the highest economic benefit for themselves and to sustain the population densities they had achieved (Bean and Lawton 1973; Lewis 1973; Shipek 1963, 1965, 1968, 1972, 1977, 1981, 1986).

It must also be recognized that by "tradition" the Indians of Southern California searched for new "knowledge-power" that could be used for the economic benefit of themselves and their band (White 1957; Shipek 1977). It must also be recognized that by constant experimentation, including the importation of plants from distant environments, they sought new information and new uses for everything that existed in their environment (Shipek 1977). As new information and new techniques became available, they were constantly incorporated into the life and economy of the Indians (Shipek 1977). It must therefore be recognized, as allowed by Public Law 280, that Indian "tradition and custom" govern Indian use of reservation land. Indian use and custom require that Indians be allowed to put the land to its highest and best economic use as they determine that use to be and to make whatever changes they require to accomplish their purpose of improving their economic status and maintaining attractive home areas.

The apparent lack of use or development is not the result of Indian tradition but rather of the improper taking of Indian agricultural and domestic water by non-Indians. Development has also been retarded by bureaucratic procedures, procrastination, and external political and economic pressures that prevented or actually destroyed nonagricultural development on reservations. Even as various court decisions during the decade of the 1970s favored reservation self-government and self-development and rejected the right of cities and counties to zone reservation lands, external political pressures were working to negate these court victories with congressional legislation to change the laws in order to remove the so-called "special privileges" of Indians and to destroy their right of self-government.[33]

Other Public Law 280 problems developed, and some were more easily handled, such as changing the marriage laws of the state of California to include the category of "Indian Custom Marriage" for all those persons married in that fashion prior to the passage of P.L. 280 (Shipek 1968a). Another was discovering the procedures for getting old-age pensions for elderly Indians who had no documentation of their age. A continuing problem has been the interaction between the various social service agencies and the Indians when the regulations under which the agencies operate were written without consideration for the special situations affecting the Indians. The problems of obtaining health services have been more or less solved with the introduction of the federal Indian Health Service in California. Reservation hunting and fishing rights were under attack from the California Department of Fish and Game, but the California Indian Legal Service aided the Indians in appealing the arrest cases that occurred, and this problem seems to have been solved. Many of these P.L. 280 problems have been described by Max Mazzetti (1980) in a monograph prepared for the Indian Justice Program of the Office of Criminal Justice Planning. Others will be described in future works.

Water Rights

Earlier sections of this work described the history of the water rights and the lack of preservation of those rights by the trustee, the United States through the agency of the Bureau of Indian Affairs. Several cases both against the government and against the taker of the water have been mentioned. The original cases, those of the San Luis Rey reservations and Soboba, were filed in 1951 as Docket 80A of the Mission Indian Claims Case, Docket 80 under the Indian Claims Commission. The commission ruled that the land claims must be heard and settled first. Therefore, work on Docket 80A was not started until late in 1964. In 1969 and 1970 the Soboba case was separated from the San Luis Rey case because Rincon and La Jolla also decided to file a case against the Escondido Mutual Water Company, which had first diverted and then dammed the San Luis Rey River above the reservations and gradually shut off all water to the reservations except storm overflow. The liability section of the Soboba case was completed and government responsibility defined in 1975, but the San Luis Rey case was settled out of court only in the fall of 1985, twenty years after the first court hearing. As of December 1986, Congress had not yet approved the settlement. An old adage is applicable to all Indian claims cases: Justice delayed is justice denied. In other words, the renewal of the economic development of reservation lands that had flourished immediately after the trust patenting but that was interrupted and effectively stopped in the 1910 to 1920 period was anticipated with the filing of the case in 1951 but was delayed for another twenty years during the case hearings. Quite obviously, the capital costs of any form of development after 1985 will be much higher than they would have been in the 1960s or earlier. Thus, while the reservations have won their cases (as the out-of-court settlement demonstrates), the return for their efforts and the potential for capital development has been effectively reduced by the lengthy delay.

The work on the second phase of the water rights cases, Docket 80A-2, had to await the completion of most of the work on 80A. Therefore this work for six more reservations has just started. How long will it take? Also, a number of other reservations had originally entered cases against the government for the loss of their aboriginal water rights as well as for the lack of protection of their reservation water. However, the present attorneys concluded that they needed to have their expenses paid as research progressed instead of carrying the expenses of the cases until the judgments or settlements, as the attorneys for the original claims cases had done. Therefore arrangements were made for each reservation or group of reservations to borrow funds from the government against the judgments the reservations would receive at the close of the case. A number of reservations, however, did not understand the excellent nature of their cases and the early history of their own water use as compared to that of their non-Indian neighbors and were therefore frightened into withdrawing from the cases. They were afraid that they could lose the case, and that the government would then hold them responsible for the debt incurred to fight for their water rights and monetary recompense for their losses due to the loss of their water. One fear repeatedly voiced was that that loan was simply another method of forcing them to sell the reservation land to repay this debt. To the best of my knowledge, a number of reservations had histories of water use and loss of water that matched those of the reservations in the San Luis Rey water case, so they had equally strong cases, but this most recent government action frightened them into withdrawing them. Other reservations may also have had equally strong cases but, being unaware of the need to file suit, had neglected to do so. In other words, all the reservations needed better access to the detailed histories and records of their own land use, the amounts or purposes of water use, the earlier level of groundwater, and the causes of the lowering of groundwater levels due to the actions of external government agencies or private parties.

At the present time, all reservations would be well advised to make every effort to have their existing water measured by their own experts, to have their present water uses recorded, and to interview all their elders concerning the immediate past uses (Shipek 1981). This is important if they are to secure and maintain even the present level of water use and essential if they are planning any future development.

CHAPTER 7

Reservation Government

AN IMPORTANT ASPECT of reservation land tenure is the Indians' ability and right to govern and to regulate the use of the community-owned land, utilities, and facilities belonging to the reservation. Easily understood rules and regulations that are not unduly burdensome to any individual or to any portion of the community are essential for maintaining the functioning of a small, closed membership community, and technically, Indian reservations have the right to govern themselves, having long been recognized as "dependent domestic nations," not omitting the necessary approval of the trustee.

Modern reservation government bears little relationship to the precontact forms of band and tribal government, in which the power and authority of the leadership were validated by the religion. After destroying the existing band governments, the bureau tried to impose a leadership subservient to the agent by having yearly elections of reservation officials who served the will of the agents. After 1900 the election of subservient "captains" gradually ceased, and the agent governed the reservations directly through a subagent, teacher, or farmer (Mission Indian Agency Records, 1900–1934, Federal Archives, Laguna Niguel). After passage of the Indian Reorganization Act, even reservations that voted to refuse the IRA provisions began to elect "spokesmen" and tribal councils. Since 1970, most reservations have developed more formal governments under articles of association or constitutions and elected chairmen and tribal councils.

Democratic elections and decisions by a majority vote were not part of the precontact government. All hierarchical positions were inherited by a direct heir if the heir proved to be qualified for the necessary training or by the nearest relative so qualified. The membership obeyed the leaders. If sufficient disagreement with the leaders' decisions developed, the band could split in two, with the minority section leaving for new territory. Under the reservation system, with the new imposed forms of government, such actions are no longer possible. Instead, the people are learning how to live under a government guided by decisions by the majority with protection for the rights of the minority.

One phenomenon that has impeded the development of modern reservation self-government has been the non-Indians' perception of Indians as totally unified and cooperative, so that any difference of opinion within one reservation, or even between reservations, has always been labeled as a negative influence. In the past, Indians who did not blindly obey the agents were labeled "hostiles," "troublemakers," or "traditionalists," in contrast to the "friendlies," "cooperative and obedient Indians," or "progressives." Since the passage of the Indian Reorganization Act of 1934, under which the Indians were supposed to develop constitutions and governmental forms modeled on those of the United States, differences of opinion have been labeled as factionalism and seemingly have been considered unhealthy by the Bureau, just as it often has been by the general public and by Indian "advocacy" organizations. This is in contrast to local, state, and national government in the rest of the United States, in which differences of opinion concerning government policies are considered normal. Lurie (1979, 1986) has ably discussed the phenomenon and has pointed out the negative effects of such labeling. I have always pointed out to those with whom I have worked that differences of opinion concerning future policy were normal and reflected thought and concern, not a negative outlook, on the part of the members. It is a lack of concern that would be negative and unhealthy. Over the long term, those reservations that have been able to develop tribal councils in which all viewpoints are represented have generally been able to function more effectively and bring more benefits to all their members than those in which one group was in total control of reservation policy and had no consideration for those with whom they disagreed.

Another major aspect of self-government is the power to enforce decisions and impose sanctions on members who are violating the democratically agreed upon rules of the society. If the power to enforce decisions and impose sanctions on its own members has been effectively removed from a society, then there is not real self-government. Some large reservations in other states have had some degree of self-government reinstituted, but not the California reservations. Some of the described conditions may only exist on reservations in states under Public Law 280.

One reservation, for example, voted to develop its community grazing land as permanent pasture. This goal required that all grazing animals be kept off the pasture for two years to allow new pasture grasses to develop properly. All members understood and agreed to this requirement. On seeing the grass developing, however, a few members turned their animals onto the pasture and destroyed the new grasses. There was no mechanism for the majority to enforce the decision to keep animals off the new pasture if this was not done voluntarily. Neither was the majority able to impose any sanction on those who destroyed the pasture. Thus any single greedy or obstructive member could potentially destroy the constructive work of all the others.

Another example of this "tragedy of the commons" (Hardin 1968) occurred several years ago. After the withdrawal of the Bureau of Indian Affairs as a result of Public Law 280, each reservation had to manage its own domestic water. Some reservations attempted to develop and maintain their own domestic water system or to maintain and manage the existing system left by the bureau. They began charging each member a small monthly fee to pay the fuel costs to run the gasoline pump and to develop a repair fund. On one reservation all but one member paid the fee, even those on welfare. But when one member (who had a good job) decided not to pay his share, the bureau officials interfered and did not allow the group to turn off his water, even though in this case the system had been developed by the group after P.L. 280 and the departure of the bureau. At one point bureau officials even offered to pay the uncooperative person's share of the costs, thus effectively destroying the constructive ability of the group to maintain its own system and to govern themselves. Another group agreed to use its limited water supply for domestic purposes only, but one member used it for extensive livestock watering, thus damaging the ability of other members to maintain reservation residence. The group was not allowed to impose any sanction for the misuse of a limited community resource.

Finally, in 1969 the responsibility for domestic water on California Indian reservations became the responsibility of the Indian Health Service, a branch of the United States Public Health Service, thereby removing all action on domestic water systems from the hands of Indian self-government in California. Thus, bureaucracy had again taken responsibility for maintaining the quantity and quality of domestic water wells. For some reservations (those that have become more adept at dealing with bureaucracy and red tape) the water systems are fairly well maintained, but for those that have not become so adept, maintenance and repairs are delayed several years, just as they were under the Bureau of Indian Affairs.

In contrast to this continual interference in band internal management and attempts to assess minor fees for services or to impose sanctions following a member's violation of agreed-upon rules, in other matters the bureau takes no action at the request of a majority of members when actions of the tribal chairman or council violate the rights of the members as a whole, as, for example, in the case of the propane tank case on Campo described earlier or other cases of obvious ballot-box stuffing. As pointed out in the discussion of the tribal use of unallotted reservations, some families have effectively taken complete economic control of all tribal assets for their individual family use, sometimes by using threats of physical violence. Yet the bureau has not interfered to protect any individual's rights or the rights of the majority in such cases of either improper or illegal action on the part of the elected council. This situation may change with succeeding generations.

In situations in which tribal constitutions and ordinances exist, bureau officials claim that all tribal actions must follow the written rules, but in disputes in which a majority of band members, following their constitution, sign proper petitions against actions of the tribal council that were taken at improper or secret meetings, often bureau officials have refused to accept any proof of impropriety on the part of tribal officials. On occasion the bureau has also refused to allow or recognize any attempt by the majority to request and hold a recall or new election, even when the majority have followed the written rules for managing such recalls.

In all disputes between band members and in other matters of self-government, the bureau officials have consistently pointed out that if the situation is not covered by written constitutional rules and ordinances, then the band may follow "traditional" customs. But such remarks are meaningless without an understanding of "traditional" government and the transformation it has undergone in the face of changing external economic and political conditions, which included enclavement by a dominant power (Shipek 1983, 1984b), and an understanding of the effects of the bureau's control over the tribal councils. The bureau does not need to veto a decision of a tribal council; in most cases it can simply take no action to implement, or to allow others to implement, an unwelcome decision.

The History of Change

In order to understand some of these events, it is necessary to summarize the sequence of the loss of traditional government forms. Prior to the 1891 Act for the Relief of the Mission Indians, the Indian agents had first attempted to appoint their own "chiefs" or "generals" to control each ethnic nationality. Failing that, they proceeded to bypass the traditional national-level leaders and to recognize only band-level leaders. Next, the agents began requiring annual elections of reservation "captains" and "judges," and they removed any elected official who did not obey them. On the more accessible reservations—those visited regularly by the agents or having a resident bureau schoolteacher—the traditional captains did not continue as the elected captains. The primary requirement for holding the position was a willingness to obey the agent, and a secondary requirement was a willingness to prevent any and all religious ceremonies and to interfere in the customary marriage practices of the people. None of these actions was compatible with the position of the traditional leader. Although some members were apparently delegated to fulfill the requirements of the agents, by 1890 most traditional leaders had ceased all open activities except the management of religious ceremonies (Sparkman 1908). Instead, they spent their time learning the new system that controlled their people and discovering new methods of protecting their members. Several were already trying out new forms of opposition before 1892, and by 1918 this opposition had crystallized into the Mission Indian Federation (Bureau of Indian Affairs Records, Federal Archives, Laguna Niguel). Depending on the proposals or actions of the agents, one side or the other became dominant at the moment, and many of the actions that were seen by the Indians as the most damaging were effectively stopped. The two sides were equally important in this interplay of forces that limited the bureau's actions. Only with the passage of P.L. 280 did the need for such opposing forces end and new, more unified forms of government begin to appear.

Among the attributes of government that all bands originally exercised was that of taxation. Traditional bands taxed their members' time and labor by requiring all of them to participate in community gathering or hunting on community land for community purposes. For example, game taken during a communal men's hunt and produce harvested by the communal women's gathering party was used to feed guests, local participants, and spectators at festivals and religious ceremonies. All band members benefited from their obligatory communal efforts by consuming both food and spiritual sustenance at the ceremony. Also, all band members gave the various band officials and specialists part of each day's harvest or hunt (Boscana 1933; Rudkin 1956). These officials reciprocated by providing their specialized skills to all band members. In other words, all band members contributed a share of their game and plant harvest to religious and secular leaders to free the latter from time-consuming subsistence tasks. This produce "tax" provided the leaders and specialists with the time necessary to work nearly fulltime at their specialties, which were indispensable to band survival.

During colonial times, Spanish missionaries imposed a labor tax on all their neophytes. In return, they distributed some food, clothing, and their own specialized ritual services to baptized Indians. As the region under Spanish control expanded, the political and military actions of traditional leaders became correspondingly limited. However, in the Indian villages of Southern California, these traditional leaders still had authority, and as the land base was reduced by the grazing of domestic animals, they developed new band irrigation projects, directed control burning and land clearing, and increased the planting of wheat and corn. They also required all members who wished to use the land or irrigation facilities to participate in the labor of preparing and maintaining the facilities and acreage.

Under the United States, all economic, military, and political power was gradually removed from the traditional leaders. By the time of the trust patenting of the reservations, the traditional leaders, as noted earlier, had "gone underground" because the Indian agents required that the captain be elected each year and also required that the elected captain obey the agent in all things (Shipek 1983, 1984b).

Next, during the early period of the reservations, before there was massive interference in the details of community life, various reservation leaders mobilized the entire community to carry out public works, which might include improving the road access into and across the reservation or constructing irrigation works or community projects, including schools, jails, chapels, and cemetery fences. In other words, reservation leaders obligated band members to work together to build things that improved the quality of everyone's life. If construction materials were needed, all band members contributed small sums or were "taxed" both in the form of cash to purchase the materials and in labor for the construction (Omish journal). At other times, all members were regularly assessed small cash amounts in order to pay one member to manage an activity for the benefit of the community.

Between 1910 and 1920 bureau officials intervened and halted reservation self-government by taking over and directly managing all governmental activity and then requiring the Indians to labor for nothing on projects that the Indians did not desire and that, understanding local conditions, they knew would be failures. As an association of Indians opposed to bureau interference and to forced unpaid labor, the Mission Indian Federation, under the traditional leadership, gained strength and began to assess all the reservation Indians heavily to support its antibureau actions and attempts to lobby Congress, as well as to support its non-Indian "counselor."

The next feature of traditional band government that disappeared under enclavement by external political powers was the existence of sanctions against the misuse of community assets or the violation of community norms. Traditional sanctions against the misuse of community assets would have varied with the seriousness of the offense. Such sanctions varied from community gossip and ridicule (a very powerful control in small closed societies) to whipping and ostracism. Very serious offenses could bring expulsion from the band or death by band execution (Boscana 1933; Bean 1972; Luomala 1978; Shipek field notes). Such sanctions and controls were validated by religious beliefs and were thus extremely powerful. Major factional disputes were solved by splitting one large band into two separate bands. In smaller bands, the dissident faction often left to become a separate band or to join another related group. Under modern reservation conditions such a split is no longer possible, nor are the Indians allowed to develop new means to solve such problems or to sanction members.

The traditional religious sanctions, which maintained generally effective control over the behavior of the population and guarded against the misuse of power or community supplies by the chief, have disappeared under the impact of external political and religious interference and control over Indian economic, political, and religious life. The milder forms of traditional sanctions have been rendered ineffective by modern external conditions, such as the ability to leave the group for the nearby cities and a lack of fear of enemy attack, and the more drastic sanctions are not allowed by the external political power of the United States, which has taken unto itself all policing powers. Further, neither the bureau nor Congress has allowed the development of new forms of internal sanctions on the California reservations or some reservations in other states.

Finally, under modern conditions the bureau has not allowed the final transformation of band internal taxation to cash even though at an earlier date the bands had on their own initiative changed the form of band taxation from labor and supplies to labor and supplies or cash.[34] As Margaret Mead pointed out in *New Lives for Old,* "While taxation without representation is tyranny, and taxation designed only to force native people to seek European employment is a form of slavery, *government without taxation is degradation*" (1956:207). To this statement I would add that self-government without the power of enforcement and of taxation is not self-government but rather continual frustration. And to paraphrase Mead, if people must continually appeal to Washington to supply the most minute local need and to enforce every local constructive action, then no self-government or self-development can occur (1956:207). A very important aspect of self-government includes the right to impose sanctions for misde-

meanors and civil offences committed by anyone within reservation boundaries and the right of the reservation members to determine the rules under which all will live and work
as a community.
Over the years, the United States government has wavered between the opposing concepts of Indian government and Indian rights, and from time to time it has implemented one or
the other, as well as every possible stage between the two ex-
tremes. One extreme has been to view Indian reservations as
dependent domestic nations with all the rights of an independent nation to govern its members within its borders. The
other extreme has been to allow the Indians no self-government. Most Indians I have known merely ask for the right,
under the Constitution, to govern themselves within the
boundaries of their reservations and to determine their membership based on a standard of ancestry. Most Indians are
well aware that the political views of the majority of the people of the United States can and will affect the rights the Indians will be allowed to exercise.

Present Conditions
Under Public Law 280, the right to have tribal courts and
tribal law enforcement agencies was removed from California
reservations. Instead, the California county sheriffs are supposed to maintain civil and criminal law on the reservations.
But the sheriffs have seldom responded in a timely and effective manner to calls by reservation members to control theft,
violence, or vandalism by either members or nonmembers, or
illegal hunting by nonmembers, all of which are covered by
criminal laws. Further, Public Law 280 apparently does not
give a sheriff the power to enforce internal civil law, reservation ordinances, or traditional rules, which therefore are
unenforceable if any member choses not to abide by an
agreed-upon course of action. When civil disputes between
Indians have been brought to local courts, the judges have
"brushed them off" and admonished them to "get along" as if
he were talking to children.
For effective self-government, the right and ability to impose

meaningful sanctions must be restored to all Indian reservations; that is, an independent judicial arm of tribal government must be allowed to develop. On small reservations, the
alternative requires that external judges must be willing to
take the time and make the effort to understand the complexities in the reservations' history and begin to untangle bureau errors as well as to adjudicate civil disputes.

Since 1965 many organizations and agencies have been formed
for the purpose of working with or for Indians on questions
concerning health, education, welfare, housing, jobs, economic development, and legal problems. These organizations vary
from governmental or quasi-governmental agencies on the
national, state, or county level to private corporations or unincorporated groups. Some are generously funded by governments or private foundations, others operate on a shoe-
string, while still others operate by attempting to channel
grant or foundation funding or contractual services for some
specific purpose purportedly to aid the reservations. Some, in
fact, primarily supply jobs and income to their operating personnel. All these organizations and agencies seek to have Indian or reservation representation on their governing body
or an Indian on their board of directors. Some expect one
Indian to speak for all the Southern California reservations.
At the other extreme, some attempt to have a board of directors composed of representatives from each of the Indian reservations or nonreservation Indian organizations in Southern California. Such non-Indian organizations and agencies
seem to believe that they will have complete communication
with all parts of the Southern California Indian communities
by having one or several such representatives on their boards.

Non-Indians attempting to work through this type of representative board or through a single Indian representative should
understand that the various Southern California Indian nationalities did not traditionally have within their sociopolitical
structures any mechanism for a band to be represented on
another body by a single member, much less for several
bands and different tribes to be represented by one person.
On the contrary, there were religious, social, political, and

economic values and constraints that required that specialists who acquired and developed a body of knowledge must keep that knowledge secret (White 1957, 1963; Shipek 1977). It was their responsibility to control that knowledge and not to make it public, but rather to use it only when appropriate and only for their own family or band. This is the exact opposite of the meaning and structure of the representative's role in American society and the American political structure. The original cultural view about the acquisition and use of knowledge still prevails among most Southern California Indians, however, and it is only now beginning to change.

Inasmuch as there is no tradition of an individual being a representative to an outside organization, neither has there been any expectation of benefit to the community from the fulfillment of such a role. Still, certain individual members of bands, at certain times and sometimes for many years, have assumed such roles and brought occasional information from the band to the outside organization and some benefits back to the band. Occasionally, individuals have brought as much as possible back to the band. However, most bands assume that such individuals are actually working for their own welfare. Normally associated with such roles are some remunerative and prestige factors, which come primarily from the outside community and are only sufficient for the individual fulfilling the role. Bands only become disgruntled when very substantial benefits accrue to the individual and his or her family and it becomes obvious that these benefits were intended by the charter of the outside organization to be widely distributed within the Indian community. Thus the majority of Indians who have served as representatives on these commissions or boards or in paid representational positions have actually been serving as private individuals. Only a very few individuals in such positions have made any effort to distribute the benefits or to serve anyone beyond their own kinship circle or, at most, their own band.

Frequently, such representatives or appointees to governmental or quasi-governmental boards and commissions are the better-educated, often city-raised, Indians who do not under-

stand reservation history, concepts, and values or the differences between the values of the Southern California Indian
groups. Consequently, such appointees often violate the beliefs and values of many reservations when they distribute
news releases or pronouncements or deliver speeches. Opposition from the reservation then develops, and either the individual is discredited or outsiders complain about Indian factionalism. Too often, one of the problems is that the
appointee has acquired and proclaimed the colonial myths
and non-Indian stereotypes about his own people.

Since the passage of the Environmental Protection Act, the National Historic Preservation Act, and the American Indian
Religious Freedom Act, some firms specializing in environmental impact assessment reports have hired an Indian in order to declare that they have cleared their report and statements with Indians. Unfortunately, such firms have often
hired persons who lack sufficient knowledge to represent
their community's religious and sociocultural values, and
even if knowledgeable, the Indian employee has the same
conflict of interest as the firm's archaeologist. Too many become more interested in keeping their jobs (just as the firms
are interested in obtaining further contracts), with the result
that the firms prepare the reports that land developers desire
rather than performing competent scientific work (Shipek
1983a) or, in the case of an Indian representative, carrying essential information back to the potentially affected Indian
community. In contrast, those firms that use a number of Indian elders as consultants for each environmental report in
each tribe's or band's territory will more effectively present
the community's traditional religious and cultural values without involving anyone in a conflict of interest. The elders are
not dependent upon the income from an occasional consul-
tancy fee, and most place their religious beliefs and values
above financial considerations. Also, each group of elders will
advise only within its own area and refuse to comment upon
another band or tribal territory.

Recently, some outside organizations have been asking that a reservation (or the tribal chairmen's association, discussed be-

low), formally elect a representative to their board. Often such an elected representative will more effectively represent the community. However, any organization or corporate body that requires such a representative from the Indian community will still have misunderstandings unless the organization realizes that even if a representative was formally elected at a band meeting, such a delegate has no authority. There are no instances in which an individual member of a band, not even the tribal chairman, may speak publicly for the band without having previously received specific authorization to speak at a particular meeting and to a particular issue. In all other instances, each Indian speaks only as an individual. He or she must return to the next band meeting, present the new problem, and request and receive specific instructions to speak on this new problem or subject. This process may take two or three months at the very least. Awareness of these conditions and their implications is essential for any person or organization attempting to deal with an Indian reservation on any legal contractual basis through intermediary governmental organizations or through an individual fulfilling the representational role.

This is not to say that the reservations cannot begin to develop the mechanisms and roles for effectively handling and distributing benefits or economic development through this type of organization. A number of attempts have been and are being made, though some are more successful than others. The bands have already demonstrated that they can organize, cooperate, and develop the governmental forms necessary to achieve their ends whenever desirable, suitable ends are available (Bean 1974; Shipek 1984). If substantial benefits remain available to Southern California reservation residents (and by this I mean those developments and programs that *the reservations* see as beneficial, not necessarily what outsiders think are benefits), this representational role and the organizational structure to handle it will continue to develop successfully.

In the past decade, the San Diego County reservations have successfully developed a tribal chairmen's association, which acts as an umbrella organization to obtain funding for various projects, especially when each reservation project would be so small that funding agencies would not be interested. The reservations had discovered that a single reservation was too small to apply and compete successfully for funds from many of the sources but that by joining together the reservations could successfully compete for funds and then allocate them proportionally to the reservations. Each reservation then managed its own project and did not interfere with the others. It must be remembered that under the federal government each reservation is a self-governing unit that jealously guards its independence and that even the tribal chairmen cannot commit themselves or their reservations to anything, no matter how apparently beneficial it might seem, until they go back to the tribal meeting, present the proposal, and receive authorization to proceed. The tribal chairmen's association has also become a forum for the non-Indian to present a proposal, idea, or matter requiring Indian action or consent. At the tribal chairmen's meeting the non-Indian will be told which specific reservation or group of reservations can or should be approached directly concerning that particular subject.

Another problem for the reservations is that of obtaining knowledgeable legal advice and representation. While some reservations have such representation at present, others do not yet have the tribal funds to have such legal advice at hand. Any contract between the tribe and an attorney must be approved by the Bureau of Indian Affairs, as must any contract between the attorney, the tribes, and a consultant or researcher on any subject, or a contractor for construction work, well digging, or another project. Frequently, the bureau puts an unrealistic limitation on what such people may be paid. This often means that the individual or firm must be willing to perform the work at a loss, or in some cases that consultants or contractors will do substandard work to stay within the cost limitations imposed by the bureau. Further, in many cases the proposed contract requires asking the permission of the bureau to develop evidence to be used against the bureau's own actions. Such proposals have been approved, and some bureau officials have cooperated and made data readily available to such consultants, but others have not.

The actual functioning of some effective and responsible tribal councils and tribal chairmen has not been discussed in this book. Rather I have concentrated upon the problems that have existed and still exist for many reservations. But some comment must be made about the careful, dedicated work of some of the tribal officials and the problems they face. Through the years, few have been fortunate enough to have their out-of-pocket expenses paid, much less received a reimbursement for the time lost from their income-producing jobs. Those on reservations that have developed some form of tribal income are at least now being reimbursed for their expenses, but the calls upon their time are so great and so complex that often their family life and income-producing jobs suffer. That they undertake these responsibilities in spite of this is evidence that many tribal officials are truly dedicated to doing the very best they can for their communities.

CHAPTER 8

Summary and Conclusions

THIS DESCRIPTION of changes in land tenure and land use patterns of the Southern California Indians has demonstrated that, contrary to tribal experience elsewhere in the United States, the allotment program did not, in itself, cause a disintegration of tribal or band structures. Nor has allotment caused more than a relatively small percentage of loss from the total allotted acreage. The allotment program in itself was not destructive but was actually desired by most Indians because it fit their major tenure concepts. The dissatisfaction with the program only developed when long-term accrued rights and family improvements were ignored by the allotting officials. In the long run, the lack of allotments, of official recognition of existing tenure rights, and of correct band membership lists on some reservations has actually been more disruptive than a knowledgeable allotment program that recognized existing rights and improvements would have been.

The greatest loss of land, depopulation, and sociopolitical disruption occurred prior to the development of trust patent reservations in 1891. Since then, the greatest problems have been caused by external agencies or persons who misunderstood the cultures and attempted to manage, to transculturate, and to "protect" or "advise" Indians on the basis of stereotyped beliefs of what Indian culture was, or is, and the belief that the advisor knows what is best for others. This reflects and continues the shortsighted and ethnocentric behavior of the earlier missionaries and Indian agents who believed they knew what was best for Indians. Ironically, rather than protecting or developing Indian resources, most Mission Indian agents and personnel were more concerned about the small portion of the population that was obtaining alcohol or "misbehaving" by not having "legal" or church marriages. Agents spent much of their time attempting to prevent Indians from enjoying and participating in their traditional ceremonies and fiestas, never understanding that profits came to the reservations from such fiestas (Mission Indian Agency Records, 1880–1940, Federal Archives, Laguna Niguel).

Problems continue to exist because of the stereotyped views of Indians as simple, easygoing hunter-gatherers who did not affect their natural environment and who had simple traditions (Bean 1968) and a totally cooperative, sharing, egalitarian culture. Those desiring to deal with Indian reservations or Indian people must understand that they are highly intelligent human beings, that each tribe and each reservation has its own culture and values arising out of differing tribal backgrounds and specific reservation histories, which were based on complex intensive land tenure, use, and land management practices that had modified the entire Southern California environment, and that these complex practices were organized and maintained by a very complex hierarchical social, political, economic, and religious structure.

Originally under their own population pressure and later under that of the Euro-American population, Southern California Indians constantly adopted new practices and sought out new types of crops and new forms of "income," not just when the older forms were no longer applicable and exploitable but continually. These Indians have a tradition of a constant search for new forms of beneficial knowledge and new forms of income. The Southern California Indian used this tradition of searching for new knowledge and new crops to survive the disruption caused by the entrance of significantly different populations—Spanish, Mexican, and Euro-American—all of whom caused drastic changes in the physical environment and brought political and economic enclavement. They have followed and are still following this tradition in order to solve the problems brought on by this enclavement and a massively increased population pressure and to maintain their reservation sovereignty in the face of external political pressures.

Finally, it must be concluded that "tribal custom" and "traditional usage" are not static forms or conditions but rather represent the constant search for additional knowledge and a willingness to change to incorporate what Indians consider to be improvements in income and the quality of life into their "traditional" culture. They have continually transformed each new possibility to fit their cultural and community values and to construct and maintain viable communities and lives for themselves.

This book has attempted to point out the need to develop a knowledge of the detailed history of each reservation and the need to collect detailed records of existing conditions and membership rolls in conjunction with the preparation of adequate plans for the future of each Indian reservation. I have also pointed to the problems that exist with the Bureau of Indian Affairs as it has functioned both in the distant past and more recently. This is in no way meant to be an argument for termination of the federal trust status. Such termination would be a disaster, not only for the Indians of each reservation but for many of the counties and communities in which the reservations are located. If tempted, the general public and state and federal legislators should remember the serious consequences of the failure of the State of California to provide adequate criminal and civil procedures and social services when these functions were transferred to it under Public Law 280 in 1953, after the state claimed to be ready and able to handle those few aspects. Major problems, some of which were created by past actions of the bureau, still exist for many reservations and must be solved before constructive action by many reservation governments can occur. Other reservations have solved some problems, but many still remain.

The need is for more careful attention to the history of each reservation, for a detailed study of the records and a clarification of the problems in order to work honestly with the entire membership to correct the past errors and, working with them, to develop plans for the future. I emphasize that working *with* the people is important. The process of conceiving or modifying general laws and regulations for all reservations at a distance—in Washington, in Sacramento, or in county seats—and by people not well acquainted with the detailed history of each reservation will continue to exacerbate the problems. To be useful and effective, plans and decisions must be made by the people of each reservation after they examine the best available technical, environmental, and social impact assessment studies, combined with an analysis of past and present conditions.

This book has been written not only for scholars but also for use by the Indian people themselves and by those who would work *with* them in the hope that the Indians themselves will be able to solve many of the problems facing them and plan for a better future. A secondary purpose is to promote an understanding on the part of the general public that the American Indians have not been given privileges not accorded to the average citizen, but rather that the Indians have generally paid more heavily and more continually than the rest of us for their status as citizens (bestowed upon them by Congress in 1924) and that only recently have they begun to secure the rights accorded to the rest of us under the Constitution and the Bill of Rights.

This work is not the final word on this topic but only an attempt to present some of the more general aspects of the problems facing the Indian reservations. I hope it will return something usable to the reservations and to the youth of the people who taught me so much and who gave me years of friendship.

Chronology of Southern California History

1540 Alarcón sails up the Gulf of California and explores the Colorado River to the Gila–Colorado confluence, hoping to contact Coronado's expedition to Cíbola.

1542 *September:* Exploring the west coast, Juan Rodríguez Cabrillo enters San Diego Bay. Indians describe Spanish who had explored inland.

1602 *November:* Exploring California coast, Sebastián Vizcaíno enters San Diego Bay.

1769 *April 11:* The ship *San Antonio* arrives at San Diego Bay.
April 29: The *San Carlos* arrives, and men of both ships camp on shore.
May 14: Fr. Juan Crespi arrives with the first overland group.
July 1: Fr. Junípero Serra arrives overland from Baja California with a group led by Gaspar de Portolá.
July 16: Mission San Diego is founded at the San Diego presidio. Overland expedition north to Monterey Bay follows Indian trade and travel route north along coast, then inland at San Juan Capistrano to pass through Los Angeles basin.

1770 *August:* Founding of Mission San Gabriel.

1772 *September:* Pedro Fages crosses mountains from San Diego to Imperial Valley in search of deserters.

1774 *December:* Mission San Diego is moved up valley about four miles to a location with better water for crops.

1775 *June:* Mission increases conversion activity, taking captains, their families, and others from several villages.
November 4: Kumeyaay revolt destroys mission. Father Jaime

is killed, and remaining Spanish flee to the presidio. Neophytes also flee away from the Spanish area. Neophytes and unbaptized Indians, some from distant villages, had united to rid area of the Spanish.

1776	*August:* Mission San Diego is rebuilt and conversions increase, primarily among coastal villagers.
1776	*September:* Mission San Juan Capistrano is founded.
1777	*June:* Repeated attacks on the Spanish are made by Kumeyaay living on the edges of the area of concentrated baptism activity.
1778	*March:* A revolt is planned by the village of Pamo but is stopped by Spanish army.
1781	Smallpox enters California with an expedition bringing settlers for the new pueblo of Los Angeles. This is followed by a Quechan revolt at Yuma that destroys the mission and the Spanish settlement there.
1782	Pedro Fages travels through Cuyamaca Mountains from Sonora to Yuma, Vallecitos, and San Diego.
1783	Epidemic spreads through San Luiseño and Kumeyaay.
1787	*March 28:* Dominican Mission San Miguel is founded at La Frontera in Baja California.
1794–1798	San Diego missionaries concentrate on gaining control of the next valleys inland, with better water supplies than Mission Valley: El Cajon, Santee, Jamacha, and Jamul.
1795	*August–September:* Fr. Juan Mariner explores from San Diego inland to Santa Ysabel and Warner's Hot Springs (Cupa) and down San Luis Rey River.
1797	*November 12:* Dominican Mission Santa Catarina is founded in the mountains of La Frontera, Baja California, among Paipai but near many Kumeyaay to the north and west.
1798	*June 13:* Mission San Luis Rey is founded. Fr. Antonio Peyri is in charge and remains head of the mission until secularization.
1810	Building of the first granary at Pala. Start of the Pala *asistencia* to Mission San Luis Rey and concentration on baptizing Indians from inland villages. Mexican war for independence from Spain begins. Missions are the sole support of settlers and soldiers for the decade, with no supplies from Mexico.

1816–1821	Mission San Diego concentrates its baptism effort in Santa Ysabel and inland.
1821–1822	Mexican revolt is successful and republic is formed.
1822	*Asistencia* of Santa Ysabel is founded and chapel built.
1825	Epidemic enters from Baja California.
1826	A proclamation of emancipation for Mission Indians capable of supporting themselves.

A policy begins for the secularization of missions and the "freeing" of Indians; i.e., the granting of mission lands to individual Mexicans and enclaving most Indian villagers as peons on ranchos. A few Indian pueblos are founded and a few hispanicized Indians receive land grants. Christian Indians are officially classed as citizens of Mexico.

"Gentiles" (unbaptized Indians) attack Santa Ysabel and San Felipe.

1827	Measles epidemic in Southern California missions.
1828	Indian populations begin leaving missions for the homes in the interior from which many had been taken.
1828–1845	Grants of mission land to Mexican individuals increase. Mexican governor appoints secular *mayordomos,* who get salaries from the income of the mission and whose extended families are supported by Indians remaining at the missions. The *mayordomos* take livestock and lands of the missions.
1832	The Indian pueblo of San Pasqual is founded.
1833	All missions are secularized by Mexican law.
1833–1840	Numerous attacks and raids on Mexicans and Mexican ranchos throughout Southern California.
1835	Founding of the Indian pueblos of San Dieguito near San Diego and Las Flores north of San Luis Rey.
1840	Revolt in Baja California by *Hutneel* (Jatiñil) against forced baptisms at Mission Guadalupe. Quechan and neophytes destroy Santa Catarina.
1846	*December:* The U.S. Army, led by General Stephen Watts Kearny, passes through Yuma, San Felipe, Warner's Valley (Cupa), Santa Ysabel, and San Pasqual. Soldiers destroy Indian houses of San Felipe for firewood and buy wheat and flour from Indians of Cupa, who then increase plantings to sell to emigrants. In the battle at San Pasqual between Mexi-

cans and U.S. Army, Kearny is aided by the San Pasqual Indians. After the battle they guide Kearny to San Diego.

Attack of San Luiseños on Mexican rancho at Pauma, followed by retaliation of Mexicans and Cahuilla allies against Temecula.

1848   The Treaty of Guadalupe Hidalgo transfers California and the Southwest to United States and guarantees existing land titles and religious freedom to Mexican citizens.

1850   *April 22:* California passes the Act for the Government and Protection of Indians, which empowers sheriffs to mark boundaries of, and protect Indian right to, land Indians "needed." State also limits other Indian rights, such as right to testify in trials. The only state constitution not to give the federal government the right to deal with Indians within the state's borders.

1850–1851   Mission Indians pay property taxes in San Diego. Some pay taxes through 1870.

1851   *Summer:* Indian commissioners making Treaties do not come to Southern California as announced. Indans angry.

November 21: Revolt of Cupa Indians, attack on Warner's Rancho.

December: Garra, leader of the Cupa revolt, is tricked by Cahuilla chief Juan Antonio and is given to San Diego citizen militia and shot.

1852   Treaties with Southern California tribes reserving to them large mountain reservations. Citizens and state legislature protest to the U.S. Senate. The treaties are shelved.

1869–1875   Temecula Indians ejected from homes.

1870   An executive order withdraws townships of San Pasqual and Pala as reservations for Southern California Indians.

1871   The executive order is canceled. The Indians of San Pasqual are evicted by the sheriff from their adobe homes.

1875   Executive order reserves are created but are too few and too late. Most Indian homes, farms, orchards, and grazing lands are already preempted by non-Indians.

1883   The Indian Homestead Act is passed. Some take homesteads. Jackson-Kinney Commission investigates condition of Mission Indians.

1891	The Act for Relief of the Mission Indians finally passes after seven years of effort in Congress. The Smiley Commission is appointed.
1891–1910	Most lands reserved by the Smiley Commission are surveyed. Only a few are allotted.
1894	Escondido Mutual Water Company begins water diversion, supposedly only the winter "surplus" from the San Luis Rey River. The contract is signed only by BIA-approved leaders of La Jolla Reservation, not by others affected.
1903	Because rancho grant court case is lost in Supreme Court decision, army moves Cupa and other villages from ranchos to land purchased for them at Pala.
1910–1912	Additional land is bought for some reservations.
1910	The Indian Irrigation Service begins taking control of irrigation on Southern California reservations.
1916	Pauma rancho is divided into orchards, and water diversion from Pauma Reservation begins.
1920–1930	Allotment of Rincon, La Jolla, and Morongo begins. Indians file suit to stop the process but lose the case.
1924	The Indian commissioner gives permission for construction of the Henshaw Dam above La Jolla Reservation; the Escondido Mutual Water Company takes all water except the six miners inches provided for Rincon. No provision is made for other reservations. Rincon seldom gets the six inches, the equivalent of 67.324674 gallons per minute.
	Congress bestows citizenship on Indians.
1929	Indians of California file suit (K-344) against the government for land lost due to U.S. Senate's tabling of 1851 treaties with California Indians. The attorney general of California is appointed as attorney for the Indians. Court awards $1.25 per acre for treaty acreage lost. The award is for $17,500,000, but value of all goods and services ever "given" Indians is offset and taken by the government, leaving $5,165,853.46, or $150.00 per capita for distribution to the Indians of California.
1934	Indian Reorganization Act is refused by most Southern California Reservations.

1946	Congress passes Indian Claims Commission Act allowing Indians to file suit for all past claims.
1948–1950	Many California cases are filed and consolidated to Indians of California: Dockets 31 and 37, except Mission Indian case (filed 1949) by seventeen Bands, Docket 80, and the Pit River case.
1951	Mission Indian Claims Case, Docket 80 before the Indians Claims Commission, is amended and twenty-nine additional bands join the case. Additional dockets are added: Docket 80A the water loss section and Dockets 80B, C, and D for financial accounting concerning the offsets, including the offset costs relating to the Soboba Indian Hospital and the Sherman Institute (an Indian boarding school) against the judgment rendered in the first Indians of California case (K-344).
1953	Public Law 280 is passed. Bureau offices are closed and only about three officials remained in the Riverside Agency office.
1954	All services except the land trust are ended immediately.
1964	Indians accept the settlement offered by the government of forty-seven cents per acre for all California land except previously settled treaty loss claim and the Mexican rancho grant land in California. Research is begun on water claims.
1965	First court hearing before the Indian Claims Commission of Docket 80A, Mission Indian Water Case.
1967–1972	Return of government programs and increased control of reservations through the Office of Economic Opportunity programs, Indian Health Service programs, and increased bureau personnel and activity.
1984	Research begun on Docket 80A-2, water losses by bands of San Luis Rey, Cuyapaipe, La Posta, Santa Rosa, Pechanga, and Morongo. Other reservations are dropped from the case.
1985	Docket 80A and case against Escondido Mutual Water Company are settled out of court. Awaiting approval by Congress as of December 1986.

APPENDIX B

Executive Order Reservations, 1875

An executive order of 1875 ordered the survey of tracts occupied by Mission Indians in Southern California. The executive order of January 7, 1876, set aside the following surveyed tracts for the use and occupancy of the Mission Indians:

Potrero (including Rincon, Gapiche,[1] and La Joya): Township 10 South, Range 1 East, sections 16, 23, 25, 26, 31, 32, 33, 34, 35, 36, and fractional sections 17, 18, 19, 20, 21, 22, 27, 28, 29.

Coahuila (Cahuilla): Township 7 South, Range 2 East, sections 25, 26, 27, 28, 33, 34, 35, 36; Township 7 South, Range 3 East, sections 26, 27, 28, 29, 30, 31, 32, 33, 34, 35; Township 8 South, Range 2 East, sections 1, 2, 3, 4; Township 8 South, Range 3 East, sections 31, 32; Township 15 South, Range 2 East, sections 2, 3, 4, 5, 6.

Capitan Grande: Township 14 South, Range 2 East, sections 25, 26, 27, 34, 35, 36; Township 14 South, Range 3 East, sections 31, 32; Township 15 South, Range 2 East, sections 1, 2, 3, 4, 5, 6, 7, 8, 9, 10; Township 15 South, Range 3 East, sections 5, 6.

Santa Ysabel (including Mesa Grande):[2] Township 11 South, Range 2 East, south half of section 21, northwest quarter and east half of section 28, and sections 25, 26, 27; Township 11 South, Range 3 East, sections 25, 26, 27, 28, 32, 33, 34, 35, 36, and fractional sections 29, 31, 32; Township 12 South, Range 2 East, sections 3, 10, 14, 15, and fractional section 13;

Township 12 South, Range 3 East, sections 1, 2, 12, and fractional sections 3, 4, 10, 11, 13, 14.

Pala: Township 9 South, Range 2 West, northeast quarter of section 33 and north half of north half of section 34.

Agua Caliente:[3] Township 10 South, Range 3 East, southwest quarter of section 23; southwest quarter of section 24, west half of section 25, and east half of section 26.

Sycuan: Township 16 south, Range 1 East, section 13.

Minaja (Iñaja): Township 13 South, Range 3 East, north quarter of section 35.

Cosmit: Township 13 South, Range 3 East, north half of northeast quarter of section 25.

Between this executive order and the 1891 Act for the Relief of the Mission Indians, some of these tracts were returned to the public domain and other tracts were added. In spite of receiving the instructions to locate and survey all lands occupied by Indians and not yet claimed by settlers, neither the 1875 surveyors nor the 1891 Smiley Commission made any attempt to fully carry out their instructions.

Notes

1. Gapiche is also spelled Ya Pech, Ya Peche, and Ya Piche. In the final trust patenting, it was recognized that Rincon was a separate band, and it was given a separate reservation. Ya Pech and La Joya (La Jolla) were adjoining villages and were left as one because they were so "jealous of each other" (Smiley Commission Report).

2. Note that the Santa Ysabel and Mesa Grande villages were totally separated by the Santa Ysabel rancho, and neither the surveyor nor the Smiley Commission separated the two as different reservations, but the reports indicate that they dealt with and visited each band separately and located the lands of each band.

3. Warner's Hot Springs. The rancho owner had the rancho resurveyed several times until he managed to include this land inside his grant boundaries.

APPENDIX C

An Act for the Relief of the Mission Indians in the
State of California

Be it enacted by the Senate and House of Representatives of the
United States of America in Congress assembled, That immediately after the passage of this act the Secretary of the Interi-
or shall appoint three disinterested persons as commissioners
to arrange a just and satisfactory settlement of the Mission
Indians residing in the State of California, upon reservations
which shall be secured to them as hereinafter provided.

Sec. 2. That it shall be the duty of said commissioners to select a
reservation for each band or village of the Mission Indians
residing within said State, which reservation shall include, as
far as practicable, the lands and villages which have been in
the actual occupation and possession of said Indians, and
which shall be sufficient in extent to meet their just requirements, which selection shall be valid when approved by the
President and Secretary of the Interior. They shall also ap-
praise the value of the improvements belonging to any person to whom valid existing rights have attached under the
public-land laws of the United States, or to the assignee of
such person, where such improvements are situated within
the limits of any reservation selected and defined by said
commissioners subject in each case to the approval of the Secretary of the Interior. In cases where the Indians are in occupation of lands within the limits of confirmed private grants,
the commissioners shall determine and define the boundaries
of such lands, and shall ascertain whether there are vacant
public lands in the vicinity to which they may be removed.

And the said commission is hereby authorized to employ a competent surveyor and the necessary assistants.

Sec. 3. That the commissioners, upon the completion of their duties, shall report the result to the Secretary of the Interior, who, if no valid objection exists, shall cause a patent to issue for each of the reservations selected by the commission and approved by him in favor of each band or village of Indians occupying any such reservation, which patents shall be of the legal effect, and declare that the United States does and will hold the land thus patented, subject to the provisions of section four of this act, for the period of twenty-five years, in trust, for the sole use and benefit of the band or village to which it is issued, and that at the expiration of said period the United States will convey the same or the remaining portion not previously patented in severalty by patent to said band or village, discharged of said trust, and free of all charge or incumbrance whatsoever: *Provided,* That no patent shall embrace any tract or tracts to which existing valid rights have attached in favor of any person under any of the United States laws providing for the disposition of the public domain, unless such person shall acquiesce in and accept the appraisal provided for in the preceding section in all respects and shall thereafter, upon demand and payment of said appraised value, execute a release of all title and claim thereto; and a separate patent, in similar form, may be issued for any such tract or tracts, at any time thereafter. Any such person shall be permitted to exercise the same right to take land under the public-land laws of the United States as though he had not made settlement on the lands embraced in said reservation; and a separate patent, in similar form, may be issued for any tract or tracts at any time after the appraised value of the improvements thereon shall have been paid: *And provided further,* That in case any land shall be selected under this act to which any railroad company is or shall hereafter be entitled to receive a patent, such railroad company shall, upon releasing all claim and title thereto, and on the approval of the President and Secretary of the Interior, be allowed to select an equal quantity of other land of like value in lieu thereof, at such place as the Secretary of the Interior shall determine: *And provided further,* That said patents declaring such lands to be held in trust as aforesaid shall be retained and kept in the Interior Department, and certified copies of the same shall be forwarded to and kept at the agency by the agent having charge of the Indians for whom such lands are to be held in trust, and said copies shall be open to inspection at such agency.

Sec. 4. That whenever any of the Indians residing upon any reservation patented under the provisions of this act shall, in the opinion of the Secretary of the Interior, be so advanced in civilization as to be capable of owning and managing land in severalty, the Secretary of the Interior may cause allotments to be made to such Indians, out of the land of such reservation, in quantity as follows: To each head of a family not more than six hundred and forty acres nor less than one hundred and sixty acres of pasture or grazing land, and in addition thereto not exceeding twenty acres, as he shall deem for the best interest of the allottee, of arable land in some suitable locality; to each single person over twenty-one years of age not less than eighty nor more than six hundred and forty acres of pasture or grazing land and not exceeding ten acres of such arable land.

Sec. 5. That upon the approval of the allotments provided for in the preceding section by the Secretary of the Interior he shall cause patents to issue therefor in the name of the allottees, which shall be of the legal effect and declare that the United States does and will hold the land thus allotted for the period of twenty-five years, in trust for the sole use and benefit of the Indian to whom such allotment shall have been made, or, in the case of his decease, of his heirs according to the laws of the State of California, and that at the expiration of said period the United States will convey the same by patent to the said Indian, or his heirs as aforesaid, in fee, discharged of said trust and free of all charge or incumbrance whatsoever. And if any conveyance shall be made of the lands set apart and allotted as herein provided, or any contract made touching the same, before the expiration of the time above mentioned, such conveyance or contract shall be absolutely null and void: *Provided,* That these patents, when issued, shall override the patent authorized to be issued to the band or village as aforesaid, and shall separate the individual allotment from the lands held in common, which proviso shall be incorporated in each of the village patents.

Sec. 6. That in cases where the lands occupied by any band or village of Indians are wholly or in part within the limits of any confirmed private grant or grants, it shall be the duty of the Attorney-General of the United States, upon request of the Secretary of the Interior, through special counsel or otherwise, to defend such Indians in the rights secured to them in the original grants from the Mexican Government, and in an act for the government and protection of Indians passed by the legislature of the State of California April twenty-second, eighteen hundred and fifty, or to bring any suit, in the name of the United States, in the Circuit Court of the United States for California, that may be found necessary to the full protection of the legal or equitable rights of any Indian or tribe of Indians in any of such lands.

Sec. 7. That each of the commissioners authorized to be appointed by the first section of this act shall be paid at the rate of eight dollars per day for the time he is actually and necessarily employed in the discharge of his duties, and necessary traveling expenses; and for the payment of the same, and of the expenses of surveying, the sum of ten thousand dollars, or so much thereof as may be necessary, is hereby appropriated out of any money in the Treasury not otherwise appropriated.

Sec. 8. That previous to the issuance of a patent for any reservation as provided in section three of this act the Secretary of the Interior may authorize any citizen of the United States, firm, or corporation to construct a flume, ditch, canal, pipe, or other appliances for the conveyance of water over, across, or through such reservation for agricultural, manufacturing, or other purposes, upon condition that the Indians owning and occupying such reservation or reservations shall, at all times during such ownership or occupation, be supplied with sufficient quantity of water for irrigating and domestic purposes upon such terms as shall be prescribed in writing by the Secretary of the Interior, and upon such other terms as he may prescribe, and may grant a right of way for rail or other roads through such reservation: *Provided,* That any individual, firm, or corporation desiring such privilege shall first give bond to the United States, in such sum as may be required by the Secretary of the Interior, with good and sufficient sureties, for the performance of such conditions and stipulations as said Secretary may require as a condition precedent to the granting of such authority: *And provided further,* That this act shall not authorize the Secretary of the Interior to grant a right of way to any railroad company through any reservation for a longer distance than ten miles. And any patent issued for any reservation upon which such privilege has been granted, or for any allotment therein, shall be subject to such privilege right of way, or easement. Subsequent to the issuance of any tribal patent, or of any individual trust patent as provided in section five of this act, any citizen of the United States, firm, or corporation may contract with the tribe, band, or individual for whose use and benefit any lands are held in trust by the United States, for the right to construct a flume, ditch, canal, pipe, or other appliances for the conveyance of water over, across, or through such lands, which contract shall not be valid unless approved by the Secretary of the Interior under such conditions as he may see fit to impose.

Approved January 12, 1891.

APPENDIX

A Typical Trust Patent

Now know Ye, That the United States of America, in consideration of the premises and in accordance with the provisions of
the third section of the said Act of Congress approved January Twelfth Eighteen hundred and ninety one, Hereby De-
clares that it does and will hold the said tracts of land selected
as aforesaid (subject to all the restrictions and conditions contained in the said Act of Congress of January Twelfth Eighteen hundred and ninety one) for the period of twenty-five
years in trust for the sole use and benefit of the said _____
Band or Village of Indians, according to the laws of California and at the expiration of the said period the United States
will convey the same as the remaining portion not patented to
individuals by patent to said _____Band or Village
of Indians as aforesaid in fee simple discharged of said trust
and free of all charge or incumbrance whatsoever, provided
that when patents are issued under the fifth section of said
Act of January Twelfth Eighteen hundred and ninety one, in
favor of individual Indians for lands covered by this patent
they will override (to the extent of the land covered thereby)
this patent, and will separate the individual allotment from
the lands held in common, and there is reserved from the
lands hereby held in trust for said _____Band or
Village of Indians a right of way thereon for ditches or canals
constructed by the authority of the United States.

[Space for the enumeration of sections, township, and range, San
    Bernardino Meridian]

In testimony Whereof I, Benjamin Harrison, President of the
    United States of America, have caused these Letters to be
    made Patent and the Seal of the General Land Office to be
    hereunto affixed.

Given under my hand at the City of
    Washington this _____
    day of _____ in the year
    of our Lord One Thousand eight
    hundred and ninety three and of
    the Independence of the United
    States the one hundred and seven-
    teenth.
By the President: Benjamin Harrison.
By M. McKeen Secretary

D. P. Roberts
Recorder of the General Land Office.

Seal

APPENDIX E

Public Law 280

AN ACT

To confer jurisdiction on the States of California, Minnesota, Nebraska, Oregon, and Wisconsin, with respect to criminal offenses and civil causes of action committed or arising on Indian reservations within such States, and for other purposes.

Be it enacted by the Senate and House of Representatives of the United States of America in Congress assembled, That chapter 53 of title 18, United States Code, is hereby amended by inserting at the end of the chapter analysis preceding section 1151 of such title the following new item:

"1162. State jurisdiction over offenses committed by or against Indians in the Indian country."

Sec. 2 Title 18, United States Code, is hereby amended by inserting in chapter 53 thereof immediately after section 1161 a new section, to be designated as section 1162, as follows:

"§1162. State jurisdiction over offenses committed by or against Indians in the Indian country.

"(a) Each of the States listed in the following table shall have jurisdiction over offenses committed by or against Indians in the areas of Indian country listed opposite the name of the State to the same extent that such State has jurisdiction over offenses committed elsewhere in the State, and the criminal laws of such State shall have the same force and effect within such Indian country as they have elsewhere within the State:

"State of	Indian country affected
California	All Indian country within the State
Minnesota	All Indian country within the State, except the Red Lake Reservation
Nebraska	All Indian country within the State
Oregon	All Indian country within the State, except the Warm Springs Reservation
Wisconsin	All Indian country within the State, except the Menominee Reservation

"(b) Nothing in this section shall authorize the alienation, encumbrance, or taxation of any real or personal property, including water rights, belonging to any Indian or any Indian tribe, band, or community that is held in trust by the United States or is subject to a restriction against alienation imposed by the United States; or shall authorize regulation of the use of such property in a manner inconsistent with any Federal treaty, agreement, or statute or with any regulation made pursuant thereto; or shall deprive any Indian or any Indian tribe, band, or community of any right, privilege, or immunity afforded under Federal treaty, agreement, or statute with respect to hunting, trapping, or fishing or the control, licensing, or regulation thereof.

"(c) The provisions of sections 1152 and 1153 of this chapter shall not be applicable within the areas of Indian country listed in subsection (a) of this section."

Sec. 3. Chapter 85 of title 28, United States Code, is hereby amended by inserting at the end of the chapter analysis preceding section 1331 of such title the following new item:

"1360. State civil jurisdiction in actions to which Indians are parties."

Sec. 4. Title 28, United State Code, is hereby amended by inserting in chapter 85 thereof immediately after section 1359 a new section, to be designated as section 1360, as follows:

"§1360. State civil jurisdiction in actions to which Indians are parties.

"(a) Each of the States listed in the following table shall have jurisdiction over civil causes of action between Indians or to which Indians are parties which arise in the areas of Indian country listed opposite the name of the State to the same extent that such State has jurisdiction over other civil causes of action, and those civil laws of such State that are of general application to private persons or private property shall have the same force and effect within such Indian country as they have elsewhere within the State:

"State of	Indian country affected
California.........	All Indian country within the State
Minnesota	All Indian country within the State, except the Red Lake Reservation
Nebraska	All Indian country within the State
Oregon	All Indian country within the State
Wisconsin.........	All Indian country within the State, except the Menominee Reservation

"(b) Nothing in this section shall authorize the alienation, encumbrance, or taxation of any real or personal property, including water rights, belonging to any Indian or any Indian tribe, band, or community that is held in trust by the United States or is subject to a restriction against alienation imposed by the United States; or shall authorize regulation of the use of such property in a manner inconsistent with any Federal treaty, agreement, or statute or with any regulation made pursuant thereto; or shall confer jurisdiction upon the State to adjudicate, in probate proceedings or otherwise, the ownership or right to possession of such property or any interest therein.

"(c) Any tribal ordinance or custom heretofore or hereafter adopted by an Indian tribe, band, or community in the exercise of any authority which it may possess shall, if not inconsistent with any applicable civil laws of the State, be given force and effect in the determination of civil causes of action pursuant to this section."

Sec. 5. Section 1 of the Act of October 5, 1949 (63 Stat. 705, ch. 604), is hereby repealed, but such repeal shall not affect any proceedings heretofore instituted under that section.

Sec. 6. Notwithstanding the provisions of any Enabling Act for the admission of a State, the consent of the United States is hereby given to the people of any State to amend, where necessary, their State constitution or existing statutes, as the case may be, to remove any legal impediment to the assumption of civil and criminal jurisdiction in accordance with the provisions of this Act: *Provided,* That the provisions of this Act shall not become effective with respect to such assumption of jurisdiction by any such State until the people thereof have appropriately amended their State constitution or statues as the case may be.

Sec. 7. The consent of the United States is hereby given to any other State not having jurisdiction with respect to criminal offenses or civil causes of action, or with respect to both, as provided for in this Act, to assume jurisdiction at such time and in such manner as the people of the State shall, by affirmative legislative action, obligate and bind the State to assumption thereof.

Approved August 15, 1953.

History and Functioning of Public Law 280

A 1958 amendment gave jurisdiction over Indian country to the territory of Alaska, and another amendment extended it to the state of Alaska when Alaska became a state.

In 1968 the Indian Civil Rights Act also amended the last section of P.L. 280 to make state assumption of jurisdiction contingent upon tribal consent. This was codified as 25 *United States Code* 1311, 1312, 1321–1326.

Further, in the last fifteen years a number of tribes have attempted to retrocede and return to tribal and federal jurisdiction. The State of Nevada, which assumed jurisdiction in 1957, pursuant to Section 7, has returned jurisdiction to the tribes. A number of the larger reservations in the states named in

the act have succeeded in acquiring retrocession for their reservations. Some members of the larger reservations in Southern California have attempted to secure retrocession, but the
members of other of the larger reservations and of the smaller reservations are not willing to have retrocession. Even
though they have been unhappy with some aspects of P.L.
280, they are not willing to return to the pre-1954 conditions
and believe that the remaining problems can be worked out
with state officials.

Section 6 did not apply to California. At the same time that P.L.
280 was being passed, another case was being tried in the San
Diego courts concerning the California Indians' right to welfare an other social services from the state (*Acosta* v. *County of
San Diego*). It was determined that the constitution of the
State of California had not expressly recognized the right of
the federal government to deal with Indians within the state
and had in fact made several laws concerning Indian rights in
1850 and 1851. Therefore, the state was responsible for ad-
ministering various forms of public welfare to Indians on the
same basis as any other citizens.

Public Law 280 Cases

During the early years after the passage of P.L. 280, Indian
individuals and groups asked the counties for various kinds
of aid to solve problems that the bureau told them were no
longer under the jurisdiction of bureau officials. The Indians
were generally ignored or told to go back to the bureau because it was not a county or state problem. After about ten
years, various cities and counties began interfering in reservation business to suit the convenience of the local government,
not the needs of the Indians. The hunting and fishing rights
cases listed below and other similar cases are discussed more
fully in the California Indian Legal Service newsletters for
the years 1969 through 1974.

Rincon Band v. *County of San Diego* (324 F. Supp. 371), San
Diego, California, 1971
The Rincon Band wanted to open a card room for playing
games not prohibited by the California penal code. These

---

card rooms are profitable in many cities in California. However, the San Diego County code prohibits them in unincorporated areas. The question was whether the county could enforce its antigambling ordinance on the reservation. The local courts decided for the county. Later, appeals courts in other cases decided such cases against the counties, and now bingo is played on many reservations.

Madrigal v. *County of Riverside,* 1973 (unreported)
This case concerned the lease of an assignment to a rock festival promoter. Construction of the facilities was stopped by the county because no permit had been obtained. Local courts decided for the county. This case was not a clear-cut county versus reservation case, because the majority of the reservation members opposed and protested the right of one member to lease an assignment without approval of the entire group.

Ricci v. *County of Riverside,* Federal District Court, 1971 (unreported)
The Ricci family wished to return to the reservation and began building their own house, using their own labor except for technical work, such as wiring. They tried unsuccessfully to find out if they needed building permits. When the house was almost complete, the county building inspector "red-tagged" it and threatened criminal prosecution because they had not applied for a building permit. The local court held that the county building code is a law of the state that, while regulating land use, does not directly conflict with federal law. The court recognized, however, that because the law had not been enforced since P.L. 280 had been passed, the Riccis had acted reasonably in assuming they did not need a permit, and the court prohibited the county from interfering with construction.

Santa Rosa Band of Indians et al. v. *Kings County et al.,* No. 74–1565
The question was whether county zoning ordinances applied and whether county permits and approval were needed for

housing, water, and sanitation facilities approved by the Bureau of Indian Affairs and the Indian Health Services. See note 22.

County of Humboldt v. *Eric W. Pearson, Jr.,* June 14, 1976
The county attempted to impose its personal property tax on the store inventory, which belonged to an Indian on the reservation. The case was dismissed.

Agua Caliente Band of Mission Indians v. *City of Palm Springs* (347 F. Supp. 42)
This reservation was created in a checkerboard pattern. Later, the city of Palm Springs was incorporated, and some reservation lands were within the city limits. The question was whether the city could validly include reservation land within the city's incorporated lands and maintain city zoning over such land. Local courts held that the lands were validly incorporated and that city zoning was applicable. The appeals court reversed the decision, stating that P.L. 280 applied to state jurisdiction and did not give jurisdiction to the city.

Quechan Tribe v. *Rowe* (350 F. Supp. 106)
For year, the tribal game warden had enforced tribal hunting and fishing regulations enacted under the tribe's Indian Reorganization Act constitution. This included selling permits to nonmembers for hunting during the dove season. The tribal warden confiscated the guns of boys who were found hunting on the reservation with no permits and who refused to purchase permits at that point. In town later the local sheriff's deputies arrested the tribal warden for grand theft. Later the charges were dropped and the tribe brought action to prevent further interference with its right to regulate hunting, fishing, and trapping on the reservation. The court decided that the tribe had the right to regulate such acts under the Indian Reorganization Act (the Wheeler-Howard Act, relating to self-government) and 18 *United States Code* 1165, and that P.L. 280 gave no jurisdiction to the state or county in this matter.

Bryan v. *Itasca County,* Minnesota, 426 U.S. 373, June 14, 1976
The court decision states that the central force of P.L. 280
was to confer on states the criminal jurisdiction with respect
to crimes involving Indians and that no other jurisdiction was
conferred.

In addition to these specified cases, a number of others occurred
involving the traditional hunting and fishing rights Indians
had always had on reservation lands. This occurred in spite
of the very specific section in P.L. 280 concerning the continuation of such traditional practices. All these cases were decided on the basis that P.L. 280 left intact the "traditional
rights" and treaty provisions in other states.

APPENDIX F

How to Research Reservation History

The following information would apply both to members interested in developing an accurate history of their reservation or in solving problems for, or planning for, their own reservation, and to outside consultants or researchers asked to work for a reservation.

1. One must first obtain permission of the tribal council (unless requested by it to do the work) and the membership. Many applied anthropologists have found that adequate planning, or the development of an accurate history and membership roll, requires detailed knowledge of present conditions and an accurate history of how the present conditions or problems developed.

After obtaining permission, read all the published histories and ethnographies of the tribe at the nearest university, museum, or cultural center library. While reading, note the length of time that the author spent in acquiring the data presented, that is, his or her length of stay with the people, the number of people interviewed, and the conditions under which they were interviewed. The longer the stay and the more people interviewed, the more apt the author is to present reliable data.

Separate the data or direct descriptive material from the author's interpretation. A number of works exist in which the two do not coincide. Also, frequently two or more works present opposing views or contradictory data that will eventually need to be reconciled or explained. Note the author's background and training in order to determine the potential for concepts, definitions, and biases that could distort the interpretation of what the author saw and heard. In reading the histories and ethnographies, remember that individuals record what they see and that what they "see" is based upon their past understanding of, and biases about, the world. For some areas and tribes, published bibliographies may exist and will provide a starting point. For California, Bean and Vane (1977) have published a listing describing what is available in various archives and museums in the state and elsewhere in the country.

2. Develop a data management system on five-by-eight-inch cards, each card recording a single topic and noting the author, title, date of publication, and page, for published works, or the person interviewed and the date and general subject for interviews. A careful filing (and cross-indexing) system must be developed for managing photocopies of all pertinent documents. If possible, a computer-based system should be used, as this will allow for greater ease and speed in managing and coordinating data from a variety of sources about any one subject. Combined with the computer, five-by-eight-inch notebooks are useful when interviewing or researching in archives. When large numbers of copies of archival documents are acquired on any subject, they should be placed in 8 1/2-by-11-inch loose-leaf notebooks labeled by reservation, subject, and date of the document. This system reduces the possibility of misfiling document copies.

3. Start interviewing older members; the more people interviewed, the better will be your understanding. Remember, however, that people see events from their own viewpoint, so do not be afraid to cross-check and requestion both books and individuals. Different tribal members may have had access to different information or may have witnessed different events and thus may be able to provide fuller or different details. Further, in many societies certain knowledge is held and "owned" or controlled privately and is not to be shared, even with other tribal members. Thus each interview must be conducted separately. Such restricted knowledge may be shared

with the interviewer only if trust is already established and the interviewer has demonstrated competence. Also, remember that each tribal member is the authority on the particular subject while you are speaking to him or her. Be respectful at all times.

Repeated interviews are essential because many types of information may be spoken about or recalled only under the proper circumstances or at the proper time of year. As indicated above, if the interviewer does not seem competent to handle a particular type of knowledge, it will not be given. If the interviewer asks inappropriate questions that the elder sees as silly or not related to past events or culture, the elder may answer the question but not tell the interviewer what actually happened. That is, if the interviewer has predetermined concepts or theories about the culture and asks questions related to those concepts but not to real events and the real culture, the elder will answer the question and make no attempt to correct the interviewer's erroneous concepts. People everywhere answer questions, but they do not necessarily tell what actually happened.

4. Next, at the local and area offices of the Bureau of Indian Affairs, check and read the general reservation records, census lists of residents, annual reports, agricultural statistics, and irrigation reports. (Written permission from the reservation is necessary in order to examine these records.)

5. The next step is to search the regional Federal Archive and the regional Federal Records Center (for Southern California, for example, this is at Laguna Niguel). Following that, a trip to the National Archives in Washington, D.C., would be valuable.

However, many of the National Archives records are now available on microfilm and can be obtained locally through various university libraries or the region's Federal Archives. The National Archives has so organized its records access that unless one has several months, it will be more efficient to hire a competent archival research firm in Washington that already knows how to use the complex set of indexes. You will need to give it sufficient information for the search. If you do go to Washington, also check with the Smithsonian Institution for pertinent records, or interviews and collections by earlier anthropologists. Other eastern museums may also have important collections of early materials.

6. Local archives should be tapped before going to Washington. Visit local central public libraries (such as the San Diego City Library, California Room) and local historical societies for references to Indians in accounts by local settlers and early explorers, and in old diaries, and local newspapers. Visit other local offices and archives for various types of old records, such as those for births, marriages, deaths, preemptions, land grants, deeds, mortgages, and water rights, at the county recorder's office; case records at the county, superior, and federal district courts; tax assessment and payment records at the tax assessor's office; copies of early county maps and surveys and early township surveys at the county engineer's office; and soil maps, agricultural records, and possibly rainfall records at the county agricultural agent's office. Some churches and missions also maintain birth, baptismal, marriage, and death records. Title insurance companies often have early records and photographs of the region. Also, annual reports to the superior officers of local missions often contain data necessary for interpreting other records. Historical societies and museums often contain old photographs that record events involving the Indians. In California, the Santa Barbara Mission Archives has copies of all the available California mission reports. In reading these records, remember that each individual records what he or she sees and that what one sees is based on one's past experiences and biases about the world.

7. Copies of old manuscript federal censuses may be found in the local or state historical society, and most local libraries are able to borrow the microfilm copies for study. Check both the population schedule and the agricultural schedule.

8. Regional archives such as Bancroft Library at the University of California-Berkeley, the California Historical Society in San Francisco, the Huntington Library in San Marino, the Southwest Museum Library in Pasadena, and the University of Arizona Library's Spanish and Mexican Archive Collection contain materials on the entire southwestern United States.

This list is not all-inclusive, and other regional institutions may be more pertinent to a local area.

9. If you are interested in the economic, and more specifically the agricultural, history of a reservation and the records of its water use, also note the practices of the neighboring non-Indian farmers and ranchers. Comparisons may be pertinent, because eastern Bureau of Indian Affairs officials and special inspectors frequently did not understand western practices and made derogatory remarks when comparing them to eastern agricultural practices (see Shipek 1977). However, often the Indians were following the best practices of the local non-Indian farmers, and they should be compared with their neighbors under like climatic, soil, and economic conditions. See the county agricultural records and the federal agricultural censuses for such material.

10. Acquire copies of the appropriate old photographs for an interpretation of cultural materials; social, religious, and political events; and environmental conditions. Whenever possible, obtain dates for the photographs and identify individuals and locations shown in them.

11. At several points in this process you will find that the information in the records makes it necessary to go back and reinterview key persons because new material and records will bring forth new understanding and new questions.

12. Most important, find copies of any laws, executive orders, administrative rulings, or court decisions relating to the particular reservation on which you are working. The California Indian Legal Service and the Native American Rights Fund attorneys are most helpful in this aspect of the research.

13. In other states, contact that state's Indian Legal Service and also find out exactly what state, county, or city agencies deal with Indian matters and concerns in any way. Obtain copies of any laws or agency regulations that may affect Indians and reservations. This is especially important in P.L. 280 states. Then interview the reservation members and the tribal council to determine how the state and local agencies actually function in relation to the Indian population.

APPENDIX G

Trust Lands in Southern California

Reservation and Date Established[a]	Tribe	Gross Acres[b]
Riverside Area Field Office		
Santa Barbara County		
Santa Ynez (1901)	Chumash	99.28
Public Domain Allotments		
San Bernardino County		
San Manuel 1893	Serrano	653.15
Twenty-Nine Palms (1875, 1895)	Chemehuevi	402.13
Riverside County		
Augustine (1893)	Cahuilla	502.29
Cabazon (1876, 1895)	Cahuilla	1,461.53
Cahuilla (1875, 1877, 1926, 1931)	Cahuilla	18,272.38

Source: Bureau of Indian Affairs Records, Riverside, California.
[a] All dates prior to 1891 are executive order dates. Those after 1891 are trust patent dates of lands as ordered by the Smiley Commission or later purchases based on congressional actions.
[b] Acreage figures may be inaccurate, beause Bureau of Indian Affairs records often change the acreage recorded with no known intervening action. The figures used here are based on 1984 figures from the BIA, which unaccountably changed acreage figures even on unallotted reservations.

Allotted Acres[b]	Population[c]		Organization[d]	Roll[e]	Est. Acreage Fee Patented
	Residents	Members			
	169	195	IRA Articles	x	
160.00					
	56	89	Non-IRA Articles		
	0	18	Non-IRA Articles		
154.86	0	2		x	122.71
308.32	25	25	Non-IRA Articles	x	698.47
	31	148			

[c] Many of the resident and membership figures are best estimates.

[d] Most reservations require action by the membership, with the tribal council and the chairman empowered only to carry out membership votes. Only Capitan Grande (Barona and Viejas) originally voted for the Indian Reorganization Act. Others, such as Cuyapaipe, did not vote and thus came under the law. All the other IRA constitutions were developed later.

[e] An x in this column means that the tribe has developed a formal roll based on enrollment regulations developed by the band and approved by the secretary of the interior.

(*continued*)

Trust Lands in Southern California

Reservation and Date Established[a]	Tribe	Gross Acres[b]
Morongo (1877, 1881, 1908)	Cahuilla Serrano	32, 247.99
Pechanga (1882, 1893)	San Luiseño	4,093.80
Ramona (1893)	Cahuilla	560.00
Santa Rosa (1907, 1937)	Cahuilla	11,092.60
Soboba (1883, 1913)	Cahuilla	5,035.68
Torres-Martinez (see Imperial County)	Cahilla	
Imperial County		
Torres-Martinez (1876, 1903)	Cahuilla	24,822.74
San Diego County		
Barona (1932)[f]	Kumeyaay	5,180.66
Campo (1893, 1907, 1911)	Kumeyaay	15,010.00
Capitan Grande[g] (1875, 1883, 1894)	Kumeyaay	15,753.40
Cuyapaipe (1893)	Kumeyaay	4,100.13
Iñaja-Cosmit (1875, 1893)	Kumeyaay	851.81
Jamul[h] (1975, 1982)	Kumeyaay	6.03
La Jolla (1875, 1892)	San Luiseño	8,228.06
La Posta (1893)	Kumeyaay	3,672.29
Los Coyotes (1889, 1900, 1914)	Cahuilla	25,049.63

[f] Purchased June 11, 1932, for the Capitan Grande people.

[g] The central valley, 7,134.46 acres, was used by the city of San Diego for a water storage dam under acts passed by Congress in 1919 and 1932. The Barona and Viejas (Baron Long) ranches, as well as some individual lands, were purchased for the members of Capitan Grande.

Allotted Acres[b]	Population[c]		Organization[d]	Roll[e]	Est. Acreage Fee Patented
	Residents	Members			
1,291.30	367	748			135.53
1,233.02	215	433			61.20
	0	3			
	25	107			
	405	555			
6,599.58	81	217		x	6,867.90
	230	304		x	
	213	160	Non-IRA Constitution		
	0	550		x	
	0	5	IRA Constitution	x	
	0	20			
	25	41			
634.00	222	246	Non-IRA Articles		111.00
	3	11	IRA Constitution	x	
	84	101			

h Former church lands amounting to 2.5 acres, including a cemetery and the approach to it. Additional land was purchased after federal recognition was obtained in 1975.   *(continued)*

Trust Lands in Southern California

Reservation and Date Established[a]	Tribe	Gross Acres[b]
Manzanita (1893)	Kumeyaay	3,579.38
Mesa Grande[i] (1875, 1883, 1893, 1925)	Kumeyaay	120.00
Pala[j] (1875, 1903, 1973)	San Luiseño, Cupeño, Kumeyaay	11,488.13
Pauma-Yuima[j] (1892, 1973)	San Luiseño	5,877.25
Rincon (1875, 1881, 1892)	San Luiseño	3,960.25
San Pasqual (1910, 1911)	Kumeyaay	1,379.58
Santa Ysabel[i] (1875, 1893, 1926)	Kumeyaay	15,526.78
Sycuan (1875, 1903)	Kumeyaay	640.00
Viejas (1932)[k]	Kumeyaay	1,609.00
Public Domain and purchased		1,300.00
Palm Springs Agency *Riverside County* Agua Caliente 1896	Cahuilla	24,463.12
Executive Order Reserved Land Kelsey Tract[l] (1907)	San Luiseño	235.00
Former Reservations[m] *San Diego County* Laguna[n] (1892)	Kumeyaay	320.00
Riverside County Mission Creek[o]	Serrano	2,560.62

[i] The figures given for Santa Ysabel represent areas designated Numbers 1, 2, and 3. Numbers 1 and 2 should have been trust patented to Mesa Grande, and the 120-acre tract should have been a homestead. An attempt has been made to sort out membership estimates.

[j] From the Mission Reserve, Pala received 3,761.4 acres, and Pauma-Yuima received 5,627.25 acres.

[k] Purchased June 11, 1932. Also, see note g, above.

[l] Correspondence indicates that this land was purchased for Pechanga, but it was nev-

Allotted Acres[b]	Population[c]		Organization[d]	Roll[e]	Est. Acreage Fee Patented
	Residents	Members			
	18	50	IRA Constitution		
	0	207	Non-IRA Articles		
1,174.29	455	475	Non-IRA Articles	x	108.00
	93	107	Non-IRA Articles		
351.81	390	390	Non-IRA Articles	x	65.89
	189	50	IRA Constitution	x	
	198	490			
259.45	52	72	Non-IRA Articles		
	217	215		x	
22,407.23 (equalized value)	119	200	Non-IRA Constitution	x	7,427.17

er trust patented to Pechanga. Pechanga members began using it immediately after its purchase for them.

[m] These are reservations where the trust patent status has been terminated by the membership.

[n] Has been fee patented to the member claiming to be the last surviving member of the reservation. Trust patented in 1892.

[o] Established by 1876 executive order; trust patented in 1921; terminated voluntarily in 1969 under the Rancheria Act, P. L. 85-671, as amended by P. L. 88-419.

NOTES

1. I agree with Bean (1978) in using the term "advocates" to designate those well-meaning individuals or organizations who will "take up battle" for an "Indian Cause"—for an individual Indian, a band, a tribe, or Indian rights in general. While some have been and are of real service, they tend to increase factionalism because frequently they contact only one faction and promote that one faction as the "real Indians." Frequently they neither investigate nor understand the full problem and see Indians only in their (the advocate's) idealized stereotypes of what an Indian is and what Indian beliefs are. Also, some even promote their own hidden advantage by advocating some course of action before the Indians or the various levels of government.
2. Throughout this study the term "bureau" will be used to indicate the Bureau of Indian Affairs and its predecessor, the Office of Indian Affairs.
3. The American Friends Service Committee (AFSC) is an action organ of the Society of Friends (Quakers). The committee ran a major relief effort in postrevolutionary Russia, and after World War II it organized thousands of young volunteers to carry out small-scale rural development projects overseas. Within the United States it provided full-time advisors for some Indian peoples in the Southwest from 1950 to 1962.
4. For this region and northern Baja California, Owen (1965, 1966) has presented an interpretation of social structure that has not been employed here, because his theory is based

upon inferences drawn from the modern conditions of refu-geeism and depopulation as if they represented aboriginal conditions.

5. In Southern California, the Spanish term "rancho" is still used to designate those rancho grants dating from the Mexican and Spanish periods, and it will be so used throughout this study. The use of this term contrasts with "ranch," which is used for those ranches developed after 1850 by American settlers.

6. The act of May 18, 1928 (45 *United States Statutes* 602), as amended April 29, 1930 (46 *United States Statutes* 264), authorized the attorney general of the state of California to file suit on behalf of the Indians of California against the United States for the value of lands lost as a result of the unratified treaties. The case was filed on August 14, 1929. On December 4, 1944, the court of claims held that the Indians of California were entitled to recover the sum of $17,053,941.98, less offsets of $12,029,099.94, and also less the expense to the state in bringing the suit, leaving a net amount of $4,996,999.84. This amounted to approximately $150 per capita for each Indian of California able to prove descent from a California Indian of 1851. The offsets consisted of the equivalent value of reservation acreage and the entire cost of any and all rations, services, equipment, and schooling received by California Indians through the intervening years. Thus the Indians of California have never been "given" anything; one way or another, they have paid for everything they have supposedly been given, even substandard, worthless goods. The claims case against the government for the improper and illegal taking of the rest of the aboriginal lands (Dockets 31 and 37, the Indians of California Calims Case; the Pitt River Case, Docket 347; and the Mission Indians Claims Case, Docket 80 before the Indian Claims Commission) was settled in 1964 when the government offered $29.1 million as a settlement for all the land claims of California Indians. The offer was accepted by a majority vote of each named docket. (The Pitt River Indians later protested the legality of the voting in their case.) Approximately $800 per

person has been distributed in this case. The law setting up the claims cases specified payment for the value of the land as of the date of taking. Since the official legal date of taking was March 3, 1851, the payment closely approximated the average per-acre value of the claimed land (at least in Southern California) as of that date.

7. The land commission demanded that all counties send their Mexican records to it for the purpose of determining the legality and accuracy of claims to Mexican rancho titles (see note 9).

8. The San Diego County tax assessment records show that from 1850 to at least 1872 San Diego County Indians were paying taxes on their personal property, cattle, sheep, and horses, and that a few paid taxes on land.

9. The San Pasqual Band has a tradition that in 1870 their old captain, Panto Duro, led a group to see Judge Benjamin Hayes in San Diego to protest intrusions on their land. A July 28, 1870, *San Diego Union* newspaper article corroborates their story and relates that they were protesting the idea of a reservation with "wild" Indians being moved onto their land. The Indians relate that Hayes took them to the courthouse and showed them documents that proved they had title to their lands and that he told them that in two months he would take Captain Panto to Washington with the papers and arrange for them to receive proper title. Unfortunately, Panto died before the trip, and Hayes did nothing more. The papers were apparently among those sent to the United States surveyor general's office in San Francisco when that office demanded all Spanish and Mexican documents from all California counties for the use of the land commission. Most counties refused to turn over their Spanish and Mexican archives, but San Diego obeyed the order. The papers were stored in the San Francisco office of the surveyor general, and most were destroyed in the San Francisco earthquake and fire of 1906. All that remains in San Diego is an index of the documents that was prepared by Judge Hayes. The most poignant entry is on page 231: "collection of papers relating to the Indian Pueblos of San Pasqual, San Dieguito, Las Flores, etc.

from 1835 to 1846." We can only speculate on what the missing documents contained and on the meaning of "etc." This entry indicates that papers relating to Indian pueblo land rights were in the hands of the land commission and that they were ignored. While in this case Judge Hayes seems to have supported the Indian title to the land, it is also a matter of record that he believed there would be no end of difficulties or any progress in the development of Southern California farmland until all Indians were gathered on reservations (Hayes Papers, Bancroft Library).

10. It is interesting that when the 1860 federal census taker went through San Diego County, he identified all the Indian villages on the major trails and roads, including Pala and San Pasqual, and named the Indians in each village (though he did not leave the main trails and thus missed about 50 percent of the Indian population). In contrast, however, in 1870, when the newspapers were proclaiming that there were no Indians in the San Pasqual and Pala valleys, the census taker identified only Mexicans and people from Europe or the eastern United States in those valleys. Some of the "Mexican" families had the same names, however, as the families identified in 1860 as Indians.

11. Feelings on this matter were still intense among the elderly Indians in the 1950s. Many told me that the worst things that ever happened to the Indians of Southern California were Helen Hunt Jackson and the reservation system, that Southern California Indians were "not like other Indians" and that each should have his own land. Others were equally adamant in their belief that all Indian homesteaders were traitors and that without reservations there would have been no Indian land.

12. It is ironic that Cave Couts, Jr., who was openly antagonistic to Helen Hunt Jackson and her purpose of preserving Indian land for Indian use (Odell 1939:179–182), was eventually hired as the surveyor to locate boundaries for the lands reserved to Indian use. See the discussion of allotments and the special case of Mesa Grande in Chapter 4 for more details. The records indicate that boundary or location disputes were

resolved in favor of settlers rather than Indians and that each additional survey of rancho, settler, or reservation lands shifted boundary lines successively inward onto the Indian-occupied lands. An accurate modern resurvey just might produce some rather interesting results.

13. Many of the 1875 and 1891 reservations did not provide even a bare minimum of subsistence farmland, and some Indians were still starving between 1891 and 1910. Later, investigative commissions purchased additional lands at Campo, along the edge of Santa Ysabel Rancho, and elsewhere to "provide more adequate farm land" for the Indians. At no time was sufficient land provided for all the Indians to maintain themselves solely by farming and stock raising, nor was first-quality farmland, such as the Indians originally owned, purchased for them.

14. The Mission Agency of the bureau was responsible for all water needs of the reservations until January 1, 1954, when it claimed that P.L. 280 had divested it of all responsibility except maintenance of the trust status. The bureau suggested that the Indians check with the county public health agency, which also disclaimed responsibility. The Indians found it impossible to get aid for their domestic water needs. In at least two cases, when the Indians attempted to hire private well-digging companies, the bureau informed the companies that they would be liable to federal penalties if they entered into a private contract with any reservation Indian.

15. Adoption by a reservation family does not carry band adoption with it. Band adoption is a separate process and must be approved by a vote of the entire membership.

16. The bureau's agents went through a reservation and simply listed all the residents on that reservation. Some persons were identified as non-Indian spouses, but not all non-Indian spouses were so identified. Some years, and sometimes for several years at a time, the agents apparently just copied a previous year's list, indicating identical ages and making the same mistakes. In some cases, various census lists have different degrees of blood listed without indicating any different source of information for making the change in the degree.

Provisions exist in most enrollment regulations so that claimants may apply who were not living on the reservation during the base year but who have other documentation to prove their right to membership.

17. Evidence from both the mission records (Shipek 1982b) and from recorded kinship terminology indicates that prior to the Spanish imposition of Catholic marriage rules, cross-cousin marriage existed. That is, marriage between children of siblings of the opposite sex (a brother and sister), or a mother's brother's daughter, or the next generation—a mother's brother's daughter's daughter. These people were not considered relatives, but rather non-kin. In contrast, parallel cousins, children of siblings of the same sex, children of two sisters or of two brothers, used the same term as was used for a biological brother or sister. In some cases, this use of the sibling term was carried to the fourth generation of descendants of sisters or of brothers. Under the Spanish and the Americans, cross cousins began to be considered as kin rather than non-kin. Thus, the Indians' rule that they should not marry anyone within five generations of kin relationship was translated into the new definition of kinship. The Spanish Catholic marriage rules that allowed marriage between second cousins conflicted with the Indian fifth-generation rule and were not adopted. Thus the mixture of the rules from the different cultural traditions has made it almost impossible for an Indian to marry another member of the same reservation, or in some cases of almost any other reservation containing tribal members, or even from any other Southern California reservation.

18. As mentioned earlier, persons could be renting houses or farms on a reservation different from their own. In other cases, they were children by a previous marriage of the non-member spouse.

19. There is no need to withdraw formally if a person decides to leave the Indian community and assimilate into the larger society; many have simply left. The purpose of a formal relinquishment of rights is to clarify membership when an individual has two possible claims to membership. For example, in the past the bureau shifted families with children from iso-

lated reservations to those that had day schools. In at least two cases, La Posta and Cuyapaipe, the children of such families were the last surviving persons eligible for membership on those reservations. The bureau finally allowed them to reclaim their original membership and required a formal relinquishment of membership rights in the reservation on which they had been raised and participated as members for years.

Another case must be mentioned. Early in the 1960s the county agency took a nine-year-old boy from his family and put him up for adoption into a non-Indian family elsewhere. As a young man, he returned and sought out the remembered kin. The band desired to have him back as a member, but the bureau refused to enroll him, claiming he was now a non-Indian, even though he was actually a full-blood Indian.

20. Several disputes between Indians on a reservation have gone to local courts, and the judgments have been less than satisfactory. In each of several cases, the judge has dismissed the case and simply admonished the Indians to get along with one another. In other cases, the judge has ignored most of the evidence, declared it too complex to understand, and told the people involved to make up, stop arguing, and work together.

21. Even as this manuscript was being completed, Congress passed another law relating to allotments. Anyone who inherits less than a 2 percent interest in an allotment automatically loses that share to the tribe. In some cases even this small an interest has great economic value to the individual, because of oil and mineral royalties or lease rights on valuable lands such as exist in Southern California. The Native American Rights Fund has already brought a case challenging this law as an unconstitutional confiscation of individual property without compensation. Congress may have been attempting to begin to protect tribal interests as against individual interests, reversing the policy of a century ago, but, as usual in Indian affairs, it did not examine all the ramifications of its action.

22. Another source of possible allotment loss resulted from P.L. 280, which closed Soboba Hospital, the only Indian hospital in Southern California. Indians were told that they should

now go to the county hospitals, where they would receive services on the same basis as any other citizen. However, they were not told the procedures necessary to gain admittance or how the charges would be assessed. In 1954 the San Diego County Hospital's charges for its services were figured on the basis of the total possible daily cost for one person multiplied by the number of days in the hospital rather than upon the actual cost of that person's care. In the case of "welfare" patients, this cost, or exaggerated cost, was placed as a lien against any property the person might own and was to be satisfied first upon the person's death before anything went to the heirs. This exaggerated figure could only be corrected if the person appealed immediately upon notification of the lien. Then the charges would be refigured on the basis of actual cost. It is not known how many Indian estates were damaged by this practice. The lien was also being improperly placed on the property of Indians who received hospital service, because the federal government was allocating funds to California counties to cover such Indian hospitalization charges.

Hospital admittance was also very difficult to obtain for Indians, because a private doctor was first required to certify that the person needed hospital care, and many Indians did not have a private doctor. Cultural differences in responses to a doctor's examination were also a cause for a failure to recognize the extreme illness of some of the Indians.

23. A recent case demonstrates this point. A young Indian couple was trying to get the water lines extended to their allotment. They had cleared the land and prepared it for an orchard and needed the irrigation water lines extended to make a success of the project. For a number of years they asked and pleaded for the extension to their allotment and were consistently told that the bureau had no funds that year to extend the water lines. Finally, in desperation, they gave up and sold their allotment to a non-Indian. The bureau immediately put in the water line. Even when a lawsuit was brought against the bureau for improperly expending its limited funds to bring water to the non-Indian before it used its funds for the

Indians, the judge approved the bureau expenditure, stating
that the water was presumed to go with the land. This judg-
ment was made even though the funds the bureau used for
the white landowner were federal appropriations explicitly
appropriated for Indian water development.

24. This was the decision of the United States Court of Appeals,
    Ninth Circuit, in the case of the *Santa Rosa Band of Indians;*
    Mark Barrios; and Pete Baga v. *Kings County; Charles Gardner,*
    Planning Director and Chairman of the Planning Commission of
    Kings County; and Kings County Planning Commission. The opin-
    ion also stated that although in Public Law 280 the United
    States had conferred on the state the criminal and civil juris-
    diction over Indian reservation trust lands, at the same time
    Congress "necessarily pre-empts and reserves to the Federal
    government or the tribe jurisdiction not so granted," and that
    the civil and criminal jurisdiction was granted to the states,
    not to the counties.

25. The adobe houses of the Indians became the first houses of
    the settlers. For many years, the San Pasqual Valley lands
    were one of the most lucrative crop and dairy-farm areas of
    San Diego County. Portions of the Indians' farm and grazing
    lands are now within the Wild Animal Park of the San Diego
    Zoo.

26. The Bureau made it quite clear that it did not want me to tes-
    tify as to the facts in the case. It claimed that I was biased.
    The bureau was unaware that I had friends on both reserva-
    tions and had determined very early not to take sides in this
    dispute any more than in other disputes between Indians but
    told both that I would provide all records and data that could
    be used to solve the problem whichever way was proved cor-
    rect. In this, as in some other disputes, much of the members'
    time and energy was engaged in the dispute rather than in
    development or any other constructive action. Too often, I
    found that most officials were not concerned with solving
    problems with correct data but instead took the easy way and
    let the disputes carry on for more generations. Note the judi-
    cial decision in this as in other cases mentioned.

I first met and became a friend of a Santa Ysabel leader who described his interpretation of the naming of the bands in the trust patents and who felt that all the land belonged to the Santa Ysabel Band. For years, no Mesa Grande people would talk to me, because they knew I had met and heard the Santa Ysabel claim first. In the course of researching San Pasqual genealogies, I began to discover the data summarized here. It took me some years to reach Mesa Grande members and let them know that I had discovered data that could be used to solve the problem.

27. The adjudication of the Pechanga case contrasts with that of the non-Indian land title case for which I did the research and in which the original grantee had sworn that as of April 4, 1871, the tidelands requested were not within two miles of any city, town, or village. Here I proved that the affidavit of the claimant (a San Diego resident) was in error (i.e., fraudulent) because National City existed as a village by that date. Here the title remained with the Port Authority and the State of California.

28. Since membership in two reservations is not permitted, inheritance of an allotment or a portion thereof on a reservation other than one's own does not confer membership in that reservation or a share of that reservation's communal assets, but ownership or inheritance of homestead lands is not considered to be under the same restriction.

29. Interestingly, the U.S. Forest Service has discovered similar problems with some of its boundaries adjoining private lands and has instituted official proceedings to recover such lands or to exchange the privately developed land for some other privately owned land adjacent to the forest.

30. This was one part of the San Luis Rey Water Case, Docket 80A. When the Pauma Reservation was purchased, only the first thirty inches of water from Pauma Creek was acquired with the land, and three inches for Yuima. However, until 1916 the reservation Indians used all the water of Pauma Creek and had their own irrigation system predating the trust patenting of the reservation. They had corn, vegetables, and highly lucrative orchards, while the ranch owner used the ranch only for sheep. Upon seeing the rich return from

the Indian orchards, the ranch owner divided the land and sold it to orchardists. The bureau had not protected Indian water use by filing under California law for the entire amount used beneficially. Instead, after 1916 the bureau agents forced the Indians to share their water with the non-Indians whenever the full thirty inches was not in the stream. The bureau put in a new, easily adjusted headgate at the diversion dam but did not protect it from tampering by the surrounding ranchers, who regularly and illegally changed the headgate to reduce the flow to Indian land and divert it to the non-Indian land. Anyone could approach the isolated headgate to change and increase the flow to the non-Indians. Gradually, the Indian orchards and crops died. Later, the state was allowed to cut off the mountain headwaters of the stream with no more than a letter of protest from the bureau.

The first hearings on this case were held in 1965, and the case was finally settled in the fall of 1985, pending congressional approval. I prepared written testimony in 1969, 1972, 1980, and 1984, was cross-examined on them in 1973 and 1981, and had a preliminary deposition taken in 1984. Pauma and Pala are receiving damages and water from the Metropolitan Water District. The Indians of Rincon and La Jolla reservations are receiving damages plus the right to a large portion of San Luis Rey River water. They plan to sell some of their water to the city of Escondido, the water that the city has been using all these years simply by taking it.

31. On Pala, the original sand and gravel plant has changed owners and lessees, and the original lease has been modified to give additional protection to the tribe. There are now more adequate controls on the lessee and a better income for the tribe. The relationship between the new lessee and the tribe has been relatively harmonious.

32. At this hearing I presented the history of the Mission Reserve and Pala Reservation, an expanded version of this and the next two paragraphs, and a short analysis of the political, economic, and bureaucratic hindrances that resulted in reservation land appearing to be unused for many years.

33. Our ancestors fought the American Revolution for the right

of self-government. We immigrated from Europe and took over the land of the nations and tribes here before us and promised them reserved areas where they could continue to govern themselves. They have seldom been allowed the rights they were promised. Even now, several organizations calling themselves some version of "Equal Rights for Everyone" are attempting to negate all Indian trust lands, trust rights, religious rights, and hunting and fishing rights (though in many cases hunting and fishing rights were the only or the primary payment to the Indians for turning almost all of their land over to the United States). Often the promised rights, as well as equal religious rights, have only recently been allowed.

34. Actually, tribes are supposed to have such taxing powers and the right to charge fees or licenses for the use of tribal property or equipment by both members and nonmembers (Cohen 1942:142–143). Thus the bureau officials have improperly interfered in these cases.

REFERENCES CITED

Books and Articles

Bean, Lowell J.

1969   The Language of Stereotype, Distortion and Prejudice: A Review of "California Indian Days" by Helen Bauer. *Indian Historian* 2(3): 6–11.

1972   Mukat's People: The Cahuilla Indians of Southern Caifornia. Berkeley and Los Angeles: University of California Press.

1973   Social Organization in Native California. Pp. 11–34 in Antap: California Indian Political and Economic Organization. Lowell J. Bean and Thomas F. King, eds. Menlo Park, Calif: Ballena Press.

1978   Morongo Indian Reservation: A Century of Adaptive Strategies. Pp. 159–236 in "American Indian Economic Development." Sam Stanley, ed. *World Anthropology.*

Bean, Lowell J., and Harry W. Lawton

1973   Some Explanations for the Rise of Cultural Complexity in Native California with Comments on Proto-Agriculture and Agriculture. Pp. v–xi, Introduction to Patterns of Indian Burning in California: Ecology and Ethno-history, by Henry T. Lewis. Menlo Park, Calif.: Ballena Press.

Bean, Lowell John, and Sylvia Brakke Vane

1977   California Indians: Primary Resources, a guide to Manuscripts, Artifacts, Documents, Serials, Music, and Illustrations. Menlo Park, Calif.: Ballena Press.

Bell, Horace
1927   Reminiscences of a Ranger. Santa Barbara, Calif.: Wallace
            Hebberd.

Boscana, Fr. Geronimo
1933   Chinigchinich. In Chinigchinich: A Revised and Annotated
            Version of Alfred Robinson's Translation of Father Geroni-
            mo Boscana's Historical Account of the Beliefs, Usages, Cus-
            toms and Extravagancies of the Indians of the Mission of San
            Juan Capistrano Called the Acagchem Tribe. Phil T. Hanna,
            ed. Santa Ana, Calif.: Fine Arts Press.

Boserup, Ester
1965   The Conditions of Agricultural Growth. Chicago: Aldine
            Atherton.

Cohen, Felix S.
1942   Handbook of Federal Indian Law. Government Printing Of-
            fice. Reprint. Albuquerque: University of New Mexico Press.
            (A more recent edition also exists.)

Dobyns, Henry F.
1966   Estimating Aboriginal Population: An Appraisal of Tech-
            niques with a New Hemisphere Estimate. *Current Anthropology*
            7(4): 395–416.
1976   Native American Historical Demography: A Critical Bibliog-
            raphy. Bloomington: Indiana University Press for the New-
            berry Library Center for the History of the American Indian.
1976a   A Brief Perspective on a Scholarly Transformation: Widow-
            ing the "Virgin Land." *Ethnohistory* 23(2): 95–104.
1981   From Fire to Flood: The Human Destruction of the Sonora
            Desert. Menlo Park, Calif.: Ballena Press.
1983   Their Number Become Thinned: Native American Popula-
            tion Dynamics in Eastern North America. Knoxville: Univer-
            sity of Tennessee Press.

Dubois, Constance
1908   The Religion of the Luiseño Indians of Southern California.

University of California Publications in American Archaeology and
Ethnology 8(3): 69–186. Berkeley and Los Angeles.

Ellison, William Henry
1919   The Federal Indian Policy in California 1846–1860. Disserta-
            tion in History. University of California-Berkeley.

Englehardt, Fr. Zephyrin, OFM
1912   The Missions and Missionaries of California. Vol. 2, Upper
            California. Part 1, General History. San Francisco: James H.
            Barry Co.
1920   The Missions and Missionaries of California. New Series. Lo-
            cal History: San Diego Mission. San Francisco: James H. Bar-
            ry Co.
1921   The Missions and Missionaries of California. New Series. Lo-
            cal History: San Luis Rey Mission. San Francisco: James H.
            Barry Co.
1922   The Missions and Missionaries of California. New Series. Lo-
            cal History: San Juan Capistrano Mission. San Francisco:
            James H. Barry Co.

Geisler, Charles, et al., eds.
1982   Indian SIA: The Social Assessment of Rapid Resource Devel-
            opment on Native Lands. *University of Michigan School of Natu-
            ral Resources, Monograph Series* 3.

Gifford, Edward W.
1918   Clans and Moieties in Southern California. *University of Cali-
            fornia Publications in American Archaeology and Ethnology* 14(2):
            155–219. Berkeley and Los Angeles.
1931   The Kamia of Imperial Valley. *Bureau of American Ethnology
            Bulletin* 97. Washington, D.C.: Smithsonian Institution.

√ Haas, Theodore H.
1957   The Legal Aspects of Indian Affairs from 1887 to 1957. In
            American Indians and American Life. *Annals of the American
            Academy of Science* 311:12–22. Philadelphia.

Hardin, Garrett
1968   The Tragedy of the Commons. *Science* 162:1243–1248.

Heizer, Robert F.
1966   Languages, Territories, and Names of California Indian Tribes. Berkeley and Los Angeles: University of California Press.

Heizer, Robert F., and Alfred L. Kroeber
1976   For Sale: California at 47 Cents Per Acre. *Journal of California Anthropology* 3(2): 38–65.

Hewes, Gordon, and Minna Hewes, eds. and trans.
1958   Indian Life at Mission San Luis Rey by Pablo Tac. Oceanside, Calif.: Old Mission San Luis Rey.

Higgs, E. S., and M. R. Jarman
1972   The Origins of Animal and Plant Husbandry. Pp. 3–13 in Papers in Economic Prehistory. E. S. Higgs, ed. Cambridge: Cambridge University Press.

Jackson, Helen Hunt, and Abbot Kinney
1885   Report on the Condition and Needs of the Mission Indians of California Made by Special Agents Helen Hunt Jackson and Abbot Kinney, 1883. Message from the President of the United States, 49th Congress, 1st Session. Ex. Doc. No. 15. Washington, D.C.: Government Printing Office.

√Johnson, Kenneth M.
1966   K-344 or Indians of California vs. the United States. Famous Trial Series No. 6. Los Angeles: Dawson's Book Store.

Kenneally, Finbar, OFM
1965   Writings of Fermin Francisco de Lasuen. Vols. 1 and 2. Washington, D.C.: Academy of American Franciscan History.

Kroeber, Alfred L.
1925   Handbook of California Indians. Washington, D.C.: Bureau

of American Ethnology, Smithsonian Institution.
1955   Nature of Landholding Groups. *Ethnohistory* 2(4): 303–314.
1962   The Nature of Landholding Groups in California. *Reports of the University of California Archaeological Survey* 56. Berkeley.

Lewis, Henry T.
1973   Patterns of Indian Burning in California: Ecology and Ethnohistory. Menlo Park, Calif.: Ballena Press.
1977   Maskuta: The Ecology of Indian Fires in Northern Alberta. *Western Canadian Journal of Anthropology* 7(1): 15–52.

Luomala, Katharine
1963   Flexibility in Sib Affiliation among the Diegueños. *Ethnology* 2(3): 282–301.
1978   Tipai-Ipai. Pp. 592–609 in Handbook of North American Indians. Vol. 8, California. Washington, D.C.: Smithsonian Institution.

Lurie, Nancy Oestreich
1979   The Will-o'-The-Wisp of Indian Unity. Pp. 325–335 in *Currents in Anthropology: Essays in Honor of Sol Tax*. R. Hinshaw, ed. The Hague: Mouton Publishers.
1986   Money, Semantics and Indian Leadership. *American Indian Quarterly Journal of American Indian Studies* 10(1): 47–63.

Mazzetti, Max
1980   Historical Overview of P.L. 280 in California. Prepared for the Office of Criminal Justice Planning, Indian Justice Program.

Mead, Margaret
1956   New Lives for Old: Cultural Transformation, Manus, 1928–1951. London: Victor Gollancz.

Odell, Ruth
1939   Helen Hunt Jackson. New York and London: D. Appleton-Century Co.

Oswald, Wendell
√1978   This Land Was Theirs. 3d ed. New York and Santa Barbara: John Wiley and Sons.

Owen, Roger
1965   The Patrilocal Band: A Linguistically and Culturally Hybrid Social Unit. *American Anthropologist* 67(3): 675–690.
1966   The Social Evolution of Northern Baja California Indian Bands. In Fourth Annual Baja California Symposium. La Asociación Culturál de las Californias. Costa Mesa, Calif.: Orange Coast College.

Painter, C. C.
1886   A Visit to the Mission Indians of Southern California and Other Western Tribes. Philadelphia: Indian Rights Association.

Ringwald, George
1967   The Agua Caliente Indians and Their Guardians. *Riverside* (Calif.) *Press-Enterprise and Riverside Daily Press.*

Rudkin, Charles, ed. and trans.
1956   Observations in California, 1772–1790, by Father Luis Sales O.P. Los Angeles: Dawson's Book Shop.

Shipek, Florence C.
1958   The Mission Reserve. Report to Pala and Pauma Reservations.
1963   Summary Report on Diegueño-Kamia Land Use to Attorney, Mission Indian Claims Case.
1965   A New Look at San Diego County Indians. Paper Presented to the First Annual San Diego County Historical Convention.
1968   The Autobiography of Delfina Cuero: As Told to Florence C. Shipek. Los Angeles: Dawson's Book Shop.
1968a   Diegueño Marriage Patterns: Request for Change in "Civil Code of California" Concerning Indian Custom Marriage. Paper Presented at Southwestern Anthropological Association Meeting. San Diego.
1969   Preliminary Testimony: Describing Water Uses and Water

	Losses of San Luis Rey River Reservations. Submitted to Federal District Court, San Diego.
1969a	Documents of San Diego History: A Unique Case. Temecula Indians vs. Holman and Seaman. *Journal of San Diego History* 15(2): 26–32.
1972	Prepared Direct Testimony, Exhibits B-50, B-51, B-52. Federal Power Commission Project No. 176, San Diego County, Calif.
1972a	Report on Jamul, Kumeyaay Band, Prepared for Indian Rights Association.
1977	A Strategy for Change: The Luiseño of Southern California. Dissertation in Anthropology. University of Hawaii (University Microfilms).
1978	History of Southern California Mission Indians. Pp. 610–618 in Handbook of North American Indians. Vol. 8, California. Washington, D.C.: Smithsonian Institution.
√ 1980	The Indians of California Claims Cases. Paper presented at a Symposium on Native American Litigation at the Annual Meeting of the Society for Applied Anthropology. Denver.
1980a	Prepared Direct Testimony. Part 1, Value of Aboriginal Water Rights of the San Luis Rey River Reservations, 1851. Part 2, History of Agriculture and Irrigation for the La Jolla, Pala, Pauma, Rincon, and San Pascual Indians of Southern California. U.S. Court of Claims, Docket 80A-1.
1981	A Native American Response to Drought as Seen in the San Diego Mission Records, 1769–1799. *Ethnohistory* 28(4): 295–312.
1982	Kumeyaay Socio-Political Structure. *Journal of California and Great Basin Anthropology* 4(2): 293–303.
1982a	Effects of Drastic Water Loss on Native American Reservations. In Indian SIA: The Social Impact Assessment of Rapid Resource Development on Native Lands. Charles Geisler et al., eds. *University of Michigan School of Natural Resources Monograph Series* 3. Ann Arbor.
1982b	Kumeyaay Socio-Political Organization: Evidence from the San Diego Mission Registers. Paper Presented at a Symposium on Mission Register Research, Southwestern Anthropological Association. Sacramento.
1983	Devolution and Enclavement in Southern California: The

San Luiseño Case. Paper Presented at the Annual Meeting of the American Society for Ethnohistory. Albuquerque.

1983a   Environmental Contract Archaeology and Ethnography: Evaluation and Impact. Paper Presented at the Annual Meeting of the Society for Applied Anthropology. San Diego.

1984a   Response. Pp. 109–122 in Final Environmental Impact Assessment for the Table Mountain Wind Energy Study. El Centro, Calif.: Bureau of Land Management.

1984b   Prepared Direct Testimony: Post–1850 Changing Leadership among the San Luiseño and the Identity of Frank Ward, Signer of 1894 Contract. *Case of Rincon Band of Mission Indians, La Jolla Band of Mission Indians, Plaintiffs* vs. *Escondido Mutual Water Co., et al., Defendants.* Federal District Court, San Diego, Calif.

1984c   Changing Role of Traditional Leadership: Southern California Reservations. Paper Presented at a Symposium on Reservations at the Annual Meeting of the American Anthropological Association. Washington, D.C.

1985   Kuuchamaa: The Kumeyaay Sacred Mountain. *Journal of California and Great Basin Anthropology* 7(1): 67–74.

1986   The Impact of Europeans upon Kumeyaay Culture. Pp. 15–25 in The Impact of European Exploration and Settlement on Local Native Americans. Cabrillo Festival Historic Seminar. San Diego: Cabrillo Historical Association.

Sparkman, Philip S.

1908   The Culture of the Luiseño Indians. *University of California Publications in American Archaeology and Ethnology* 8(4): 187–234. Berkeley and Los Angeles.

Spicer, Edward H.

1962   Cycles of Conquest: Impact of Spain, Mexico, and the United States on the Indians of the Southwest, 1533–1960. Tucson: University of Arizona Press.

Spier, Leslie

1923   Southern Diegueño Customs. *University of California Publications in American Archaeology and Ethnology* 20(16): 297–358. Berkeley.

Steward, Julian H.
1938   Basin-Plateau Aboriginal Socio-Political Groups. Washington,
           D.C.: Bureau of American Ethnology, Smithsonian Institu-
           tion.
1955   Theory of Culture Change. Urbana: University of Illinois
           Press.

Stoffle, Richard F., and Henry F. Dobyns
1983   Nuvagantu. Nevada Indian Comments on the Intermountain
           Power Project. Reno: Bureau of Land Management.

Strong, W. D.
1929   Aboriginal Society in Southern California. Banning, Calif.:
           Malki Museum Press, Morongo Indian Reservation. 1972 Re-
           print ed. of *University of California Publications in American Ar-
           chaeology and Ethnology* 26.

Sutton, Imre
1965   Land Tenure and Changing Occupance on Indian Reserva-
           tions in Southern California. Dissertation in Geography. Uni-
           versity of California-Los Angeles.
1967   Private Property in Land among Reservation Indians in
           Southern California. *Yearbook: Association of Pacific Coast Geog-
           raphers* 29:66–89.

Tac, Pablo
1958   Indian Life and Customs at Mission San Luis Rey: A Record
           of California Mission Life Written by Pablo Tac, an Indian
           Neophyte about 1835. Minna Hewes and Gordon Hewes,
           eds. and trans. Oceanside, Calif.: Old Mission San Luis Rey.

Welch, Patrick
1984   Draft Environmental Assessment for the Table Mountain
           Study Area: Wind Energy Development. El Centro, Calif.:
           Bureau of Land Management.

White, Raymond C.
1957   The Luiseño Theory of Knowledge. *American Anthropologist*
           59(1): 1–19.

1963   Luiseño Social Organization. *University of California Publica-*
               tions in American Archaeology and Ethnology 48(2): 91–194.
               Berkeley and Los Angeles.

Wolcott, Marjorie Tisdale
1929   Pioneer Notes from the Diaries of Judge Benjamin Hayes.
               Los Angeles: Privately printed.

Government Documents: United States
1856–1940   Annual Reports of the Commissioner of Indian Affairs to the
               Secretary of the Interior. Washington, D.C.: Government
               Printing Office. (Cited as ARCIA.)
1860   U.S. Federal Census. Manuscript Census of San Diego Coun-
               ty. Schedule 1, Population. Schedule 4, Agriculture. Serra
               Museum, San Diego Historical Association, San Diego.
1902   Preliminary Report of the Warner's Ranch Indian Advisory
               Commission presenting the Commission's Findings and the
               Commission's Recommendation for the Purchase of a Suita-
               ble Tract of Land in Southern California for the Warner's
               Ranch Indians and such other Mission Indians as may not be
               provided with suitable lands elsewhere. Los Angeles, Calif.
               Original copies at the Southwest Museum, Los Angeles, and
               the Museum of Man, San Diego.
1937   Location and Character of Indian Lands in California. Pre-
               pared by Jesse Garcia and Philip J. Webster, Land Use Plan-
               ning Section and Land Utilization Division of the Resettle-
               ment Administration, U.S. Department of Agriculture.
1949   Program for the Termination of Indian Bureau Activities in
               the State of California. Submitted to the Commissioner of In-
               dian Affairs. Prepared by the California Indian Agency, Sac-
               ramento.

Government Documents: California
1852   The Majority and Minority Reports of the Special Committee
               to Inquire into the treaties made by the United States Indian
               Commissioners with the Indians of California. Journal of the
               Proceedings of the Senate of the State of California of the
               Third Session of the Legislature begun on the fifth of Janu-

ary, 1852 and ended on the fourth of May 1852 at the cities of Vallejo and Sacramento. A. F. Fitch and Co. and V. E. Geiger and Co., State Printer, San Francisco. Minority Report Written by J. J. Warner of Warner's Ranch, San Diego County.

1955   Progress Report to the Legislature by the Senate Interim Committee on California Indian Affairs. Senate Resolution 115. Sacramento.

1957   Progress Report to the Legislature by the Senate Interim Committee on California Indian Affairs. Senate Resolution 124. Sacramento.

1959   Progress Report to the Legislature by the Senate Interim Committee on California Indian Affairs. Senate Resolution 171. Sacramento.

1960   Senate Fact Finding Committee on Natural Resources. Hearing of the California Subcommittee on Indian Affairs on Proposed Legislation for Federal Termination. Sacramento.

Newspapers

San Diego Herald, May 29, 1851, to April 7, 1860.
San Diego Weekly World, July 27, 1872, to July 19, 1873.
San Diego Daily World, July 25, 1872, to May 30, 1874.
San Diego Bulletin, August 21, 1869, to July 20, 1872.
San Diego Union, 1868 through 1903.

Unpublished Journals in Author's Possession:

Calac, Saturnino
    Journal. 1866–1900, Rincon Reservation.
Omish, Gregorio
    Journal. 1894–1908, Rincon Reservation.

Manuscript Collections:

Basic Records of Land Grants in California. Bancroft Library, Berkeley, Calif.
California State Papers, 1835–1839. Microfilm. Bancroft Library, Berkeley, Calif. (Originals are in California State Archives, Sacramento.
Couts, Cave

Papers. Huntington Library, San Marino, Calif.

Hayes, Judge Benjamin
Papers. Bancroft Library, Berkeley, Calif.

Hayes, Judge Benjamin
Index to the Records of San Diego County Sent to the Surveyor General's Office, San Francisco. Serra Library, San Diego Historical Association, San Diego, Calif.

Mariner, Fr. Juan
Journal of Exploration from San Diego through Cupa and Pala and Down San Luis Rey River, 1795. Written by Grihalva. Bancroft Library, Berkeley, Calif.

Smiley, Albert K.
Papers. Redlands Public Library, Redlands, Calif.

Unclassified Expediente No. 163. The Indians of the Pueblo of Las Flores Claiming Lands Thereon, 1844: Bowen Indices. Bancroft Library, Berkeley, Calif. (Original is in California State Archives, Sacramento.)

Unclassified Expediente No. 206. Indians of San Luis Rey, Mission Lands, 1843: Bowen Indices. Bancroft Library, Berkeley, Calif. (Original is in California State Archives, Sacramento.)

Government Archives: United States

Bureau of Indian Affairs, Mission Indian Agency Records, 1855–1970, Federal Archives and Federal Records Center, Laguna Niguel, California.

General Land Office, Los Angeles District Land Office, Federal Archives and Federal Records Center, Laguna Niguel, California.
Index to Letters, 1860–1890
Letter Book No. 1
Miscellaneous Boxes of Claims Filed

Office (later Bureau) of Indian Affairs, National Archives, Washington, D.C.
Jackson, Helen Hunt, Papers
Mission Indian Agency Records
Smiley, Albert K., Papers

Government Archives: Local

San Diego County Clerk's Office
  Board of Equalization Records
  County Board of Supervisors Records
  Court Records, 1850–1900
San Diego County Recorder's Office
  Books of Grants
  Books of Miscellaneous Recordings
  Books of Mortgages
  Books of Pre-emptions
  Books of Vital Statistics
  Books of Water Claims
San Diego County Tax Assessor's Office
  Tax Assessment Records, 1850–1890

INDEX

Acts: Act for the Government and Protection of Indians, 1850, 31, 34; Act for the Relief of Mission Indians, 1891, 9, 22, 31, 38–39, 49, 63, 74, 84, 141; Act to Ascertain and Settle the Private Land Claims, 1851, 30–31; American Indian Religious Freedom Act, 1978, 14–15, 83, 148; Environmental Protection Act, 15, 82–83, 148; General Allotment Act, 2, 49, 73, 106; Indian Homestead Act of 1883, 37; Indian Reorganization Act, 136–37; National Historic Preservation Act, 148

Adoption. by family, 197; by band, 63, 71

Advocates, xi, 3, 34–35, 37–39, 120, 137, 152; self-serving, 38–39

Agriculture (*See also* Fire; Water; Land use): agricultural land taken, 20, 21, 31–37, 42–43, 71, 85, 91; cash crops, 33, 54–56; crops lost, 55–58, 72; destroyed by non-Indian actions, 132–33; development, 122–25; emergency plant foods, 33, 55; European style or crops, 19, 22–25, 27–28, 32–36; federal census of 1860, 32; non-Indian farms, 22, 29, 91; permanent-field intensive concepts, 18; plant husbandry, 11; precontact resource management and agriculture, 11–18, 85, 131; prereservation, 21,

27–28, 31–39, 85; reservation, 22, 49, 54–58, 85–87, 122, 123; records, 27, 32; subsistence, 20, 22, 25, 49, 53

Agua Caliente Band, 88–90, 130; guardianships, 90

Agua Tibia Wild Area, 62, 130

Aid to Dependent Children, 87, 120

All Mission Indian Housing Authority. *See* Housing

Allotment (*See also* Inheritance), 1–2, 22, 46–54, 55, 73–79; antagonism to incorrect survey, 47–49, 53, 152; court cases, 53, 88–89; confiscated improvements, 47–49, 50, 53; equal-sized rectangle (cadastral), 47, 50; farmland, dry and irrigated, 47, 53, 74; General Allotment Act, 2, 49, 73, 106; house sites, 47, 54; mortgage, 74, 75, 85, 114–16; originally desired, 46; petitioned for, 47–48, 50, 86, 152; possible prejudice to land recovery cases, 48–49; problems of Agua Caliente, 88–89; of Torres Martinez, 86–88; public domain allotments (*See also* Homesteads) 107; refused allotments, 48, 53; sales of, 65, 74, 75, 76, 77–78, 87, 89, 121; title to improvements wanted, 46–49; water liens, 58

American Friends Service Committee, xiii, xiv

American Indian Religious Freedom
Act of 1978 (*See also* Sacred lands),
14–15, 83, 148
AMIHA. *See* Housing
Animal husbandry (*See also* Grazing):
non-Indian, 19, 24–25; Indian con-
trolled, 23, 27–28, 33, 54
Animal resource management, pre-
Spanish, 11
Archaeological exploitation, 15
Army forced Indian removal (*See* Pala
Articles of association, 137
Assets of reservation stolen, 127
Assignments, 53, 67–69, 77, 78, 79,
116; improvements abandoned on,
55; inheritance of (*See also* Salgado
assignment use case), 78–79; lost im-
provements under allotment, 53;
mapping needed, 69; on allotted re-
servations, 77–79
Avocado land, valuable, 109, 113, 123

Baja California (*See also* Kumeyaay), 20,
103
Band (*See also* Tribe; Reservation), 1–9;
defined, 3, 9; enterprises, 122–25;
meetings, 114, 149; organization, 99,
101; precontact organization, 3–8,
13–17; territory, 13–15, 40, 97–99
Baptized Indians, 23, 24, 25
Barker v. Harvey (*See also* Pala; Cupeño),
42, 102
Barona (*See also* Capitan Grande), 46,
71, 73; new developments, 59, 123
Baron Long (*See also* Viejas, Capitan
Grande), 71–73, 123
Battle of San Pasqual, 28
Bean, Lowell J., testimony, 99–100, 124
Bingo, 59, 123–24
Blake Sea, 6, 84, 86–88
Blood, degree of, 64, 94, 96–97, 118–
19; of Band, 64, 94–96
Boscana, Fr. Geronimo, 20
Boundaries: cannot contract for own
surveys, 113; discrepancies in, 39–
40, 42, 47–49, 111–14; homestead,

112–13; Indians object to incorrect,
36, 47–50, 53; precontact, 5–6, 13,
97; resurveys needed, 114; section
sizes small, 112
Building codes, attempts to impose, 1,
130
Bureau of Indian Affairs (BIA): business practices, 89–90; and federal
trust status, 154; tribal management
of moneys, 120
Bureau of Land Management (BLM),
45, 46, 105
Byrne v. Alas et al. (*See also* San Jacinto),
42

Cadastral land survey system, 47–48
Cahuilla: bands, 4–5, 11, 12; lineage, 6–
7; missionized, 24; reservations, 46,
85, 186–90
Calac, Oligario, 36, 101
California: environmental laws, 83; failure of state, 129, 154; legislature,
30–31; Supreme Court, 42; water
law, 123
California Indian claims cases: Indians
of California case K-344 (*See also*
Treaties with Indians, 1851–52), 30–
31, 121, 194; Indians of California
claims case dockets 31-37, xv, 32,
121; 194; Mission Indian claims cases (*See also* Water), Land Claims
Docket 80, xiv–xv, 32, 57, 133, 194;
Docket 80A and 80A-2 (*See* Water);
Pitt River case docket 347, xv, 194
California Indian Legal Services (CILS),
81, 90, 104, 133
California Inter-Tribal Council, xvii
Campo, 9; purchased land added, 45;
BLM land, 46; propane tank prob-
lem, 125–26, 139; leaf mold, 127–
28; water case, 56–57
Capitan. *See* Captain
Capitan Grande (*See also* Irrigation;
Barona; Viejas), 48, 127; part for
dam, 71–73, under national leader,
101; refugee bands supposed to

join, 40, 103; water case, 57
Captain: band leader, 3–9, 15, 16, 38, 136, 141; subservience to agent required, 136, 141–43; traditional powers, 141, 142; originally under generals, 101
Catholic Church, (*See also* Franciscan missions; Missions), 25; forced conversion to, 19–20; inherited allotment, 75; patronage lands (*See also* Jamul; Santa Ynez), 102–5; property, 29–30; rituals, 20; school, 79; sold land for reservation (*See also* Pauma), 43
Cemetery: sacred area, 13–14, 66, 69, 79; cremation, 14; looting, 128, 130; home area of Jamul, Santa Ynez, 103–5
Censuses of reservations, 64, 65, 66, 70, 93–96, 119
Ceremonies, traditional forbidden, 141, 153
Chairman. *See* Tribal chairmen
Checkerboard reservations (*See also* Coachella Valley reservations), 85, 88
Chiefs (*See also* General; Tribal chairmen), 4–5, 13, 14, 141; power removed, 142; status and power, 15–16
Churches: on reservations, 69, 79; Indian pueblo, 93
Citizen status, 28, 107–8, 128, 155; Mexican, 21; Spanish, 19
Civil law and disputes (*See also* Public Law 280), 67–68, 69, 70, 145–46
Climate, 8, 12, 15, 21; droughts, 8, 21, 23, 33, 37, 55–56, 57, 58 72; floods, 58
Coachella Valley reservations, 50, 53, 73, 84–90, 112
Colonial government institutions, 19; Mexican 21, 25–28; Spanish, 20–21, 23–25; U.S., 21–22, 28–40
Confiscation of private property (*See also* Allotment), 49, 53

Congress (*See also* Acts), 9, 22, 31, 37–38, 43, 50, 58, 71, 74, 89, 104–5, 109, 110, 123, 124, 129, 132, 133, 143, 144; executive order reservations, 61–63; Duncan Hunter, 45
Constitutions of reservations, 63–64, 104, 109, 136–38, 140
Contract work, on reservations, 113–14, 150
Controlled burning. *See* Fire
Coronado Bay Company, 104
Cosmit (*See also* Iñaha), 40; boundary changed, 113
Cota, Manuel, 35
County governments: attempts to control reservations, 1, 2, 3; fear of reservations, 126; reservations suffer from, 126
Courier system, traditional, 13
Court of Claims (*See also* Water cases), 57
Couts, Cave, subagent, 29;
Couts, Cave Jr. (surveyor), 47–48, 92
Crafts, mission craft specialists, 19–20, 24
Criminal law. (*See also* Public Law 280; Sheriff)
Cuca (*See also* Ranch; San Luiseño), 27, eviction of band, 43
Culture (*See also* Values; Traditional custom): cultural centers, museums, 79, 120; affected by housing program, 117; child training, 117
Cupa, 30
Cupeño (*See also* Pala; Garra revolt), 30; at Pala, 53; forced to move, 42–45; in missions, 23–24; opposition ot environmental assessment report, 1976, 83–84; pre-Spanish, 4, 5, 8, 11–18
Cuyapaipe, 71, 84

Dams. *See* Water
Dawes Act. *See* Allotments
Death (*See also* Population; Cemetery); personal property burned upon, 16;

rates increased at missions, 23
Degree of blood. *See* Blood, degree of
Democratic elections, 137; agreed upon rules, 136, 138
Department of Interior, 29
Dependent domestic nations, 136, 145
Desert resources, 6, 7, 33
Development (*See also* Water), 60; capital costs increased, 133–34; continual adaptation, 2–3, 33, 131–32, 154; economic development, 3, 62, 69, 89, 90; formal organization required, 99; hidden costs, 125; health and safety codes, 125, 126, 128, 129; planning for, 3, 118, 119, 122, 154; plans frustrated, 100–2; 109–10; new development, 122–27; new programs, 99, 111; proposals refused, 124–25; retarded by others, 62, 86–90, 101, 132; water post–1970, 58–59
Diegueño. *See* Kumeyaay
Differences of opinion as political norm (*See also* Factionalism), 137–38
Disabled persons, 55, 120
Disease. *See* Population; Death rates
Dispossessed families, 33, 37
Dominican missions, 20
Droughts. *See* Climate
Duro: Cenon, 98–99; Panto, 91

Ecological knowledge, xi–xii, 5, 6, 7, 8
Economic adaptation. *See* Development
Education: Catholic, 22, 79; cultural training, 117; mission, 23–24; preschool, 79; transculturation schools, 22; training for hierarchy, 6, 7, 137
Egalitarian. *See* Stereotyped beliefs about Indians
Elders: at mission, 20, 24; care of, 117; train youth, 117; knowledge of past, 135; per capita distribution to, 120–21; housing, 115; for environmental impact work, 148
Elections, 66, 136, 142; Bureau controlled, 93–95; committee, 99; delegates, 114; not traditional, 137
Elkwanon. *See* Santa Ysabel
Emigrant routes, 33
Enclavement, 26, 153–54
Enrollment (*See also* Membership; San Pasqual), xiii–xiv, 119; regulations, 63–66; enrollment problems, 93–97; Mission Creek, 109
Environment (*See also* Land use; Agriculture): drastic changes in, 80, 153; knowledge of, xi–xii; managed, xi–xii, 3, 11, 130–31; distant resources, 6, 7
Environmental impact assessment and reports, 82–84, 148
Environmental Protection Act, 15, 82–83, 148
Environmentalist organizations, 3, 62, 130–31
Equal-sized rectangular farms. *See* Cadastral land survey system
Escondido Mutual Water Company, xv, xvi, 122, 133
Estudillo, Francisco, Indian Agent, 101
Ethnocentric behavior, 152–53
Eviction, 42, 48, 91
Executive order reservations: 1870 order, 34; cancelled 1871, 35–36, 91; 1875 order, 36–37, 38, 43; addition to, 48; errors in 1875 order, 97–99, 100–101; Kelsey Tract, 62–63; 102; Mission Reserve, 60–62
Expediente of Paome and Cuca 1843, 27–28

Factionalism, 137, 148
Family lands. *See* Tenure
Federal programs or grants (*See also* Development; Housing): recognition of band, 41, 104; regulations, 111
Federal Register, 95
Fee patent title (*See also* Out-of-trust), 65, 73–74, 108–9
Fiestas, 79, 93, 153

Fire: traditional use of, 6, 11–12, 17, 142; controlled burning, 80
Fireplaces for heating, 117
Firewood, 66, 117
Foote, Kate (first allotting agent), 47–48, 53
Franciscan missions/missionaries (See also Missions), 19, 21, 23–25

Garra revolt, 30
General (See also Chiefs), 13, 101, 141
General Land Office. See United States: General Land Office
Government. See Political structure; Leadership
Grazing land, 33; not allotted, 47, 79; range management, 80, 138; tribal fees, 79, 80; trespass by non-Indians, 79–80, 127

Hayes, Judge Benjamin, 91
Health and safety codes. See Development
Health service (See also Indian Health Service): clinics on reservations, 79; county hospitals, 129, 132, 199–200; precontact, 14, 16
Henshaw Dam (See also Water; Docket 80A), 122
Highway access. See Roads
Hispanicized Indians, 21, 26
Holes in reservations, 121–22
Homesteads (See also Public domain allotments), 1, 37, 38, 92–93; absorbed into reservations, 38–39, 48, 98–99, 107; boundary problems, 112–13; bought for some Capitan Grande members, 71–72; history of, 106–8; non-Indian, 32, 34, 36, 102, 121; roads, 109; sale of, 108–9; valuable, 109, 113
Housing: AMIHA, 114–18; at Barona, Viejas, 72; development pressure, 118–19; eligibility, 114, 115; Federal Housing Authority (FHA), 116; financing, 75, 114, 116; Housing Improvement Program, 116; Housing, Urban Development, 114, 118; inspections, 117–18; loss to Indian ownership, 115; need for, 111; nonmember potential use, 114; planning for, 118–19; siting rules, 116; substandard construction, 45, 116, 130; tribal, 115, 120; visiting rules, 117
Hunting and fishing rights, 132–33
Hunting territory, 13; grazing right equated, 80
Hunting-gathering, incorrect stereotype, 11, 18, 153
Hupa, 90

Imperial Valley Irrigation District (See also Coachella Valley reservations), 88
Iñaha (Inyaha), 101, 113
Income property, 90, 106
Indian Health Service (See also Health service; Water), 58–59, 132, 139
Indian Homestead Act of 1883. See Acts
Indian Reorganization Act (IRA), 136–37
Indian Rights Association, 37, 39, 104
Indians of California claims cases. See California Indian claims cases
Inheritance, 1, 2, 6, 7, 121; by church, 75; homestead, 107–9; kinship terminology, 77; reservation, 66–69, 72, 74, 76–79; non-Indian spouse, 76, 108, 121; reservation membership, 64–66; traditional, 15, 16, 17, 25, 28, 33; leadership positions, 137
Ipai. See Kumeyaay
Irrigation (See also Agriculture; Water), 54–55, 92; bureau controlled, 56–58, 85–88; on Capitan Grande, 72; developed by Band, 58, 72, 85, 142–43; reimbursable basis, 58; Pechanga lacked, 54; pre-Spanish, 12, 17, 85; rights of way for, 84

Leases on reservation, 66, 68, 124–26; Agua Caliente, 89–90; Coachella Valley, 86
Legal counsel, 150
Los Angeles, Pueblo (*See also* Metropolitan Water District of Los Angeles), 21
Los Conejos (*See also* Capitan Grande), 71
Los Coyotes, 45, 59, 123
Lummis, Charles F. (*See also* Pala), 44

Marriage, 64–65, 141; state law problem, 132
Mataguay, 42–44, 101
Mazzetti (PL 280), 133
Medical resources. *See* Health service
Membership (*See also* Enrollment), 108, 152; ineligible children, 118; inheritance, 63, 65, 76–77; marriage effects, 65; for allotment, 49, 53; for planning, 119; relinquished, 77; rights, 66–67; rolls, 109, 119
Mesa Grande (Mesa Chiquita), 35, 45, 46, 81, 92; boundary problems, 49–50; Department of Interior title investigation, 99–100; trust title problems, 40, 97–102
Metes and bounds survey (*See also* Cadastral land survey system), 47
Metropolitan Water District of Los Angeles, xv, 57
Mexican settlement (*See also* Pueblos; Ranchos): governors, 25–27; independence, 25; Indian land use under, 26–28; Indians protest abuses, 26–27; Indian water, 26–27; laws, 26, 27, 30–32, 42; military posts, guards, 26; policy, 21, 25; records, 21, 26; revolution, 21; stripped missions and Indians of land, 21, 25
Military (*See also* Presidios; Revolts and raids by Indians): band boundary defense, 13; Spanish, 20–21, 25
Mission Agency, 22

Mission Creek Reservation, terminated, 109–10
Mission Indian Federation (*See also* Opposition organizations), xiv, xvii, 53, 129, 141; taxation by, 143
Mission Indian Land Claims Case. *See* California Indian Claims Cases
Mission Reserve (*See also* Executive Order; Pala; Pauma), 44, 60–62, 130
Missions (*See also* San Diego; San Gabriel; San Luis Rey; San Juan Capistrano; Santa Ynez): agriculture, 23–24; asistencias, 25; communal life taught, 20, 25; communal forced labor, 25; crop and grazing areas, 24–27; disease (*See also* Population), 23; Franciscan, 19, 24–25; labor tax, 25; policy, 19–20, 23; properties, 29; records, xv; rituals, 20; sanitation, 23; secularized and dismantled, 21, 25–27; secular mayordomos, 25–26, 29; supplied army, 21
Money, shell, paid to hierarchy, 6, 7
Monterey Bay Presidio. *See* Colonial government institutions
Morongo, 9, 79, 90; BLM land, 46; opposed allotments, 50, 53; refugees from Cupa, 45; water, 56, 59, 84
Morse, Joseph B. *See* Smiley Commission
Mountain resources, 6–7, 33
Mutewheer. *See* Duro

Named descent groups. *See* Kinship
National Historic Preservation Act, 148
National level tribal organization (*See also* Leadership; Tenure; Political structure), 4–5; land, 13
Natural environment (*See also* Agriculture; Irrigation; Stereotyped beliefs about Indians; Land use), xi, xii, 3, 11, 62, 127, 130–32, 153
Neophyte. *See* Baptized Indian
Net (also noot, nuut), 3, 6
Non-Indian spouse. *See* Inheritance

Nonreservation village. *See* Jamul
Noot (nuut) (*See also* Captain), 3, 6–7
Noria (Puerta Ignoria), 44
Noxious businesses, 74, 83, 126

Ocean resources, 6, 7, 33
Old-age pension, 87, 120, 132
Omish, Gregorio, 67
Opposition organizations (*See also* Mission Indian Federation), 49–50
Orchards. *See* Land use; Avocado land, valuable
Ordinances, 114, 138
Out-of-trust: allotments, 2, 53, 73–74, 75, 77–78, 108–9, 115, 121; bands desire to buy back, 121–22; funds, 120–22

Painter, C. C. *See* Smiley Commission
Paiute Ghost Dance, 50
Pala (*See also* San Luiseño; Water cases: Docket 80A; Cupeño). 9, 75, 101; allotment, 53–54; BLM land, 46; death rate increased at, 45; development, 120, 122; executive order, 34–37, 91; forced migration to, 44–45; history differs, 53–54; lands containing minerals removed, 45; land purchased for Cupa evictees, 41–45, 50; Mission Reserve, 60–62, 130; Mexican pueblo, 27, 30; sand and gravel, 122, 124; sewer system, 128; tribal housing, 115; tribal land, 79; water, 56, 59, 84
Palm Springs: city of, 88–90, 130; reservation. *See* Agua Caliente Band
Pamo. *See* Mesa Grande
Parrish churches, 21, 25
Patrilineage. *See* Kinship
Patronage lands. *See* Jamul; Santa Ynez
Pauma (Paome) (*See also* Barker v. Harvey; Water cases: Docket 80A): land purchased for, 43; Mexican period, 27–28; Mission Reserve, 60–

62, 130; water case, xv, 56, 59, 84, 123
Peaceful settled Indians, 28–29, 31–32, 36, 91
Pechanga, 84; allotment, 47–48; BLM land, 46; evicted from Temecula, 48; farms, 54; Kelsey Tract, 62; land stolen, 42, 102, 114; trash dump beside, 126
Pio Pico, 27
Pitt River case, xv
Political structure (*See also* Leadership; Opposition organization; Tribal): Bureau interference in, 138–41; constitutions, 137; leadership forced underground, 136; modern self-government, 9, 66, 111, 136, 145, 149–50; national level destroyed, 5; transformed to modern, 140–45
—precontact: band, 1, 3–9, 136–37, 140; hierarchical, 3–9, 137, 153; leader trained, 6–7, 137; national level, 4–5, 13,101; religion validated, 3–4, 136; reservation, 9; status and power differential, 6, 7, 8, 9, 15–16; tribal, 136, 137
Population: density, 8, 12, 17–18, 153; depopulation and disease, 8, 23, 131, 152; Pala death rate increased, 45; pressure, 118–19
Pothunting (*See also* Cemetery: looting), 15, 130
Potrero (*See also* San Luiseño), 100
Power to enforce ordinances (*See also* Sanctions), 138–40
Preemption by settlers, 32–36
Presidios (*See also* San Diego; Monterey), 19, 20
Propane: gas stoves, 117; tank lease (*See also* Campo), 125, 139
Property tax. *See* Taxation
Public Domain allotments (*See also* Homesteads), 1, 37
Public lands, 32, 34, 36, 45–46, 61

Public Law 280, xii-xiii, 1, 87, 90, 130–33, 145, 154; lack of law enforcement under, 70, 127–30; no internal sanctions under, 138–39; opposition organization no longer needed, 141

Pueblo (*See also* Pala; San Pasqual; Las Flores; San Dieguito): Indian, 21, 26–28, 32, 40, 91; Spanish and Mexican (*See also* San Diego, Los Angeles, San Juan Capistrano), 20–21, 32

Puerta de San Felipe, 44

Puerta Ignoria (Noria), 44

Puerta La Cruz, 43–44

Pul (plural of puplum) (*See also* Shaman; Specialist), 6

Raids. *See* Revolts and raids by Indians

Railroad land (*See also* checkerboard reservations), 85

Ranch: Rancho, 29–30, 35, 101, 104, 112; enclaved villages, 26, 29, 30, 31, 32, 35, 41–43, 48; forced labor on, 25–26, 33; Indian rancho grants, 27, 43; Indian title cases (*See also* Cupeño), 42; Mexican, 25–27; Spanish, 20–21

Rancheria Act, 22, 110

Rancherias (villages), 13, 15, 17, 33, 37

Rancho California, 102, 126

Rations for Indians, 33, 55

Refugees, 9, 24, 37, 43, 45, 49, 91–92

Religion (*See also* Sacred lands; American Indian Religious Freedom Act) ceremonies, 6, 7; constraints on, 141, 144, 153; forced conversion, 14–15, 19–20, 24; validated leadership, 3–4

Recreation, 3, 79, 86–87, 122–23

Removal of all Indians proposed, 30

Rent (*See also* Salgado): allotments, 54, 55, 56, 74–75; houses on reservation, 69–70, 115; traditional use, 17

Rentiers, 106, 115

Representation, to other organizations

(*See also* Elections: delegates), 146–49

Reservations (*See also* Executive order; Specific topics), 1, 22, 34–40; complex individual histories, 153–55; incorrect trust title (*See also* Mesa Grande), 40; mislocated (*See also* Cosmit; San Pasqual), 40, 93; single family reservations, 71; stolen lands (*See also* Boundaries; Pechanga); sole survivor claim, 109

Resources: ocean, 6,7; mountain, 6, 7, 8; desert, 6, 7

Revolts and raids by Indians, 21, 26, 28–29; Garra revolt, 30

Rights-of-way, 46, 69, 79, 80–84; across allotment, 82; Indian homesteads need, 108,109; for utilities, 82

Rincon (*See also* San Luiseño; Water cases), 35, 43, 59, 90, 100–101, 130; allotment desired then opposed, 47, 51, 52, 53, BLM Land, 46; development, 123, 124; Mexican period, 28; tribal land, 79; water case, xv-xvi, 56–58, 84, 133

Riverside, 22, 87, 126, 130

Roads: pre-Spanish, 13; prereservation, 80; reservation, 80–84; modern, 3, 33, 56, 108, 109, 118, 122, 123

Sacred lands, 13–15, 16, 17; altar, 14; band sacred mountains for solstice and sun watcher ceremonies, 14; ceremonial areas, 13, 14; cemetery (*See also* Cemetery), 14, 15; creation locations, 14; healing areas, 14; national sacred mountains, 14–15: Kuuchamaa, 14; Signal Mountain, 15; Table Mountain, 14; Tecate Peak, 14; Wee'ishpa, 14

Safety code. *See* Development: health and safety codes

Sales, Fr. Luis, Dominican missionary, 20